EUROPE IN DECAY

A Study in Disintegration

1936–1940

BY

Sir Lewis Bernstein

L. B. NAMIER, F.B.A.

PROFESSOR OF MODERN HISTORY IN THE
UNIVERSITY OF MANCHESTER
HON. FELLOW OF BALLIOL COLLEGE, OXFORD

GLOUCESTER, MASS.

PETER SMITH

1963

First Published, 1949

Reprinted, 1963
By Permission of Sir Lewis Namier

PREFACE

BEFORE I had finished writing, and re-writing, *Diplomatic Prelude, 1938–1939*, I realized that it would not be possible to continue bringing it up to date as if it were a yearly almanac. I therefore added a section, " Episodes and Men ", " to serve as a ' revelation ' bag — not in the sense of ' revelations ' but of expansive capacity " ; it was " to provide packing space " for material complementary to the book but which could not be incorporated in it. Two years have passed since I finished writing *Diplomatic Prelude*, and more than a year since it was published. During that time books bearing on its subject have been appearing at such a rate that my essays about them fill by now this new volume. I do not mean to attempt re-writing *Diplomatic Prelude* till the most important collections of documents for the pre-war years are published ; and then I will somewhat enlarge the period covered by it. In the meantime I propose to keep myself and my readers up to date by continuing a critical analysis of the most important new publications — volumes of documents, memoirs, and monographs — adding occasionally essays on particular subjects ; and whenever there is enough to hand, I will reprint them in book form. Works of a technical military character, or mainly concerned with the period after 1940, are outside my province.

I have to thank the editors and owners of *The Times Literary Supplement*, *The Listener*, *The National Review*, and *The United Nations World* for permission to reprint essays, or parts of essays, which appeared in their columns.

L. B. NAMIER

60 THE GRAMPIANS
LONDON, W.6
June 27, 1949

CONTENTS

MEMOIRS BORN OF DEFEAT

DEFEAT produces, as a rule, an earlier and richer crop of memoirs than victory. In those who can let results speak for them there is not, unless they are writers by nature, the same urge to explain. But when a great inheritance seems in jeopardy, when disasters and suffering descend upon the nation, it asks for the reasons and calls to account those who had been entrusted with the conduct of its affairs. In France, after the defeat of 1940, the inquest was started in the form of State Trials, first in the Court House of Riom, and next in the prosecutions of collaborators. But there is a natural wish in the defendants, or in material witnesses, to continue their evidence and to expand it in narratives unhampered by legal procedure and more readable than proceedings in court. Nor has the liberation of France, and the way in which it came about, improved the psychological setting for those concerned in the defeat. Under the impact of irreparable defeat, questions of individual failure or justification would recede before the overpowering problems of the national fate and survival, and individuals would be less interesting even to themselves. But when the previous setting has in appearance been restored without achievements commensurate with the preceding failure, when liberation has come without spiritual deliverance for the nation, attention reverts to the scene of disaster and tends to deal with it in individual terms. Still, unless the author is a man of exceptional stature, an apologia seldom makes pleasant reading. In attempts at self-justification men excuse themselves and accuse others, select their facts and set their memory working to establish a case. Claims to objectivity and detachment, solemn affirmations that theirs is an unvarnished account

I

of strict veracity, tend to render self-vindications even more distasteful. Few men emerge with enhanced prestige from such disquisitions and wrangles.

The historian studying the memoirs of M. Bonnet, M. Flandin, or General Gamelin — to mention a few outstanding through the position they held in crucial periods and the ingenuity they now display — will examine their statements, allegations, and pleas in the light of accumulating evidence, and try to fit them into the structure which gradually arises. But as he proceeds, big outlines appear which dwarf the persons, actions, and responsibility of the men who so hotly discuss great historic processes in terms of their individual lives and performances. The temptation for them is well-nigh irresistible. Yet if only they got away from their own persons, or rather saw them in their true proportions and setting, and turned to the historic tragedy of their nation, their own lives and failures would appear as what they are: as part of the tragedy.

From a Europe in ruin and misery, demoralized and debased, one thinks back to the days of French preponderance. France was heir to Rome, and a Roman universality attached to what she created. Her language was that of civilized European society, and her art was, and is, the art of modern Europe. Spiritually the Great Revolution was a battle for the freedom and dignity of man. And seldom was conquest so productive of good as in the Napoleonic period. The two nations flanking the Continent — Britain at the gate of the Western world and Russia at that of Eurasia — defeated the bid for a French-dominated Europe. Yet with Napoleon's defeat vanished what was probably the only chance of uniting Europe to its cultural gain.

The predominance of France, which had rested on her numerical strength and on Germany's disunion, was no longer possible after 1870. What France now desired was a restoration of her territorial integrity, impaired by the loss of Alsace-Lorraine, and the security required for a good life — a nation cannot live in an ivory tower with Germany for neighbour. Even in the period from 1871 to 1904, there was a cleavage in the attitude of France to Europe and war: on the surface, noisy talk about *revanche*; deeper down, a resigned pacifism which grew as the years went by. The Franco-Russian alliance was a security measure; the Anglo-French Entente, to begin with, a mere clearance of old discords. Germany's aggressive bluster and the very real threat behind it brought the three Powers together, and next changed the character of their agreements. Each of the three, in its own sphere, had to defend its independence against the growing weight and impact of Germany. But while Britain was protected by the seas, and Russia by her vast spaces, France was well-nigh a hostage of the Germans, named by them as such: she was the one they would pounce upon and hold to ransom. Twice, or rather three times, in the 19th century had she suffered invasion by foreign armies: she had now to choose between collaboration with the Germans and resistance, between playing second fiddle to an overbearing Germany and facing a new invasion by the Germanic hordes. Rouvier and Caillaux favoured collaboration, and in the two Morocco crises, during which they were Premiers, the stand which Britain took at the side of France was firmer than that of France herself. But Britain's loyalty to the Entente would have been even more reassuring had she been less slow in facing up to her moral obligation of having an army fit to help France if attacked by the Germans. Clemenceau, foremost among the champions of resistance, said to Mr. Wickham Steed in 1908: " You are hopelessly unprepared. . . . You could smash the German fleet and make a lovely hole in the water. But in 1870 there was no German fleet, which did not prevent

3

the Prussians from entering Paris."

France fought with ardour in the war of 1914: this was the last fierce flare-up of feelings born of the defeat of 1870. But when victory came, it was, in Mr. Churchill's words, a haggard France that greeted its dawn. " Worn down, doubly decimated, but undisputed masters of the hour, the French nation peered into the future in thankful wonder and haunting dread."[1] The loss of one and a quarter million men, irreplaceable in a stationary population, and the abnormally low number of births during the war years, " the hollow years ", were a poignant reality. Yet victory revived memories of past greatness (too much memory is a deadly danger in politics). The circumstances of 1919 assigned to France once more the part of the predominant military Power on the Continent; she resumed her former position of a " protecting Power ". She could not renounce that distinction which victory thrust on her, nor could she sustain its burden, not being prepared again to pay the price of war. Satellites clustered to her; but what she sought in those alliances was a safe retreat — her own inclination, the outcome of excessive suffering, being to withdraw into an impregnable shell. Still, the " Maginot mentality " was incompatible with the rôle *d'une puissance protectrice*: a fatal contradiction.

The more the fruits of victory proved illusory, the stronger grew in France the determination to husband that unique treasure, her human material: truly, there was nothing worth its sacrifice. Disillusioned and civilized, with an intense analytical awareness, the French had lost that primitive *élan* which carries men into battle. In the spiritual sphere there was a growth of individualism; in the material, of selfishness. And in the absence of a potent common purpose uniting the nation, social divisions, which during the preceding one hundred and

[1] *The Gathering Storm*, pages 5 and 9-10.

fifty years had repeatedly resulted in civil war, became accentuated, inhibiting still further national action. But the creative leaders, or servants, of a nation merely focus the spirit that is in it. There is a Jewish legend that the Burning Bush, from which the voice of God spoke to Moses, was the nation of Israel gathered at the foot of Mount Sinai. Statesmen and generals can hardly plan as much as a sensible policy unless the voice of the nation speaks clearly to them. Correct conclusions are seldom reached, still less acted upon, in cold logic unsupported by a burning passion; and the most amazing lapses from elementary common sense will occur in work done against the background of contradictory impulses in the nation.

British statesmen, foremost Mr. Lloyd George, realized the weakness of the French system of alliances with secondary Powers, and would not endorse them, either directly or through the League of Nations. Locarno marks a turning away of France from her satellites toward Britain : a significant and not altogether healthy symptom. There was growing reliance on Britain, although this country had disarmed and was pressing France to do likewise. Until the spring of 1939, the influence which the British Government exerted, or tried to exert, on France with regard to Germany was mostly unsound : which justifies the conscious tenderness that Mr. Churchill showed to France in June 1940 and voices in his book, but hardly the reproaches which certain French statesmen address to this country in their memoirs. For they would not have sought British advice, whose character they could gauge beforehand, nor would they have acted upon it, had it not answered their own unavowed inclinations.

The outstanding case is that of the remilitarization of the Rhineland, in March 1936. On the flimsiest of pre-texts Hitler violated the Locarno Treaty which he had repeatedly promised to observe. His army was as yet utterly unfit to stand up to the French. Had France taken immediate military action, Hitler would have suffered a fatal check which might have brought down his régime, and would, in any case, have put an end to his treaty infringements. But the French Government consulted the British, and then let themselves in for negotiations which left to Hitler the gains of his insane *coup*. He could now build against France his Western wall; he advanced by a hundred miles his starting-point for an offensive against her; and he exposed a debility of purpose in the French which deeply impressed both the Germans and France's satellites. There was in France a paralysis of will which it is difficult to explain in terms of reason. Even men who understood how much was at stake, and how little risk there was in acting, failed to act.

The position was more difficult at the time of Munich, but not desperate; not nearly as bad as in September 1939. Again the British exercised a restraining influence on the French Government, which at times wished, and at times begged, to be restrained. The long and the short of M. Bonnet's argument is that France was fully determined to stand by her obligations to Czechoslovakia, but would have courted disaster had she done so; and that he, Foreign Minister since April 1938, had tried his best to reconstruct a front against German aggression, but was let down by everybody. Few who have read Mr. Churchill's estimate of the situation at that time, or Mr. Wheeler-Bennett's history of Munich, or, last but not least, the *Documents on British Foreign Policy*, will accept M. Bonnet's elaborate explanations. But the crowds which acclaimed M. Daladier and Mr. Chamberlain on their return from Munich showed once more that these Prime Ministers represented the spirit of the period.

Changes in political atmosphere are more easily registered than explained; and public opinion, certainly in this country and probably also in France, without necessarily revising its view of Munich, would have refused to countenance its repetition. For years there had been enough in Hitler's words and actions to provoke indignation; this, vocal at first, seemed to flag as he gained force. Prague revived it — there was now the feeling that everyone was in danger. Poland was the object of his next operation. Again the French were moved by contradictory feelings, openly admitted by M. Bonnet and M. Noël, French Ambassador to Warsaw, and implicitly by General Gamelin. On the one hand, they did not relish the prospect of going to war over Poland, and would gladly have loosened the ties between the two countries, taking Poland's action in Teschen for excuse. On the other hand, they felt that they might need her if Hitler turned against the West, and therefore did not want to drive her into his camp. But they now set to work to gain Russia's support, and in the ensuing negotiations went ahead of Britain in trying to meet Russian wishes. Poland was to relieve German pressure on France, and Russia to reduce French commitments in Poland.

But unless Russia's help was secured, the position would be exceedingly difficult. In May 1939 General Gamelin signed a military protocol with the Poles, promising them to open an offensive on the sixteenth day of mobilization. The circumstances and significance of that protocol, and of a parallel political agreement, have given rise to bitter and pointless controversy. What emerges is that the French, to make sure that the Poles would resist a German attack which might otherwise turn against France and catch her unprepared, led the Poles to expect more than France proposed to perform: in the Committee of National Defence on August 23, General Gamelin explained that the French would " not be able to assume the offensive in less than about two years ". There was a complete acceptance of the defensive, though during the German offensive in Poland only forty-two half-equipped and half-trained German divisions guarded Germany's long front from the North Sea to Switzerland. On August 26 Mr. Churchill saw General Georges, Gamelin's chief assistant. "He produced all the figures of the French and German armies", writes Mr. Churchill, "and classified the divisions in quality. The result impressed me so much that . . . I said : 'But you are the masters'. He replied : 'The Germans have a very strong army, and we shall never be allowed to strike first. If they attack, both our countries will rally to their duty.' " [1]

To sum up : Had France had a different neighbour in the East, she would have settled down to a peaceful existence rendered glorious by undiminished cultural achievements. Circumstances forced her into the war of 1914, and next thrust on her a pre-eminence and a burden greater than she could bear. To abdicate would not even have been safe. She had therefore to carry on, against her deepest inclinations. Hence the contradictions and chaos. And there is a great deal to be said in defence of the French statesmen and generals of the inter-war period, but on a plane different from that on which most of them choose to argue their case.

[1] *Op. cit.* page 312.

FLANDIN

PIERRE-ÉTIENNE FLANDIN was born in 1889; he entered
the Chamber of Deputies in 1914 and continued in it till
1940; he sat in nine Cabinets; was Prime Minister from
November 8, 1934, till May 30, 1935, and as such concluded the Rome Agreement, the Stresa Pact, and the
Franco-Soviet Pact; he was Foreign Minister from
January 24 to June 2, 1936 — *i.e.* during the remilitarization of the Rhineland; and again under Vichy, from
December 14, 1940, to February 10, 1941. He was
arrested by the Free French in Algiers in October 1943,
and kept in prison for twenty-five months; tried by the
High Court of Justice in July 1946, he was sentenced to
five years of " national indignity " but was granted an
immediate reprieve, and therefore released without loss
of citizen's rights. The main charge was that of having
held office under Vichy. His defence was that having,
to the intense annoyance of the Germans, displaced Laval
(arrested by Vichy the previous day), he tried to steer
towards a covert understanding with the allies, prevented
an expedition against the Free French in Equatorial
Africa, and was forced by the Germans to resign. A letter
from Mr. Winston Churchill confirmed that the change
from Laval to M. Flandin had been welcome and useful
to the allies, and helped to clear his record. This, combined with the merely nominal verdict, closes the
" criminal " side of the case. There remains the case of
M. Flandin the politician, to be argued before the tribunal
of history in terms and by methods applied in this country
to the record of statesmen ever since the vindictive, and
mostly unfair, weapon of impeachment was discarded.
The available material is now enriched by M. Flandin's

evidence before the High Court [1] and his book on *French Policy, 1919–1940*. [2]

" This book was written in prison . . . between December 1943 and May 1944 ", says M. Flandin, in his introduction : he does not claim that it is a history and he disclaims its being polemical or an apologia, but adds that the reader " will not be surprised to find in it numerous personal recollections ". " I have somewhat the impression ", remarked the presiding judge at M. Flandin's trial, after having listened for two hours to his disquisitions on international affairs, 1919–1936, " that you are allowing this to become a history lecture, interesting, no doubt, and useful . . . but we are in a law-court." It is natural for a statesman in court to deal with the background of his actions, and thus widen the incidence of responsibility, and for one writing in prison, to plead his cause ; while affected impersonality and strained digressive ease are apt to be trying. With a more direct approach M. Flandin's book would be more convincing for the reader and more useful to the historian. But what stands out both in M. Flandin's book and evidence is that the crisis connected with the remilitarization of the Rhineland was the turning-point of his foreign policy ; and no wonder : it was a turning-point in history — *le relais où les destins changèrent de chevaux*.

Still, he himself was a principal in the crisis : what was his part, what were his conclusions, how did he apply them, and how does he view them now ? During the Rhineland negotiations of March 1936, M. Flandin lunched one day with some Members in the House of Commons, and a note of his conversation made at the time is reproduced in Mr. Boothby's autobiography. [3] He said that had he obtained

[1] *Le Procès Flandin devant la Haute Cour de Justice, 23-26 juillet 1946*. Librairie de Médicis. Paris, 1947.
[2] Pierre-Étienne Flandin, *Politique française, 1919–1940* (Histoire contemporaine). Paris : Les Éditions nouvelles.
[3] *I Fight to Live*, pages 136-7.

the approval of the British Government he would have
acted; that he had every reason to suppose that " the
Germans would have withdrawn without firing a shot ";
but that now the German occupation must be regarded
as a *fait accompli*.

> This completely changed the European situation.
> The French alliance with the Little Entente was now
> valueless.   In future they could not hope to give
> effective assistance to Poland, Czechoslovakia, Yugo-
> slavia, or Rumania, in the event of German aggression.
> " So far as I am concerned," he added, " this means
> a fundamental reorientation of French policy.   In my
> opinion, the last chance of saving central and eastern
> Europe from German domination has been thrown
> away.   So far as France is concerned we shall have
> to make the best terms with Germany we can get,
> and leave the rest of Europe to her fate."   He spoke
> with a cold passion which impressed us all; and I
> am quite sure he meant what he said.

One-third of M. Flandin's book, labelled " The Reign
of Illusions ", covers the years before 1935.   France
emerged from the war " fraternally united to her allies ",
and entered upon the " most pacific and least ambitious
period of her history ".

> Confidence in the League of Nations, collabora-
> tion and alliance with England; an international
> organization to assure peace, to guarantee the security
> of France, and to maintain the *status quo* in Europe;
> enforcement of the Peace Treaties, payment of
> reparations, disarmament of Germany — such were,
> after November 11, 1918, the aims which guided
> French foreign policy.

She therefore desired to endow the League with coercive
force; while the Anglo-Saxons conceived of it merely as
a " moral power " and deemed this sufficient.

> The sovereignty of the member States was to
> remain complete in all spheres and circumstances.

Thus theories which had made the fame of Jean-Jacques Rousseau were transferred from the individual to the collective plane. Nations were by nature good, honest, just, and peace-loving. Nothing had been lacking except a written international code. Now that a moral power received the mission and authority to expound that law, it would be automatically respected, and no one would think of infringing it.

But did not the difference largely turn on how much either side wished to see enforced? France and her satellites claimed finality for the new territorial status of Europe, while the Covenant drafted by the Anglo-Saxons admitted the possibility of treaty revision. Having failed to make the Covenant suit her needs and views, France found herself the " prisoner of her own policy ". " All States whose existence or interests were endangered, gathered to her, not to bring aid but to receive protection." M. Flandin admits that the policy of the French military chiefs " in helping Poland to enlarge her territory [in the east] beyond what was assigned to her at the Peace Conference was probably neither wise nor far-sighted ", and that he himself had never thought her a suitable ally : though opposed to Bolshevism, he would have preferred Russia (to whom he would not have refused frontier revisions). Indeed, were M. Flandin to sift his various arguments, he would find sounder explanations for British hesitancy than idyllic naivety.

Anyhow with M. Flandin " Utopian pacifism " soon loses its innocence and becomes an " epidemic sickness of mind and will ", engendered by laziness, cowardice, and self-indulgence. It reaches its climax in 1935,

> when China is left to shift for herself, America enacts her neutrality laws, England concludes a separate naval agreement with Hitler, and the sectarian blindness of the pacifists, by applying sanctions to Italy, destroys the only dam which, after Stresa, is being

raised against the European Imperialism of the Third Reich in full flush of rearmament.

Treacle and vinegar, home truths and dangerous half-truths, alternate in M. Flandin's narrative, and a strong case is often spoiled by acrimony: for France had undoubtedly a strong case as regards reparations and disarmament. While " Germany scientifically organized her insolvency ", and blubbered (*larmoyait*) at international conferences, " the British and American delegates vied in generosity to her ". This solicitude, M. Flandin suggests, was heightened by concern for the huge dollar and sterling loans granted to her: in 1931, to help the American bankers, President Hoover imposed a moratorium; and in 1932 an end was put to reparations. Now Schacht found it " as easy to finance an intensive rearmament programme as he had found it impossible to finance reparations ".

Germany had never honestly disarmed, but at Locarno the report of the control commission exposing her default was ignored by Chamberlain and Briand to enable her to enter the League. Next, schemes for " general disarmament " helped her to rearm; and this vertiginous course was pursued in spite of danger signals from within Germany. In November Hitler scored a great electoral success, and in December the principle of " equal rights " with France was conceded. In January 1933 he took office, and in March MacDonald presented a new disarmament plan at Geneva. In November he secured a 95 per cent vote, and in January 1934 Britain produced yet another plan. An impressive series: till M. Flandin caps it with a juxtaposition of Hitler's massacres on June 30, 1934, and Britain's refusal in July to guarantee the European territorial *status quo*! Or, again, he discerns in naval parity between France and Italy, as laid down at the Washington Conference, a British move to render France dependent on Britain.

13

Thus the Anglo-Saxons willed it that on sea France should at best be Italy's equal in the Mediterranean; on land, Germany's on her Eastern frontier. But in fact, French commitments in distant seas spelled inferiority in the Mediterranean; and Germany's army potential, inferiority on the Rhine.

This leads up to 1935–1939, and so does the account of France's allies in eastern Europe. Here her need of a second front against Germany blended with a " noble passion to guarantee the independence and integrity of the small Continental nations ". But the French system was based on grievous miscalculations; it brought no honour or profit to France, and disaster to her allies. M. Flandin writes with hardly veiled dislike about the Czechs and Poles, and continues in retrospect the campaigns which he carried on in 1938 and 1939 against succouring them. He praises the " heroism of the Polish armies ", and belittles their part in the defence of France : " the Polish forces formed on May 10 an incomplete division which was not fully trained " ; in reality at that date one complete division was in the *zone des armées*, joined later by another division and an armoured brigade, while two divisions were in process of formation. But his errors where Poles or Czechs are concerned are almost invariably to their disadvantage : a sure sign of bias. (And mistakes abound in the book : wrong dates, inaccurate statistics, bad demography, even slips in names — Sir Neville Chamberlain, Sir Eric Philipps, François Poncet, Schusnigg, Zalewski, etc. etc.).

M. Flandin is undoubtedly right in thinking that co-operation with the U.S.S.R. would have been sounder policy (this was the view held throughout by Lloyd George, the bugbear not of Polish politicians only) ; and he claims to have " saved the Franco-Russian entente from shipwreck " — " I met therein with intense ill-will from M. Laval [his Foreign Minister] . . . but forced him to

sign the Franco-Soviet Pact ". He does not add that
it was a different Pact from the one Barthou had drafted,
and merely blames M. Blum and his successors of the
Front Populaire for having made so little of it. M.
Flandin's attitude towards Russia is indeed in line with
the French tradition " which does not encumber the
conduct of foreign policy with ideological or sentimental
impediments ", and the remarkably rosy, even lyrical,
picture which he draws of conditions inside the U.S.S.R.
reminds the reader of stories told about *batiushka* Tsar
and the *moujiks* some forty or fifty years ago.

> Very few mistakes were made in the three five-
> year plans of 1927, 1932, and 1937. The enthusi-
> astic support of the people for the gigantic work of
> industrializing Russia was gained by a deliberate
> enlistment of the political idealism of one section,
> and of the patriotic faith of another. In the colossal
> factories which sprang up like mushrooms across the
> entire country and into Siberia . . . the one took
> pride in the success of the Soviet régime, while the
> other watched with admiration the growth of power
> and wealth of Holy Mother Russia.

And so on. But how much zeal for co-operation with the
U.S.S.R. was shown by M. Flandin during the decisive
period, February 1938 to August 1939 ?

When Barthou died in October 1934, his place at the
Quai d'Orsay was taken by Laval, who was retained by
M. Flandin in his Cabinet of November 8 : pressed to
form it in a single day, he says he had to keep on most
members of the preceding Government, " and especially
M. Laval ", though he disapproved of Laval's policy of a
Franco-German *rapprochement*.

> You may ask [said M. Flandin at his trial] how
> two different policies can co-exist within a Govern-
> ment. I shall give you the reason. . . . At that
> time the idea of co-operation with Germany for the

sake of European peace was not peculiar to Laval but was held all over Europe, and anyhow in London by, say, 80 per cent.

Thus Laval's presence had its uses. Screened by his policy "against the thunder-bolts of Anglo-Saxon pro-German super-pacifists", writes M. Flandin, "I meant to continue the policy . . . of obstructing German ambitions" by means of understandings with Britain, Italy, and Russia. Over the Saar plebiscite Laval had his way, and tried to turn it to account: "He let Berlin know that he would raise no difficulty or claim on that occasion" — and was repaid, on March 16, 1935, by Hitler's repudiation of the military clauses of Versailles. But, averse to anything suggesting an "encirclement" of Germany, he had apparently to be forced into the other negotiations. M. Flandin made him go to Rome in January 1935 and negotiate "a general clearing of mutual grievances " — " the principal clause . . . contained a renunciation by France of her economic treaty rights in Abyssinia ". And in a footnote:

> It is often said that there were secret clauses. This is absolutely wrong. M. Laval, on his return from Rome, informed me of the course the negotiations had taken which, he said, had been very difficult. It was only a private conversation with Mussolini which removed the last differences. Did he in that talk, as is alleged, promise Mussolini a "free hand " in Abyssinia ?

M. Flandin does not think so: at no time was such a promise cited to him by the Italians. [1]   But according to

---

[1] A very different story is incidentally told in Ciano's *Diario, 1937–1938* (December 24, 1938; page 313). When Lord Perth told him that day of Laval having asserted that only an economic conquest of Abyssinia had been conceded by France, Ciano claims to have replied: "This is wrong. I told Perth that the French were fully informed of our plan for territorial conquest. I told him also of a talk I had in Paris with Flandin in May 1935, in which he gave me advice about a suitable way for starting a conflict. He suggested that we should provoke a revolt of the Ras against the Negus which would serve as pretext for intervention."

General Gamelin, Badoglio told him in September 1935, that Mussolini claimed to have been given a "free hand" by Laval; in November 1935, Laval, then Prime Minister, told the Council of National Defence: "I have a secret treaty with Mussolini, and have done well to have it"; and in 1940 he claimed in the Secret Committee of the Senate to have said to Mussolini: "Henceforth you have a free hand but . . . *sur le plan pacifique*".[1] M. Paul-Boncour states[2] that Laval once offered to prove to him by the minutes of the talk in Rome that it was only about "economic penetration".

> But [asks M. Paul-Boncour], what was said in the *tête-à-tête* during the evening party at the Palazzo Farnese . . .? We shall never know. Perhaps they said nothing to each other. . . . But if they did speak of Abyssinia, and if then . . . by a shrug of the shoulder or a wink of the eye — Vandervelde who knew them both well was sure it was thus that it must have happened — M. Laval allowed M. Mussolini to understand that he would not be too severe should a military expedition be attempted . . .

In short, the secrets of the much vaunted "diplomacy by conference" of the League period will never be known. Moreover, Laval was Prime Minister and Foreign Minister while the Abyssinian crisis was acute — June 1935 to January 1936; M. Flandin was only "Minister of State", and Laval "consulted his colleagues as little as possible" on the conduct of foreign affairs.

> The custom had grown up that a Premier who held the Foreign Office would report to the Cabinet on his foreign policy but not consult them beforehand.

When on January 24, 1936, in Sarraut's Cabinet, M. Flandin assumed the Foreign Office, "I had", he says, "but one preoccupation: the Rhineland". Here he expected Hitler to try his next *coup*. When in London

[1] *Servir*, ii. 172, 179, and 182.   [2] *Entre les deux guerres*, iii. 14-16.

for the funeral of King George V, M. Flandin asked Mr. Baldwin in Mr. Eden's presence what line Britain would take should Germany thus break the Locarno agreement. Mr. Baldwin replied by inquiring what decision had been reached by the French Government. " I could merely express my personal opinion : that it would resist." Back in Paris, M. Flandin put the question to the first meeting of the Sarraut Cabinet. " I had the impression that my colleagues thought me too much in a hurry, but I obtained that the Supreme Military Committee should be summoned to examine what measures ought to be taken. . . ." And at the trial :

> The Cabinet accepted my proposal to tell the British Government that France would not agree to a reoccupation of the Rhineland. But I said this was not enough, that a decision without a plan of action was of small value, and that I would not take the risk of France backing out after having told the British Government that she would act. . . .

The Supreme Military Committee met a few days later ; the Service Ministers and their advisers were reticent, and when asked by M. Flandin " what military measures could be taken immediately . . . the War Minister explained . . . that the French Army had been given an entirely defensive character and had nothing prepared . . . for a military intervention such as I had suggested " ; the Minister of Marine said that the co-operation of the British Navy was needed for blockading Germany ; and the Air Minister that bombardment from the air would be an act of war.

> It was perhaps unique in French history that the Foreign Minister . . . should take the bellicose line while the Service Ministers did not think of fighting for the Rhineland. On my expressing astonishment at the negative attitude of my colleagues, General Gamelin intervened and said that the General Staff

was an executive organ, and that it was for the
Government to decide; their decision would be
carried out. . . .

M. Flandin reported to the Cabinet and, as he was
starting for Geneva, asked what answer he should carry
to Mr. Eden : he was authorized to say that " the French
Government would place all its forces . . . at the disposal of the League of Nations to oppose by force a violation of treaties ", and he was to invoke British aid under
the Locarno Treaty. To this Mr. Eden replied that he
would report to his Government, and send their answer
through the diplomatic channels. (No precise dates of
meetings, talks, etc., are given in M. Flandin's book.)

But Hitler acted first. The French Chamber of
Deputies having ratified the pact with the U.S.S.R. on
February 27, Neurath, on March 7, presented a memorandum to the Ambassadors of the Locarno Powers
declaring that treaty annulled by the Franco-Soviet Pact,
and offering the usual flummery of long-term non-
aggression pacts, a demilitarized zone on both sides of
the frontier (thus scrapping the Maginot Line), and
ultimately Germany's re-entry into the League ! At noon
Hitler announced that the German troops were on the
march. When the Cabinet met in Paris, writes M. Flandin,

> there was pitiful confusion. I reported on the situa-
> tion and said that I had immediately notified the
> Secretary of the League of Nations. It was, unfor-
> tunately, an obligation under the Locarno Treaty
> to have contraventions established by the League
> Council; and I knew that in London great import-
> ance was attached to that procedure, even by friends
> most determined to stand by the Locarno Treaty. I
> asked what military measures were envisaged and
> when they would be carried out, though I reported
> that the British Government insistently urged us not
> to take any measure prejudicing the future before
> the representatives of the Locarno guarantors had

met. Whereupon the War Minister stated, to my utter stupefaction, that all that was envisaged was to man the Maginot Line and to move two divisions from the Rhône Valley to the eastern frontier. He added that for action in the Rhineland the General Staff demanded a general mobilization.

This provoked turmoil in the Cabinet. A general mobilization six weeks before a general election, what folly! declared some of my colleagues. . . . Finally only four of us were for immediate military action: the Premier M. Sarraut, M. Mandel, M. Paul-Boncour, and myself. . . . The Cabinet would await reactions, at home and abroad.

But at home politicians were pre-occupied with the forth-coming elections: the Right denounced the Soviet Pact as the source of evil, and the Left Laval's Abyssinian policy. In Belgium the young King, the Flemings, and the Socialists were turning " neutral ", and the Prime Minister, M. van Zeeland, " acted the super-pacifist ". In England the Press was finding excuses for Hitler. M. Sarraut tried to rouse French public opinion, and declared in a broadcast, prepared by the Quai d'Orsay: " We are not willing to let Strasbourg come under the fire of the German guns ". But the response was poor. " Decidedly," remarks M. Flandin, " France had lost *le sens national*."

" On March 6 [it should be 10] the Conference of the Locarno Powers opened in Paris." M. Flandin explained that France unaided could force the Germans to withdraw, but that she would adhere to the League procedure. Not her security alone was at stake, but also her ability to fulfil, across a re-fortified Rhineland, obligations assumed within the League framework towards Austria, Czechoslovakia, and Poland. The territorial status of Europe was endangered. Mr. Eden, " who himself seemed to share my views ", repeated the warning of the British Government against any irretrievable step: they did not mean to evade their Locarno obligations, but thought the conflict could be settled by negotiation. Belgium, " as much interested in a demilitarized Rhineland as France ", supported Britain.

> I then pleaded with all my strength . . . that any adjournment of action would almost certainly result in final inaction. I declared that all delay in the *riposte* practically signified acquiescence. . . . Negotiations . . . would be futile, or rather would sanction a new renunciation [*abandon*] ; and this one will be decisive, for it will engender an entire series of new renunciations.

As the British delegates lacked authority to go any farther, M. Flandin referred to his own Government. He warned them against getting bogged in negotiations ; under Locarno France was free to act after a contravention of the demilitarization clauses was established, " or perhaps even before, though this was disputed by Britain " ; anyhow, preparatory measures (a decision to mobilize) should be taken immediately, though it might be already too late.

> But we must face the fact that England will disapprove, and Belgium will disavow our action. The Cabinet must consider whether, in the present and future interest of France, the risk should be taken of negotiating or of a serious disagreement with England. For my part, I continued to favour resistance.

Again the Service Ministers aired their difficulties, and the trimmers their doubts : why court difficulties when the English undertake to negotiate the evacuation of the Rhineland ? M. Flandin and M. Paul-Boncour were sent to London to act " for the best interests of France ". The game was lost, and M. Flandin had foreseen it. But on March 18-19 he obtained a reaffirmation of Locarno and what he describes as tantamount to an Anglo-French military alliance. (M. Flandin, in his references to the *Text of Proposals* of March 19, and the covering *Correspondence* of April 1, 1936 — published in this country as Cmd. 5134 and 5149 — tends to ascribe to them more of a treaty character than the documents warrant.) Under that agreement, writes M. Flandin, any fortification of the Rhineland would immediately reopen " the question of military intervention by France and the guaranteeing Powers, Britain and Italy ".

> I have always been asking myself why my successors in office never, to my knowledge, invoked the London Agreement, especially when work on the Siegfried Line was started. I had been careful to draw M. Blum's particular attention to this capital point in the London Agreement.

It might be thought that an answer was contained in M. Flandin's own foregoing observations. But while frequent changes of Government hamper policy, they enable ex-Ministers freely to discourse on how they would have managed the situation they bequeathed to their successors.

In the Rhineland crisis M. Flandin had a difficult hand to play. He was let down by the military : General Gamelin's cautious language and elaborate explanations fail to hide his negative attitude ; even now he adduces thickly padded figures of Germany's military strength in 1936 ; [1] and the remark which he records that he made to the Staff,[2] " Whatever the cost, no one must be able to say that the Army did not dare to march ", gives the game away. In the Cabinet temporizing weakness prevailed, while the country was rent politically and was " Maginot-minded ". The League was a *salle des pas perdus*. In Britain, Government and public opinion alike favoured appeasement. And yet — did not M. Flandin himself play to weakness? Before he had ever spoken to the military or to the British, he assumed that France might " back out ". And in February, according to General

[1] See *Servir*, ii. 199, 201, and 208-11.   [2] *Ibid.* pages 203-4.

Gamelin, the Foreign Office inquired what conditions would need to be exacted should the Government decide to admit a limited remilitarization of the Rhineland.[1] In the reply which M. Flandin gave to Mr. Eden, again before the Germans had moved, the responsibility was passed on to the League; whereas M. Paul-Boncour, its greatest champion in France and Minister for League Affairs, having quoted the relevant paragraphs of the Locarno Treaty, writes:[2]

> We need not have asked either Allies or League; we should have acted *first*. *After* having acted, *after* having replied to an occupation contravening the treaty by the only nethod whereby it could be met immediately, that is by checking it, we ought to have gone to Geneva or The Hague to argue the case, if a case was brought up.

Nor was there any point in asking London, unless dissuasion was invited. But what was it in fact that M. Flandin asked of Great Britain on March 7, the day on which an immediate military *riposte* to Hitler was imperative? Did he propose such action or did he suggest a preliminary meeting of the Locarno Powers in Paris to concert about the case to be put before the League Council? If this was what he asked for (as the available evidence seems to indicate), then it was he himself who gave away the case at the decisive hour; and his subsequent objurgations and imprecations seem to have been better calculated to establish his alibi for the future than to produce effective action. He himself admits: ". . . we could have forced Britain's hand. The Locarno Treaty gave us the right to act. . . . I believe Britain would have stood by her engagements. . . ." But this, he thinks, would have been the end of the Entente: which does not prevent him from blaming his successors for not trying to force Britain's hand over Austria in 1938, under

[1] *Ibid.* page 197.   [2] *Entre les deux guerres*, iii. 32.

far worse conditions; and in the supreme crisis of August–
September 1939, M. Flandin was ready to dissociate
himself from Britain altogether. Nor does he, in searching the international horizon, mention the offer made by
Poland on the very day of reoccupation to mobilize
immediately; it only appears during the London Conference, prefaced: " Le Colonel Beck, dont la mauvaise foi
éclatait. . . ." And a hundred pages farther M. Flandin
slips in the incidental remark that it was " under cover (*à
l'abri*) " of the German-Polish Treaty of 1934 that " in
1936 Hitler remilitarized the Rhineland " !

The centre for action lay in the French Cabinet —
did M. Flandin give them a steady, determined lead ?
No minutes were kept. But M. Paul-Boncour, a witness
not unfriendly to M. Flandin, writes about its meeting of
March 10 : [1]

> I still see and hear M. Flandin summing up con-
> clusions without a vote being taken : with his arm
> in a sling, after a serious accident of which he bravely
> bore the consequences, he inclined his tall figure
> towards the Premier, next to whom he was seated :
> " I see, Mr. Prime Minister, one must not insist."
>
> Wherein he was wrong. The Premier would have
> been happy if the Minister best qualified to do so,
> had insisted and made the Government speak out
> and give effect to his [Sarraut's] broadcast of two
> days before. . . .

And according to M. Sarraut,[2] when M. Flandin spoke of
the choice before France, and of Britain being " forced
to follow us " but doing so " ungraciously and with dis-
approval " :

> " *Qu'importe !* " exclaimed Mandel. " If we don't
> act, a few years hence England and America, having
> changed their view, will charge us with having
> through cowardice lost Europe, and perhaps the
> world, which will be much more serious."

[1] *Entre les deux guerres*, iii. 35.
[2] Quoted after Reynaud, *La France a sauvé l'Europe*, i. 553-4 n.

M. Reynaud said, early in 1937, that in the Rhineland crisis the Government had taken " a middle line between action and inaction : they talked ". Indeed, every argument which could be adduced in favour of military intervention was put forward by M. Flandin, then and since : but he did not enforce action as Clemenceau or Poincaré would have done (or Mandel, not handicapped by being a Jew). And M. Flandin himself remarked at his trial : " You would, at bottom, be justified in saying to me : ' If this was your view, why, *quand même*, did you not march into the Rhineland ? ' "

His reply, in court and in his book, seems hardly sufficient. He finishes by talking, for short, about " the British veto ". But can the gravest responsibilities be shifted ?

The Front Populaire having won the general election of May 1936, M. Flandin was henceforth in opposition. From a visit to Berlin in December 1937, he returned convinced that Germany meant action, and he gave to the Agence Radio a " deliberately Sibylline " statement on the choice which the French Government and nation would soon have to face ; but he says nothing in his book about the very outspoken campaign which he now started for a radical change in French foreign policy. For instance, in his speech at Bordeaux, on February 13, 1938, he advocated *rapprochement* with Germany and Italy as the alternative to rearmament, which, he said, served the purpose of the Communists, also in that it prepared the ruin of public finances ; and he named no conditions for his suggested *détente*. On February 12 Herr Schuschnigg was ordered at Berchtesgaden to take the Austrian Nazis into his Government, and on the 27th M. Flandin wrote in the *Sunday Times* :

. . . the problem of peace or war can no longer be shelved. And for the French public it is and will be as follows :

Should France allow herself to be inveigled into a war as a result of her adhesion to an ideological *bloc*, falsely named the camp of democracies, against the totalitarian States, *i.e.*, Germany and Italy?

He was urging a settlement with Italy — but one with Germany was also part of his new gospel of " realism ". In an interview published in the *Temps* on March 3, he asks : " Is it impossible to think of a solution for Germany which would not necessarily be colonial and which would solve the problem of her surplus-population (*des excédents allemands*) ? " And the interviewer wondered whether M. Flandin thought of South America or of the Ukraine — " knowing that he would not answer, we did not ask." M. Flandin, at his trial, claimed to have been the only one in Parliament on February 26 " to demand action in Austria " ; but the Paris correspondent of *The Times* reporting the debate speaks about M. Flandin's doctrine " which appeared to involve the utter renunciation of French influence or interest outside the national borders ".

M. Flandin describes " the surrender of Vienna " as " much more shameful " than Munich, recalls the obligations under innumerable treaties to uphold Austria's " independence ", and expatiates on the international alignment which there was in 1938 for action against Germany — " even Italy could not have stood aside ". Mussolini " awaited offers ", but Chamberlain " sacrificed Eden too late ", while France did nothing, though her " interest in the international arena demanded a *rapprochement* with Italy, be it at the cost of a change of the [Governmental] majority at home ".[1] " No doubt, just as in 1936, England would not have followed France in 1938 in a trial of strength with Germany over Austria . . . but there was nothing against trying." And though the military superiority of France was no longer what it had

---

[1] *I.e.* a change of the combination of parties on which the Government was based.

been in 1936, this was the time " for strong and quick action " if the Versailles settlement was to be restored; and even if England would not face the risk of war, it was the duty of France, exposed to the main impact of the German armies, to meet it in time. But then one may well ask why all these considerations had not *a fortiori* made M. Flandin act over the Rhineland? He propounds the argument that the unilateral Locarno guarantees created " a kind of subordination of France to Britain's will ", from which he freed her by the reciprocal " treaty " of March 18, 1936. Clever, perhaps, but hardly convincing. Nor does M. Flandin's assertion seem credible that Italy, even after having abandoned Austria to Hitler, " was ripe for a great deal ", and that " throughout April Mussolini awaited in vain a serious offer from France ".[1] " Rome ", says M. Flandin, " would go to the highest bidder, and where the risk was least "; but he does not say what offers the Western Powers could have made to Mussolini comparable to those of Hitler, nor how in view of the Rhineland fiasco, Spain, the *Anschluss*, and their own failure to rearm, they could have convinced him of their superior strength and daring.

At the end of February, a week before Hitler entered Vienna, M. Flandin wrote, looking ahead to the crisis next but one: ". . . since the Communist Party disposes of numerous and various sources of publicity, an attempt will be made to exploit national and even nationalist feeling against Hitler's claims in respect of Czechoslovakia ".[2] And on June 12 he referred in terms of indignant surprise to reports that a general mobilization order had been prepared in France at the end of May during the crisis over Czechoslovakia — an unwarranted

[1] Ciano writes in his *Diario, 1937–1938* (April 20, 1938), page 161: " Talks with Piccio [Air Attaché in Paris]: Flandin sends word that, if we wish it, he is ready to put forward his candidature for the Rome Embassy." The Italian reply is not given.

[2] *Sunday Times*, February 27, 1938.

step unless France herself were attacked or until every method of conciliation and arbitration had been exhausted. But on June 18 Hitler wrote in one of his secret army directives : " I will decide to take action against Czechoslovakia only if I am firmly convinced, as in the case of the demilitarized zone and the entry into Austria, that France will not march and therefore England will not intervene ". When, between Godesberg and Munich, it seemed that the Western Powers would make a stand against Hitler, on September 28 M. Flandin put out the placard addressed " Au Peuple français " which started : " Peuple français, on te trompe. Je prends pour moi seul le risque de te le dire " ; he alleged that " a clever mechanism " had been set up " for weeks or months past to render war inevitable ", and argued that whether the German troops entered the Sudetenland before or after the frontier had been drawn was a mere "question of procedure". After Munich he sent telegrams to Chamberlain, Daladier, Hitler, and Mussolini, warmly congratulating them on peace having been preserved : and now he defends the one to Hitler by pointing to the other three, but fails to explain why Hitler, who alone had endangered peace and had been bought off by the sacrifice of an allied nation, should have been included in the congratulations.

But to Flandin (and the Germans) Czechoslovakia " was a factitious and artificial creation of the peace treaties ". By 1938 Germany was superior to France on land and in the air ; the League of Nations had ceased to count ; the British " alliance " of 1936 covered direct aggression against France only. " The most elementary prudence should have made France revise her engagements." Moreover, through the Runciman mission, Britain had " assumed full responsibility for the events which were to result in the Munich agreement " ; and the joint *démarche* of the Western Powers in Prague on

September 21 postulated "a partial dismemberment of Czechoslovakia " —

> from that moment there could be no question of France giving military assistance to Czechoslovakia under the treaties of 1924 and 1925, as German aggression would have been provoked by Czechoslovakia not accepting conditions deemed satisfactory by Great Britain and France. This is a capital point, for it destroys the perfidious insinuation, so often repeated, that France broke her word to Czechoslovakia. Moreover, both treaties were fitted into the framework of the Covenant. A previous appeal to the League Council . . . formed an absolute obligation incumbent on Czechoslovakia, from which France could not have released her.

France herself had adhered to that procedure over the Rhineland. " There was therefore no breach of any French engagement towards Czechoslovakia." How simple it all is, and how much fuss there was about nothing !

And here is M. Flandin's peroration :

> Frenchmen who, having formed an independent judgment on the indisputable unpreparedness of their country for war, tried to defer it so as to gain time for the nation to brace itself, to re-arm, and to find allies and indispensable supports, will be able to assert that they served better the interests of France, and ultimately of a world coalition against Hitler, than those converts to a belated *bellicisme* who, playing Hitler's game, were to involve France, Europe, and the world in one of the greatest catastrophes in human history.

Hitler would, of course, have waited till France was ready.

It was towards Russia, says M. Flandin, " the greatest Continental Empire in the world ", that " our eyes should have turned ". Russia's help could have restored the balance. But early in 1940, during the Russo-Finnish

War, M. Flandin, in a secret session of the Chamber of Deputies, demanded immediate military action against Russia — " in vain ", he complains.

M. Léon Noël, French Ambassador in Warsaw, when commenting on Hitler's speech of April 28, 1939, pointed out that Hitler placed Danzig in the foreground expecting that Britain and France would think it too insignificant to warrant Polish resistance, but that Danzig was neither the cause nor object of the conflict (which assertion Hitler himself confirmed in the secret address to his commanders-in-chief on May 23). Still, in M. Flandin's book the chapter on German-Polish relations, March–August 1939, bears the title : " Danzig ". And though he himself admits that " Danzig was merely a façade ", he alleges that this is how the problem presented itself to French public opinion :

> Will you fight to prevent Danzig, which does not belong to Poland but is a German city under League control, from rejoining the German community in accordance with the wish of its population ? Do you want war because the Poles refuse to let a German *autostrade*, which will link up two German provinces, pass across their territory . . . ?

If it was a fight for freedom and civilization, " no one had taken the trouble of saying so to the French people " (there were on this occasion no placards, " Peuple français, on te trompe "). M. Flandin says that Hitler's proposals of April 28 rather surprised the world by their moderation.

> For four months Hitler's offer remained before the public for consideration and criticism. By an incredible default on the part of the British and French Governments, it evoked no discussion or counter-proposal.

But even the terms of Ribbentrop's " gabbled Note " of August 30 were for M. Flandin " comparatively moderate " ; they " should have served as a basis for negotiation ", and " every endeavour should have been made by London and Paris to obtain from the Polish Government the immediate dispatch of a plenipotentiary to Berlin " — a repetition of the Schuschnigg and Hacha performances.

It would be as idle as it would be impossible to try to follow up M. Flandin's contradictions, misstatements, and distortions, especially in the chapters on March–September 1939. But here is an example of history rewritten : Ribbentrop was disappointed in his hopes that the Franco-German *rapprochement* of December 1938 would result in economic *pourparlers* ; the British Government, too, was averse to economic negotiations with Germany ; Hitler, " blockaded financially and economically, seems to have resolved upon war ".

> On March 1, Dr. Funk made the Reichsbank guarantee German exports. . . . The American Government replied by raising the tariff on German imports to the U.S.A. by 25 per cent. Thereupon Hitler decides (*Hitler décide, alors*) to lay hands on the riches of Bohemia, and especially on her considerable resources in foreign exchange and gold.

About the outbreak of war, M. Flandin's thesis is roughly this : The French Government were being deceived by stories of Hitler's " bluffing " : in reality war at that juncture " served the interests of Germany " ; " the majority of Frenchmen, if consulted, would probably have rejected war " ; the French Government let itself be dragged along by the British, who sometimes even took it upon themselves to speak for France ; there was something approaching sabotage of the Italian mediation of August 31–September 2 ; the French Government violated the Constitution in declaring war without a vote of Parliament : " had there been a vote on September 2, the Government would have been disavowed " ; before going to war they ought to have brought the matter before the League of Nations — and here follows once more the story of the Rhineland. In a private talk with Daladier on August 27, " I begged him ", writes Flandin, " not to let himself be dragged into war. . . . And I pointed out to him that he would be held doubly responsible having been War Minister for so many years (. . . five out of the seven preceding the war)."

About the Armistice M. Flandin says that " its terms were not harder . . . than those imposed on the Germans " in 1918. " It did not prejudge the future; no territorial cessions, no renunciations. . . . Only the occupation payments were heavier." But before the world France was " charged with having acted egotistically and harmed her ally, Great Britain ", when in reality Britain gained by the provisional neutralization of the African coast; though some disappointment was naturally felt in Britain when the Germans were thus enabled to turn immediately against her.

> But we, too, had experienced similar bitter disappointments in the preceding battle which settled the fate of France; we had awaited in vain the British fighter force which saved England in September, 1940, and which perhaps would not have saved France in May, 1940.

Perhaps there is some difference between trying to stop an invasion across the Channel and an advance across the plains of Northern France. M. Reynaud, then Premier, tells the story. At the meeting with Mr. Churchill, on May 31, he pressed for additional air support; " and henceforth," he writes, " not a day passed without my taking up again, often several times, the plea for an increase in British help, especially, of course, by the R.A.F." On June 10 Mr. Churchill replied: " We are giving you all the support we can in this great battle, short of ruining the capacity of this country to continue the war ". And looking back, M. Reynaud writes : [1]

> Subsequent events have proved that Churchill would have committed the greatest mistake if in the Battle of France he had sacrificed all his air force, which, a few weeks later, was indispensable for the defence of England against the German air offensive. I am not certain today that I then sufficiently reckoned with that danger which bore on the fate of France as much as on that of England. . . . But in the first days of June I was entirely taken up with the battle which we fought in defence of Paris. . . . The event has proved that the Prime Minister went as far as the care of our great common interests allowed him to go.

M. Flandin's book benefits no cause which he may have had at heart in writing it.

[1] *La France a sauvé l'Europe*, ii. 270.

REYNAUD

It was a tragic choice that France had to face in August–
September 1939, and the title of M. Reynaud's book,
La France a sauvé l'Europe,[1] is a reply to the would-be
Munichois of that summer and defeatists of the next who,
exploiting the post-war torment, try to resume, by way of
covert counter-attack, the argument of the Riom court-
house. In 1940 France, the nation which dominated the
continent of Europe when Europe was supreme in the
world, suffered the most catastrophic and humiliating defeat
in all her history, hardly set off by the subsequent allied
victory. The Second World War hastened developments
which were inherent in the progressing redistribution of
population and resources; but for France they are stamped
by the *débâcle* brought on by her moral and material unpreparedness in 1939. There is a case to answer.

> In the proceedings which it behoves France to
> open against herself [writes M. Reynaud] I come
> forward to testify.
> Deputy since 1919 (barring 1924–28), several
> times Minister, and Prime Minister at the moment
> of the disaster, I have seen and heard much. I also
> assumed responsibilities, before and during the war.
> I deny none. I have accounts to render. I shall
> render them. . . .
> After the liberation of the land comes that of the
> spirit . . . France needs to know. . . .
> . . . Let us work to restore to our people a sense
> of greatness. . . .
> . . . It is our last chance.

"After 1918 the French soul bore the impress of
martyrdom, not of victory." But, through the loss of the

[1] Paul Reynaud, *La France a sauvé l'Europe*. Two vols. Paris: Flam-
marion.

élite, martyrdom enfeebles a nation, and " a moral flexion had already started about the end of the last century ". France wanted peace, but not the means which secure it. Locarno was the game of an ostrich — " there was an element of Munich in Locarno ". Then came the rise of Hitler, and the gradual decline of France : lassitude, the wishful illusion of exclusive defence " under shelter of the Maginot Line ", hence *la démission de la France*. Even worse — ultra-pacifism which declared : " slavery rather than war " ; and a patriotism conditional on one's own side being in power : " Hitler rather than Blum ". There was inter-action between moral decline and material failure. When war came France had neither the allies she needed, nor the fortifications, nor the arms. How had this come about ? M. Reynaud attempts to answer the question.

Great Britain was for France " a necessary but insufficient ally ".

> To-day [wrote M. Reynaud in 1937], we need, as we did in 1914, instantaneous and powerful succour in the first hour. . . . If the French subordinate the imperative requirements of their foreign policy to their internal quarrels . . . it will be vain to shed tears when Russia comes to an agreement with Germany, which is not an imaginary danger.

Barthou meant the Franco-Russian Pact to provide for immediate aid and assistance in case of unprovoked aggression by a European Power against either country. His successor Laval deleted that clause : not to give Stalin the decision about peace, he gave Hitler the decision about war.

> The treaty of May 2, 1935, concluded by the Flandin-Laval Government, is the most confused and ineffective document ever produced by French diplomacy.

The Contracting Parties made their action depend on the decision of the League Council, which provision rendered the treaty meaningless. Russia desired a military convention with France. In July 1935 her Ambassador raised the question with Colonel Fabry, War Minister in Laval's Cabinet. " Fabry refused . . . without consulting . . . either the Council of National Defence or the Supreme Military Committee." General Maurin, War Minister when the Pact was signed, and again during the remilitarization of the Rhineland, said in Cabinet, as Laval was starting for Moscow: " From the military point of view the Russian alliance is devoid of interest ". Pétain objected to it, for it would make Communism an " admissible doctrine " ; and some, because the Germans would feel " encircled ".

" Domestic politics determined the attitude of the majority of Frenchmen in foreign politics, whether towards Italy or towards Russia."

> Was an alliance with Fascist Italy possible? What could we offer to Mussolini? The *status quo*. But such fare would not have satisfied either his personal ambitions or the needs of a régime which required prestige.

Moreover, Mussolini would always go with whom he thought stronger. There was therefore no chance of retaining him in the Stresa camp after France had shown weakness.

> Do you see Machiavelli espousing weakness? A beautiful subject for a tapestry! The camp of weakness and the *status quo* meant to Mussolini taking risks without profit. But what prospects of booty there were in the camp of force!

It would therefore have been to the interest of France to bring him down over Abyssinia, as it would have been to bring down Hitler over the Rhineland.

France failed to fortify her frontier; M. Reynaud blames Pétain; while War Ministers changed, he was a fixture of the inter-war period. In 1922 Joffre proposed to establish a series of " fortified regions ", from Dunkirk to Belfort. " Pétain opposed it, and Joffre had to resign." Pétain believed in " the continuous battlefield " of trench warfare. But in 1927 he agreed to two fortified sectors on the Alsace-Lorraine frontier. The Maginot Line was started — cover for eighty out of 450 miles of frontier: the northern plain remained open. In 1932, prompted by Weygand and Gamelin, Tardieu wanted to fortify it. Pétain objected — " it would mean leaving the Belgian Army to itself ". (But Gamelin points out that what the Belgians dreaded most was that the Maginot Line would divert the Germans to the unfortified north and make them march once more across Belgium.[1]) In 1934 Pétain, then War Minister, explained to the Army Committee of the Senate that in the north the frontier was too close to the objects to be covered — " it is necessary to advance into Belgium ". " Lille will be protected by Belgian fortifications." With his full concurrence the doctrine of " systematic defence " was adopted by successive French Governments : " it answered the secret desire of a nation exhausted by the heavy losses of the preceding war ". " The legend was born of the war of concrete walls, a war without tears : which was to turn into the ' phoney war '." France imagined she had a cuirass; she had but bits of one, and even these were not proof against the new weapons. But " to say to an army : ' You shall fight only from behind concrete', means to kill its morale ". " To have given France a *defensive* army is one of the most serious signs of our intellectual and moral declension during the inter-war period."

France required either a Maginot Line from the North Sea to the Swiss border, with a properly equipped defens-

[1] *Servir*, ii. 68-9.

ive army, or a European policy of balance of power;
that is, adequate allies in the East and an offensive striking
force capable of succouring such allies. But France had
weak allies in the East and no army fit to relieve them;
there was a contradiction between her foreign and her
military policy. And her own fortifications were so
incomplete that her army, organized for defence, was
doomed to encounter the powerful German offensive in
the open plains of Belgium. " Future historians will
wonder at so much incoherence."

" Our heavy losses before Sebastopol produced General
Frossard's fatal doctrine of systematic defence which led
to the catastrophe of 1870." By way of reaction, on the
eve of 1914 a school arose which preached a systematic
offensive, " of advancing, always advancing, regardless of
losses. . . . The influence of that school was considerable
. . . as is seen in the initial offensives of August 1914."
But the great leaders arrived at a synthesis. Pétain alone,
through " the sarcastic pessimism and the defeatism which
. . . underlie his nature . . . was inclined to revert to
the defensive of General Frossard "; and " a man never
gives up a doctrine or a faith which answers the basic
needs of his nature ". *Le feu tue* remained his slogan, and
the unassailable continuous front his doctrine : he believed
in the decisive superiority of the defence. In his *Instructions* of 1921 he assigned a merely accessory rôle to tanks —
" they facilitate the advance of the infantry ". Meanwhile the Maginot Line engendered a legend, and " systematic defence " became a cherished tenet of the French
nation. In 1934 Pétain became War Minister in Dou-
mergue's great Coalition Government, while Weygand
was Commander-in-Chief; and they did nothing to
render the French Army fit to resist the rising Nazi
danger. " Victories are apt to burden an army with the
reign *des vieillards glorieux*." Its doctrine remained unchanged. In 1936 new directives were issued revising

those of 1921 : while professing to take account of the technical progress, they still adhered to " the body of doctrine fixed on the morrow of victory by eminent chiefs who had held high commands ". Tanks, it was thought, would be countered by anti-tank weapons, as the infantry was by machine-guns in the previous war, and would be able to attack only under cover of massed artillery fire. In 1938 General Chauvineau published a book, *Is an Invasion still Possible?*, with an introduction by Pétain praising him for having " shown that a continuous front answers both the lessons of history and the nature of the arms and fortifications ". Here are a few of Chauvineau's dicta : " A war of movement . . . is no longer possible in France. Mechanization has killed it." " Railways and motor transport have rendered fronts unassailable." " A break-through is chimerical." " The tanks, which were to have reinstated short wars, are a signal failure." A motorized attack against a continuous front " will bite the dust ". The terrors of war evoked in the last ten years " are based on a complete misconception of military possibilities ". The book, with Pétain's introduction, was republished in 1940.

In June 1936 M. Blum, on assuming the Premiership, inquired about the state of the French Army ; Pétain replied that it was " in perfect condition and fit to face any army ". And General Weygand said, in a speech on July 4, 1939 :

> You ask me how I feel about the French Army. I shall tell you frankly, solely concerned with the truth, which in no way embarrasses me. I believe that the French Army is of greater intrinsic value than ever in its history : its armament is of the first quality, its fortifications are of the first order, its morale is excellent, and its leadership outstanding. None of us desires war, but I affirm that if forced to win a new victory, we shall win it.

And Daladier, in the Council of National Defence, on
August 23, 1939 :

> France had agreed to make a massive effort for
> the sake of a fortified system protecting her frontiers.
> . . . Now that France is called upon to struggle
> alone for several months, we are in a position to
> appreciate the security which we derive from the
> existence of our fortifications.

M. Reynaud was one of the very few who did not
pin their faith to the defensive system. In July 1924 he
published an article : " Have we the army of our needs
or the army of our habits ? " To enforce the peace
treaties it should be able to go " fast and far " — shock
troops for offensive action. And in the army debate of
March 15, 1935, he said :

> A country should have the army of its policy.
> Have we perhaps abandoned the policy of assistance
> and pacts ? Or do we consider that we can claim
> assistance in London, but need not carry it to Vienna,
> Prague, or Brussels ?

The War Minister, General Maurin, replied :

> How can anyone believe that we still think of an
> offensive after having spent milliards on a fortified
> barrier ? Should we be so mad as to go beyond that
> barrier, in search of I don't know what adventure ?

In 1936 General de Gaulle published his book, *Vers
l'armée de métier*, a plea for an armoured corps, a specialized,
independent striking force : distinguished not so much by
the number and type of its tanks as by the way in which
they were to be employed. Even before the book appeared
M. Reynaud had become the Parliamentary exponent of
General de Gaulle's military doctrine. On March 28,
1935, he tabled a motion for a " specialized corps " of
long-service professional soldiers, 100,000 men strong,
comprising six divisions with a total of 3000 tanks ; to be
completed not later than April 15, 1940. " Our great

military chiefs ", writes M. Reynaud, " unanimously declared against my motion." General Gamelin, the most open-minded among them, told him : " We are moving in your direction ; don't hustle the Army ".

On March 7, 1936, Hitler reoccupied the Rhineland and started building his Siegfried Line. On October 14 Belgium denounced her military agreement with France and reverted to " neutrality ". This produced a new strategic position. Hitler knew that the Western Powers would not violate Dutch or Belgian neutrality, which therefore offered perfect cover for the northern, more vulnerable, part of the Rhineland and the Ruhr ; but it was equally certain that Hitler would respect neutrality only as long as it suited him. The Western Powers would now have to wait with entering Belgium till after the Germans had done so : the plan of an initial French con-centration behind the Antwerp–Liège–Arlon line was no longer feasible. The system was breaking down ; and yet there was no change in French military conceptions. Parallel was the failure with regard to the French Air Force : scarcity of aircraft and an erroneous conception concerning the modes of employing them.

Lastly there was the defective organization of the Service Ministries and High Command. A Minister of National Defence was appointed without proper staff, and he, whose task it should have been to co-ordinate the three services, usually held also the War Office (more-over, 1938–1940, M. Daladier combined the two with the Premiership). There was no Ministry of Supplies or Munitions. General Gamelin was Chief of Staff of National Defence, Commander-in-Chief of all land forces, and Commander-in-Chief of the North-Eastern front — again an impossible accumulation of functions. Since the summer of 1936 he had wished to be relieved of the command of the armies. But it was not till January 1940 that General Georges replaced him as Commander-in-

Chief of the North-Eastern Front, and even then with incomplete powers; there were entangled responsibilities and divided authority.

M. Reynaud, Minister of Finance in 1930, was a member of the Parliamentary Finance Committee. During his speech on army organization, on March 15, 1935, General Maurin, Minister for War, remarked to M. Mandel: " So M. Paul Reynaud now busies himself with military problems? What would people say if I dabbled in financial questions? " Then a chance came to M. Reynaud of removing to the Army Committee, and even of becoming its chairman.

> Was I wrong in not making the exchange? Had I become Chairman of the Army Committee, and worked on military problems as I did on currency and economics, could I have made my ideas prevail? I can't say. But I then thought that economic recovery was a precondition of military recovery.

M. Reynaud's economic ideas resembled those of Lord Keynes: he was opposed to a rigid gold standard and favoured devaluation and economic expansion. What he does not seem to have sufficiently appreciated was that in the 1930's the expansionist stimulus once supplied by the building of pyramids and of medieval cathedrals or by the discovery of useless gold, could most easily have been obtained by rearming. Had he convinced the French of the need of preparing against the German danger he might have realized his ideas of full employment and economic expansion. On November 2, 1938, he became Minister of Finance in M. Daladier's Government and so remained till he replaced Daladier as Premier in 1940.

In 1939 motives of honour and self-preservation made France enter the war; yet fearing heavy losses and another invasion, and conscious of her own inferiority in numbers and armament, she did so *à contre-cœur*. Hence the " phoney war " with its absurd contradictions, its timidity in action and the rashness of its plans. The High Command tried to save appearances amid apprehensive evasions, and to keep up morale while warding off the hour of supreme ordeal. In September 1939 there was sham fighting in the Saar, and no action in the air to relieve Poland, for, said General Gamelin, were they to attack objectives other than the troops themselves, this might produce " an immediate German reaction which would seriously hamper our concentration ".[1] And the R.A.F. was long stopped from bombing the Ruhr or mining German rivers for fear of reprisals.[2] But expeditions were planned to Finland and Scandinavia, Salonica and Constantinople, and against Baku and Batum, to deprive Germany of iron and oil and to open up new theatres of war : diversions from the French front which were to " pin down and use up " German forces. Meantime, it was hoped to make up deficiencies in armament and to obtain substantial British reinforcements. General Gamelin writes : [3]

> France, from a feeling of justice, deeply sympathized with Finland. Public opinion, on the whole, wished us to succour her, overlooking that this meant to provoke Russia. As M. Reynaud states in his book, Parliament . . . pushed towards intervention — perhaps influenced by the future " Vichyites ". M. Daladier, a wise man, was not enthusiastic, and the British Government, especially Mr. Churchill, even less so. We Servicemen, British and French, were not for provoking Russia — except perhaps Admiral Darlan. But, I admit, we should have wished to be able to support Norway against a German attack, of which we felt the danger, and hoped that this would postpone the hour of the offensive against us.

[1] In the War Council on September 8; see *Servir*, iii. 51.
[2] See below, page 167.   [3] *Servir*, iii. 205.

In fact, an expedition across Scandinavia was being prepared when, on March 12, 1940, Finland signed the
armistice : and this brought down the Daladier Government. M. Reynaud took office on March 21.

Whatever doubts Gamelin evinced in crises, or now
recounts in his memoirs, the problem as conceived in his
" Note on the Conduct of the War " of March 16, 1940,[1]
was how to draw out the Germans and make them fight :
in the West, a tightened blockade might cause them " to
precipitate matters and invade Holland and Belgium "
(he himself now describes the sentence as unfortunate
" for we did not envisage *an immediate affair* ") ; in Scandinavia, if deprived of the iron ore, they might attempt
" armed intervention " ; an air bombardment of Baku
or Batum would affect their oil supplies ; their rivers
should be mined. None the less Hitler's invasion of
Norway caught the allies napping. Gamelin blamed the
British : theirs was the command in the North. " Have
you given them proxy for letting yourself be beaten ? "
inquired M. Reynaud. His relations with Gamelin were
not happy, nor with Daladier, who remained Minister of
Defence and for War. In the War Council of April 9 (of
which there is no minute) Darlan proposed to counter the
German move in the North by entering Belgium ; he was
supported by Daladier, Gamelin, and Georges ; Reynaud
claims to have pointed to Germany's superiority in
numbers and air force. Gamelin, while accepting Reynaud's contention that he was opposed to an advance into
Belgium, asserts that he never heard him say so. After a
meeting of the War Cabinet on April 12, at which Gamelin
was severely criticized by Reynaud, Gamelin handed his

[1] Reynaud gives its gist in volume ii, 20-21 ; it is not included in the
great mass of military documents printed by Gamelin, who seems to resent
the prominence given to it by Reynaud : " une note . . . dont M. le
président P. Reynaud fait état dans son ouvrage " (*Servir*, iii. 216-17) ; and
he tries to play down its importance.

resignation to Daladier,[1] but was persuaded to stay. On May 9 Reynaud demanded his removal; Daladier objected, which brought on a Cabinet crisis. This was resolved the next day by the German invasion of the Low Countries. Reynaud wrote to Gamelin: " Mon général, la bataille est engagée. Une seule chose compte: la gagner. Nous y travaillerons tous, d'un même cœur." Gamelin replied: " Monsieur le président, à votre lettre de ce jour je ne vois qu'une réponse: seule compte la France ". [2]

Interesting documents and material for the weeks which followed are printed by M. Reynaud. The reasons of the disaster are now hardly in dispute, merely their relative importance. The unpreparedness of France was intellectual, material, and moral; an obsolete doctrine of war, a wrong strategy, poor use of effectives and material, a very inferior air force, and a military morale undermined by war-weariness, pacifism, and subversive propaganda both from the Right and the Left. By May 15 a breach of about 50 miles had been made in the French front, from Sedan to Namur; by the 17th, seven Panzer divisions were approaching St.-Quentin and Cambrai: could they be stopped — where and how? That day M. Reynaud summoned Pétain from Spain and Weygand from Syria — a crisis opened in the Government and the High Command. Pétain's glory had grown as the years went by — the one survivor of victory — " a lonely giant " — an image rather than a man — described by the Press as " the noblest and most humane of our

---

[1] Gamelin wrongly dates the meeting of the War Cabinet " April 13 " (*Servir*, i. 6); its minutes are published both in Reynaud (ii. 33-9) and in P. Baudouin, *Neuf Mois au gouvernement*, pages 26-33, with the correct date of April 12, 6 P.M. While the text of these minutes in the two books is otherwise the same, the first paragraph is lacking in Reynaud without any mark of omission: it mentions the need of intervening " soit dans le nord de l'Europe, soit dans la mer Noire et au sud du Caucase ".

[2] *Servir*, i. 6-7.

military chiefs ", as the embodiment of the " sublime and victorious resistance of Verdun " ; while Weygand was " Foch's man " and claimed to possess his " secrets ". M. Reynaud took over Defence and War, Pétain became Vice-Premier, Daladier was moved to the Foreign Office, Mandel, the strongest man in the Government, went to the Home Office, and Weygand replaced Gamelin. On May 19, the last day of his " military existence ", Gamelin went to see Georges at his H.Q., and wrote out a " Personal and Secret Instruction " which starts : " Without wishing to intervene in the conduct of the battle now in progress . . ." ; but which he, none the less, describes as an " order " and as " the only solution fit to save the situation ".[1] The transaction, minutely analysed by the two Commanders, does not gain in the re-telling.

When on May 23 the Germans reached the Channel, forty allied divisions in Flanders were " like a cut flower in a vase " ; and as soon as Weygand lost hope of effecting a junction between them and the armies on the Somme he started talking armistice (the need of " an army in being " to preserve internal order was a consideration which throughout seems to have preoccupied his, and Pétain's, thoughts). In the War Council of May 25[2] the two urged broaching the subject of an armistice to the British Government, and on the 29th, in a written note,

[1] *Servir*, i. 3-12, and iii. 427-35 ; Reynaud, ii. 135-45.
[2] For minutes of the meeting, taken by Baudouin, see *Neuf Mois au gouvernement*, pages 81-9 ; Reynaud says that they " contain mistakes " which he would have corrected " had the text been submitted to me, as it should have been " (ii. 181 n.). The first part of the minutes, covering six of Baudouin's eight pages, is also in Albert Kammerer, *La Vérité sur l'armistice*, pages 393-6 ; and the last four are in Weygand's *Conversations with his Son*, pages 83-5. There are a few minor divergencies between the three texts, and about the middle of the fifth page in Baudouin, part of a sentence is lacking. The English editions of Baudouin and Weygand, produced by the same publishers, appear with two different translations of the same minutes.

Weygand demanded that Britain be told that, should the new front on the Somme and the Aisne fail to hold, France might have to quit. M. Reynaud, convinced that Britain would not give in, wanted France to stand by the engagement of March 28, 1940 (not to negotiate a separate armistice or peace), and to continue the fight be it from a redoubt in Brittany or from North Africa. His book supplies extensive documentation for those days, and also for the last absurd attempt to buy off Mussolini.[1]

Pétain and Weygand, called in to lead the resistance, became the chief *capitulards*. Here is M. Reynaud's description of Pétain: " A man of limited intelligence, on his own admission lacking memory and imagination, with no faith in France, the author of the military policy which was our ruin ". But he claims: " It is only gradually, in my prisons, that through successive disclosures his true face was revealed to me ". Now M. Reynaud fills scores of pages with condemnations of Pétain, going back to Clemenceau, Poincaré, Lloyd George, Joffre, and Foch. But was all this extensive knowledge of what competent judges had said or written about Pétain during the previous twenty-odd years acquired by him only after 1940 ? Had he, who gave so much serious thought to army matters, remained ignorant of the military policy of that " inter-war fixture " ? Was it not rather that he paid excessive regard to the voice of the public? (That tendency seems to be borne out by his copious quotations

[1] Both in 1939 and during the critical days of 1940, Laval tried to have himself sent to Rome, imagining that he was in France the man best suited to talk to Mussolini; whereas in fact Mussolini bore him a grudge, and wished to see him least of all. He remembered the controversy over the Abyssinian agreement, but foremost his dislike was caused by his having read a wire in which Laval " boasted of having obtained Mussolini's signature to the Franco-Italian Agreement of January 1935, without even having to make the territorial concessions in Africa which the French Government had authorized him to make ". (See Mario Toscano, " Fonti per la storia della guerra ", *Rivista Storica Italiana*, vol. lx, No. 1, 1948.) The wire, sent from Rome, was deciphered by the Italians.

of what others said about his own actions or person.)
But that he was not a good judge of men is shown by
many of his ministerial appointments. When he realized whither the two " military glories ", of whom he
could no longer rid himself, were steering, he decided to
remove from his Cabinet ministers who were likely to
favour an armistice ; and under pressure from the Senate
he also decided to remove Daladier. He himself took over
the Foreign Office and made M. Baudouin his Under-
Secretary : because " he was *persona grata* with the
Italians " ! He brought into the Cabinet M. Bouthillier
(who in November 1940 was to indict *les bellicistes*, and
M. Reynaud as their chief) and M. Prouvost : later office-
holders under Pétain ; besides, he retained five ministers
who reappear in Pétain's first Cabinet.

On June 5 opened the Battle of France. The French
lacked reserves and air support, and turned for them to
this country which, after Dunkirk, had nothing to spare.
Correspondence which passed during those days between
M. Reynaud and Mr. Churchill is reproduced in the book.
M. Reynaud wired on June 8 : " It is incumbent on me
to demand that you should, like ourselves, throw all your
forces into the battle ". Mr. Churchill replied the same
night : " We are giving you all the support we can in
this great battle, short of ruining the capacity of this
country to continue the war. . . ." The 52nd Lowland
Division and the 1st Canadian Division were sent across,
the R.A.F., not yet reformed after the Flanders campaign,
was once more heavily engaged. But more than one-
third of the allied forces having been lost, the German
superiority in numbers was overwhelming. By June 9 all
hope of holding the Somme-Aisne front had vanished,
and on the morning of the 10th Weygand wrote to
M. Reynaud that the disaster, apprehended in his note
of May 29, was imminent : " The final break in our

defensive lines may occur any moment ", after which the disintegration of the French Armies will be " merely a question of time ". The same day the Lower Seine was forced by the Germans, and Paris had to be evacuated ; M. Reynaud addressed his famous message to President Roosevelt :

> We shall fight before Paris, fight behind Paris, shut ourselves up in one of our provinces, and if they drive us out, go to North Africa, and, if need be, to our American possessions.

On June 11 the Allied Supreme Council met at Briare, on the Loire. Weygand declared that he could not guarantee the front to hold another day, nor could he any longer intervene in the battle as Commander-in-Chief, for he had no more reserves at his disposal. " The French Army is reduced by a superior armament. Light-heartedly was the war entered upon in 1939, without suspecting the power of the German armament." (Weygand now chose to forget what he and Pétain had previously said on the matter in contradiction to General de Gaulle and M. Reynaud.) The demand for increased air support from Britain was raised once more as the only means which might still save the situation. Mr. Churchill replied that British hesitations did not spring from an ill-conceived egotism but from the deep conviction that it would be impossible to continue the war if the R.A.F. was destroyed bit by bit. If the defensive front broke, argued Weygand, all France would be overrun ; and then " one asks oneself whether she would be able to continue the war ". M. Reynaud intervened : " The continuation of the war is a political problem, and has to be decided by the Government ". Mr. Churchill declared that in no case would Britain give up the struggle, and M. Reynaud that " the determination of the French Government is not inferior ".

After the Council M. Reynaud said to Pétain and Weygand that if France separated from Britain she would, now and probably in the future, have to face Germany unaided. Weygand replied : " The country will never forgive you if, in order to keep faith with England, you refuse a possible peace ". Reynaud writes :

> Obviously what mattered to Weygand, and also to Pétain, was to put an end to the sufferings of war. But the independence of France? Her moral greatness? Fidelity to her pledged word? The figure she would make among the nations after such a betrayal? Nothing of this seemed to count.

The same day, at the Cabinet meeting at Cangé in Touraine, Weygand again demanded an armistice : otherwise everything would go to pieces. Mr. Churchill was now to be invited to the Cabinet meeting, to discuss the question. The next day the Allied Supreme Council met at Tours.[1] Mr. Churchill said that Britain would not waste time on idle recriminations, but would continue to cherish the cause of France, and in case of victory would restore her to " power and dignity ". He did not release France from her engagement : in fact, M. Reynaud never asked him to do so but assured him that France would continue the struggle ; and Mr. Churchill, having to leave for London, did not attend the meeting of the French Cabinet, in which the *capitulards* were growing in number. And it was now contended that to leave France, even with a view to continued resistance, would be desertion.

At the next Cabinet at Bordeaux, on June 15, still more Ministers on humanitarian grounds favoured an armistice ; M. Reynaud replied, as he had to Weygand, that a simple military order to " cease fire " would be even more effective, without implying political surrender. The Cabinet agreed, but Weygand again refused to give such

---

[1] For a fuller analysis of that meeting of the Allied Supreme Council, see below, pages 53-7.

an order as " dishonouring " the French Army, although
M. Reynaud had offered to assume the responsibility for
it in writing. Then M. Chautemps, while declaring himself convinced that the German armistice conditions would
prove unacceptable, demanded that the attempt be made
in order to convince the French people that the Government had no choice but to leave the country. Thirteen
Ministers were with Chautemps, and only six against —
though this was clearly entering the road to surrender.
M. Reynaud thereupon handed his resignation to the
President of the Republic, but was persuaded to stay :
Britain's consent to the armistice inquiry was to be asked.
At the next Cabinet, in the morning of June 16, the Presidents of the two Chambers declared for removing to
North Africa with a view to further resistance ; after they
had left Pétain read out his own letter of resignation in
protest against the delay in suing for an armistice ; he was
answered by M. Reynaud that after the question had been
put to Britain her reply had to be awaited.

In the early afternoon a first telegram arrived from
London which agreed to France asking for armistice terms,
but on condition that, pending negotiations, the French
fleet was sent to British ports ; moreover, the British
Government, being determined to continue the fight,
completely dissociated themselves from any such inquiry.
It was pointed out in a second telegram that the condition was in the French, as much as in the British, interest. M. Reynaud objected that such a removal of the
French fleet would deliver North Africa to the Italian
fleet. An hour later a third telegram from London
cancelled the two previous ones ; and next came Mr.
Churchill's offer of constitutional union between Britain
and France, which, however, proved to have little appeal
for the French Cabinet. But M. Reynaud continued to
oppose an armistice : " You have raised a statue on the
Place de la Concorde to Albert I for his fidelity to his

allies. To-day you have the choice : Albert I or Leopold III." Finding himself heavily outnumbered he announced the resignation of the entire Cabinet. The same night President Lebrun consulted the Presidents of the two Chambers ; they advised him to entrust M. Reynaud with the formation of a new Cabinet ; but he turned to Pétain. This meant armistice and separate peace, with all that implied.

> . . . the question whether Britain would hold out, as I maintained [writes M. Reynaud] or whether the Ministers would in three or four weeks have to return to France to be treated as *fuyards*, counted for a great deal. Once again our military glories were wrong on matters concerning their own profession. And once again they got the better of me.

M. Reynaud had for years urged on France the right course of action, as Mr. Churchill had on this country ; neither was listened to in time — power and responsibility came to both when disaster could no longer be averted. Still, Britain was protected by " the great anti-tank ditch " of the Channel : without it Mr. Churchill could hardly have succeeded. M. Reynaud found himself in a much more difficult, indeed in a well-nigh hopeless, position. But anyhow was he the man for times of disaster ? Though possessed of a quick intelligence, insight, and excellent analytical powers, responsive to ideas, hard-working, energetic, and moved by a sincere patriotic desire to serve, he hardly seems to have been equal to a crisis of the first magnitude. He seems to lack detachment, and a sense of perspective and proportion ; restless and uneasy, he is exceedingly argumentative and prolix. As an author he has failed to master his material ; or else his book of 1200 pages would have been reduced to a third and the number of its readers multiplied at least tenfold. The book abounds in digressions and repetitions ; it is

not formless, but its outlines are overlaid with masses of
irrelevant matter and overgrown with the weeds of dead
controversy. Sometimes it resembles an album into which
its owner sticks reports of his own speeches, favourable
references to himself, and criticisms of his opponents ; such
a collection may be treasured but should not be printed.
M. Reynaud had a strong case and a good cause ; but by
a wrong approach and presentation he has in his book
deprived his person and record of the tragic greatness
which could have been theirs.

NOTE

The account of the Allied Supreme Council at Tours,
given above on page 50, is based entirely on M. Reynaud's
book, the only source available when that account was
written. But two other authoritative books of memoirs
published since put a somewhat different complexion on
certain phases of the discussion. A careful comparison of
the three accounts seems necessary.

Here are the relevant passages from M. Reynaud (ii.
320-323) :

> J'apprends à Churchill et à ses collègues que Weygand
> a demandé la veille au gouvernement de solliciter un
> armistice de l'ennemi et je fais le tableau le plus
> sombre de la situation, exposant la thèse des partisans
> de l'armistice. . . . Et tout en déclarant que, per-
> sonnellement, je ne capitulerai jamais, je pose la
> question qui aurait été posée par mes adversaires,
> les partisans de l'armistice, sur l'attitude qu'aurait
> l'Angleterre à l'égard de la France si, un jour, un
> gouvernement français le demandait. . . .
>
> Churchill me répond qu'en tout cas, l'Angleterre
> ne perdrait pas son temps en vaines récriminations,
> *ce qui ne signifie pas, dit-il, qu'il dégage la France de son
> engagement du 28 mars,* ce que je ne lui avais pas
> demandé.

And after a private consultation with his colleagues (Lords Halifax and Beaverbrook), " il me dit qu'ils partagent son sentiment ".

The previous day it had been decided to invite Mr. Churchill to attend the French Cabinet. When M. Reynaud now rejoined his colleagues, there was considerable dissatisfaction on hearing that they would not meet the British Ministers. Reynaud told them " que le conseil n'a pas qualité pour disposer du Premier ministre britannique ", and informed them of the first part of Mr. Churchill's reply, " à savoir que l'Angleterre ne perdrait pas son temps en vaines récriminations "; to which M. Reynaud added " que la question de la capitulation ne se pose pas, car la France restera dans la guerre ".

But the question of an armistice could hardly have been treated by M. Reynaud in quite so theoretical and remote a manner as he now seems to suggest: nor would Mr. Churchill have answered a question which had never been put to him, still less would he have sought, in private consultation, the opinions of his colleagues about it. M. Baudouin, Secretary to the French War Cabinet and Under-Secretary for Foreign Affairs, has published his own notes of the meeting in his book *Neuf Mois au gouvernement*, pages 154-159 (in English translation, *The Private Diaries of Paul Baudouin*, pages 102-105). Here the dividing line between what M. Reynaud says on behalf of others, and what he says as from himself is much less clear, and while declaring that he himself would not negotiate or conclude a separate armistice, he seems to suggest that objective circumstances might prove such as to render it advisable:

M. Paul Reynaud: . . . Le général Weygand a fait remarquer hier soir au Conseil que dans la lutte commune la France a été mise en avant et a été complètement sacrifiée. Il est maintenant matériellement impossible de continuer cette lutte. La Grande-

Bretagne accepterait-elle de délier la France de son engagement? Voilà la première question. Nous devons l'examiner immédiatement.

Mr. Churchill replied that he understood how much France had suffered; that England's turn was coming now; that she was determined to fight to the bitter end; and that France should go on fighting, be it a guerilla war.

M. Paul Reynaud: Je n'ai pas demandé à l'Angleterre ce qu'elle allait faire et comment elle voyait l'avenir. Je lui demande: si un gouvernement français disait au gouvernement anglais: 'Vous allez continuer à vous battre, mais d'une part la France ne peut plus continuer la lutte, et, d'autre part, la France ne peut pas être totalement abandonée à la domination allemande. Dans ce cas, faut-il que la France prolonge avec des moyens misérables une lutte sans espoir qui ne fera que rendre plus dure, plus impitoyable la domination allemande? Faut-il que le gouvernement français abandonne la terre de France et la laisse tout entière foulée par les rudes talons des vainqueurs? Est-ce que, dans ce cas, la Grande-Bretagne n'estimerait pas que la France peut lui dire: 'Mon sacrifice a été si grand, si total, que je vous demande de m'autoriser à me retirer du combat par un armistice séparé, tout en maintenant la solidarité qui existe d'après nos accords. J'insiste, répète M. Paul Reynaud, un armistice ne détruirait pas la solidarité qui existe entre la France et la Grande-Bretagne.'

M. Winston Churchill: En tout cas, nous ne ferons pas de récriminations. Dans une pareille hypothèse, des récriminations seraient vaines, et on ne les adresse pas à un associé malheureux.

. . . Quelle que soit l'attitude de la France qui s'est sacrifiée dans la lutte contre l'adversaire commun, quelle que doive être cette attitude après sa défaite, la Grande-Bretagne restaurera la France dans tous les cas, dans sa puissance et dans sa grandeur. La Grande-Bretagne chérira toujours la France.

Now these were M. Baudouin's own notes, and not an agreed official minute — he himself writes : " Voici la copie de mes notes prises au cours de ce Conseil " (which is hardly rendered accurately in the English translation : " Here is a copy of the minutes of the meeting ") ; and M. Reynaud questions, for instance, the accuracy of M. Baudouin's minute of the War Committee on May 25, 1940 (ii. 181, footnote). M. Baudouin strongly supported the armistice policy, and might tend to over-emphasize whatever was said on that side. But on this occasion it is possible to check his minute by extracts from the official British minute of that meeting now published by Mr. Churchill (*Their Finest Hour*, pages 160-161) :

> M. Reynaud replied that he had never doubted England's determination. He was, however, anxious to know how the British Government would react in a certain contingency. The French Government — the present one or another — might say : ' We know you will carry on. We would also, if we saw any hope of a victory. But we see no sufficient hopes of an early victory. We cannot count on American help. *There is no light at the end of the tunnel*. We cannot abandon our people to indefinite German domination. We must come to terms. We have no choice. . . .' It was already too late to organise a redoubt in Brittany. Nowhere would a genuine French Government have a hope of escaping capture on French soil. . . . The question to Britain would therefore take the form : ' Will you acknowledge that France has given her best, her youth and life-blood ; that she can do no more ; and that she is entitled, having nothing further to contribute to the common cause, to enter into a separate peace while maintaining the solidarity implicit in the solemn agreement entered into three months previously ? '
>
> Mr. Churchill said that in no case would Britain waste time and energy in reproaches and recriminations. That did not mean that she would consent to action contrary to the recent agreement. . . . If

England won the war, France would be restored in her dignity and in her greatness.

About the meeting of the French Cabinet, M. Baudouin writes (*The Private Diaries*, pages 106-107):

> . . . it was with astonishment that I heard the Prime Minister . . . give an inaccurate account of his interview with the British ministers, and declare that he had only told Mr. Churchill of the decision of the French Government not to take the advice of General Weygand.

And further:

> The Prime Minister was very embarrassed, said that Mr. Winston Churchill was in a hurry to return to England, and declared that he had not had an opportunity of asking him to address the Council of Ministers.

But Mr. Churchill writes (page 162):

> After our departure . . . M. Reynaud met his Cabinet. . . . They were vexed that I and my colleagues had not come there to join them. We should have been willing to do so, no matter how late we had to fly home. But we were never invited; nor did we know there was to be a French Cabinet meeting.

BONNET

THE second and concluding volume of the memoirs [1] of
M. Bonnet, French Foreign Minister, April 10, 1938–September 15, 1939, starts with a blare of self-praise —

> . . . here closes a historical account based on a
> documentation whose width and precision have
> already amazed my readers. . . .
> My book is an objective statement of facts. When
> presenting . . . the diplomatic transactions of a
> great nation, it is obviously easy to insist on certain
> aspects, to dwell on details, to give prominence to
> some negotiations and slur over others, in short to
> adjust the account to the taste of the day. I have not
> done so. Not wishing to leave anything unclear, I
> have taken care to explain not my measures alone
> but also the intention and thought which inspired
> them. . . .
> . . . Firm in my convictions, quiet in mind, having nothing to hide, to disown, or to regret in what
> we have done, I can here testify to the truth.

A great many files of the French Foreign Office were
destroyed in May–June 1940, to avoid capture by the
Germans. M. Bonnet managed to save his own copies.

> These texts, unique and irreplaceable, authentic
> and numbered copies identical with those which have
> been destroyed, have enabled me to draw up an account, free of errors or gaps, of the events in which I
> took part between April 1938, and September 15, 1939.

Unfortunately the French Yellow Book on 1938–1939
was not published as originally prepared by M. Girard,
Deputy-Archivist of the Quai d'Orsay, under the direction of M. Coulondre, late Ambassador in Berlin; but
pruned and weeded by political hands. If a copy of the

---

[1] Georges Bonnet, *Fin d'une Europe. De Munich à la guerre.* Bibliothèque
du Cheval Ailé. Geneva.

original survives, one might wish the missing documents were printed even now. For a few years will be required before a publication of French pre-war diplomatic documents can start. A careful search is being made; material is being gathered from French Embassy archives; and M. Bonnet, if asked, will no doubt place his own at the disposal of the French Government.

The testimony of a man who held M. Bonnet's key position in 1938–1939 is in itself of importance, and so are the documents which he has chosen to publish. But his handling of them astonishes by its negligence and vagueness. His transcription, where it can be checked, proves defective. Thus of half a dozen passages quoted from the Yellow Book on pages 248-254, not one is accurately reproduced. Omissions are not marked, and words are changed; either because M. Bonnet fails to appreciate the importance of meticulous accuracy, or because he is incapable of it. He inserts documents which serve " as evidence ", and adds that the hurried reader " may content himself with the summary which each time precedes the published telegram ". But take pages 176-179, dealing with the early stages of the 1939 negotiations with the U.S.S.R.: M. Bonnet claims to have proposed to M. Souritz, Russian Ambassador in Paris, to " widen and define (*d'élargir et préciser*) the Franco-Soviet Pact " ; while in his own telegram to the French Embassy in Moscow, which he quotes in evidence, he is seen merely urging that the U.S.S.R., in its own interest, should give effective assistance to Poland and Rumania, and thus preserve them from German ascendancy. And he seems unaware of the divergence which there is between his summary and the text.

The story continues :

A few days later, on April 9, I asked Daladier to summon the Committee of National Defence in order to put before it the absolute need of concluding a *military* alliance with the U.S.S.R. This was a bold move. Since the Franco-Soviet Pact was signed in 1935, never had a Government agreed to enter into Staff conversations with the U.S.S.R., although the question was occasionally raised.

M. Reynaud is cited as witness to this "bold move" though, not having been a member of the Committee, he cannot speak from personal knowledge. More to the point is Bonnet's quotation from the official minute of the Committee:

> M. Georges Bonnet has inquired with the U.S.S.R. what they could do for Poland and Rumania. Conversations on the subject will be started without delay by our diplomatic representative in Moscow. M. Georges Bonnet asks that our military attaché should start similar talks on the subject with Marshal Voroshilov. This is agreed to.

But nothing is said of a "military alliance" with Russia, not even in the full text of the minute, which runs into almost five pages in General Gamelin's memoirs.[1] The width of interpretation which M. Bonnet puts on his documents suggests an amazing capacity for self-deception.

"Bonnet," wrote Neville Chamberlain on May 1, 1938, ". . . is clever, but ambitious and an intriguer. The French are not very fortunate in their foreign secretaries."[2] Judgments on Bonnet by his colleagues or officials tend to be even severer — seldom was a statesman so little trusted while in office, or has since met with so much disparagement; its volume, and sometimes its venom, would be fit to secure a sympathetic hearing for his defence, were not such feelings quickly dispelled by his own glib, over-eager, uneasy discourse: invariably

[1] *Servir*, ii. 403-7. [2] Feiling, *op. cit.* page 353.

blameless, and successful where his own endeavours sufficed, he knows only of other men's faults or torts, and with a smirky vivacity recounts the story of his eighteen months at the Quai d'Orsay. Craving for approval and devoid of clear, firm purpose, intelligent and unstable, Bonnet vacillates, and both his policy and personality seem determined by events in which the initiative is never his. As France was circumstanced his task was unenviable, and even at the time he seems to have been pre-occupied with his own risks and liabilities; but a prefabricated defence is distasteful and unconvincing. " Bonnet is preparing his Yellow Book ", remarked Mandel to Reynaud, when listening to him in the Cabinet meeting of September 1, 1939.[1] What alibis and testimonials he now produces ! " I have not spent any length of time in Germany since 1927, when Stresemann was in office, and, not having been at Munich, I never saw either Hitler or Mussolini. On the contrary, I went to Moscow in 1934, and spent almost two months in the U.S.S.R. . . ." And he winds up his story with the farewell letter which, when removed from the Quai d'Orsay, he received from Lord Halifax, and with an obituary compliment paid to him in Cabinet by M. Daladier.

When, on the morning after Munich, Chamberlain, without saying a word to Daladier, got Hitler to sign the egregious joint declaration, the French appeasers felt outdistanced and hastened to contrive the Franco-German Declaration of December 6, which Bonnet still tries to furbish up into a French diplomatic success. How the evil-minded tried to foil him ! The talk started on October 18-22 ; then there was silence : Nazi extremists urged Hitler " not to accept any commitments towards France ". But on November 5 the German

[1] Reynaud, *op. cit.* i. 598.

Ambassador, Count Welczek, brought Bonnet a text in which hardly any modifications seemed required. Two days later Herr vom Rath was murdered in Paris, and negotiations were not resumed till November 19. The text was submitted to the French Cabinet on the 23rd, and received its unanimous approval (for a different story see Zay, one of the Ministers present, *Souvenirs et solitude*, pages 168-170). Ribbentrop was to come to Paris. Then a general strike of a political character was proclaimed in France for November 30, and the German Government, comprehendingly, postponed the visit to December 6. Next, Mussolini, to prevent a Franco-German *rapprochement*, staged the " Nizza, Corsica, Tunisia ! " demonstration in the Italian Chamber. None the less Ribbentrop came to Paris and publicly acknowledged " that Alsace-Lorraine was French, and should remain French ". " Was that an empty gesture ? Was there not reason for self-congratulation upon it ? Did it not usefully remedy the diplomatic disequilibrium produced by the Hitler-Chamberlain declaration of October 1 [read : September 30] ? " " What would not have been Bismarck's or Bülow's joy had a French Minister been found to come to Berlin and publicly hold such language to the French ? " On December 6 Bonnet pulled off what had proved beyond Bismarck's capacity !

But M. Bidault wrote in the Catholic *Aube* on December 7 :

> One would like to know if for once Germany really intends to respect her signature. For if not, there is every reason to believe that our frontier is being recognized and guaranteed so that other frontiers in Europe may be destroyed.

M. Bonnet protests :

> In signing that Declaration . . . we abandoned nothing and no one. Our treaties were upheld. The interests of France and of her allies were completely safeguarded.

And he claims to have insisted from the outset on a
" reservation concerning the treaties which France had
signed ". But the Declaration merely speaks of the
" special relations " of the Contracting Parties to Third
Powers: which fits Anglo-French and German-Italian
relations rather than the Franco-Polish alliance and the
Franco-Soviet Pact. And, indeed, on December 8, *Le
Temps*, a newspaper close to the Quai d'Orsay and
especially to M. Bonnet, argued that the reservation
proved the Axis and the Franco-British accord to retain
all their value, but did not mention the treaties with
Poland and Russia, which were generally supposed to
have lost interest for France. When, however, in July
1939 Ribbentrop asserted that the " Third Powers " were
Britain and Italy, but not Poland, and that M. Bonnet
had spoken to him about the radical change which Munich
had produced in the French attitude to Eastern Europe,
M. Bonnet denied it; and he denies it again in his book.

He tries to show how at every step he had kept France's
eastern allies informed of his negotiations with Germany.
But the reader has merely to compare the account which
M. Bonnet now gives of his talk with Souritz on November
22, 1938 (page 31), with his contemporary minute, to
which he himself refers (document No. 27 in the Yellow
Book), to discover curious discrepancies. Now he says,
for instance, that he showed the Russian Ambassador the
text of the Declaration, whereas in his minute Souritz,
after the interview, applies for it over the telephone, and
M. Bonnet refuses to give it, " as it had not been communicated to anyone ". Similarly, the account in the
book of his talk with Ribbentrop on December 6, differs
markedly from that given in his own circular telegram of
December 17, 1938, which he now claims to have been
sent " to all our [diplomatic] missions "; but in the
Yellow Book it is marked as sent only to London, Berlin,
Brussels, Rome, Barcelona, and Prague. Moscow and

Warsaw were wisely omitted : for in the account (of about
700 words) Poland is never mentioned, and Russia only
once — when Ribbentrop remarks that French policy
towards her seemed " a survival of the Versailles policy of
encirclement ", and M. Bonnet replies that it was the
refusal of other Powers to join which had given it a
bilateral character.

Even if the talk of December 6 (at which the German
Ambassador and the Secretary-General of the French
Foreign Office were present) had been such as M. Bonnet
now makes it, what about his *tête-à-têtes* with Ribbentrop ?
He refers on page 39 to the talk of December 6 as his " only
conversation with Ribbentrop " ; and on page 45, more
guardedly, as "the first and last I had with the German
Minister on political subjects ". But, in the Senate Committee for Foreign Affairs, on December 17, 1938, M.
Bonnet spoke of the cordial character of his talks with
Ribbentrop on December 6 and 7 ; and, similarly, in his
letter to Ribbentrop of July 21, 1939, he refers to " what
passed between us on December 6 and 7 " (words deleted
on page 254 of his book). To reinforce his present contention M. Bonnet supplies a chart of Ribbentrop's movements on December 7 ; *inter alia* : " A la fin de l'après-
midi on lui fit visiter le Musée du Louvre ". And who
could know better ? For M. Bonnet himself accompanied
Ribbentrop ; they entered the Louvre at 5.20 P.M. by the
Porte Donon and, leaving at 6.30 by the Porte des Arts,
went back to the Hôtel Crillon, where M. Bonnet remained
about 40 minutes, " during which time ", wrote the Paris
correspondent of *The Times* on December 7, " the question of economic relations, yesterday only touched on in
principle, received a more detailed examination ". The
same night, at a reception in the German Embassy,
" Ribbentrop ", writes M. Bonnet, " had long talks with
many French politicians and numerous foreign diplomatists " ; and *The Times* correspondent, on December 8 :

" M. Bonnet and Herr von Ribbentrop had the last of their diplomatic talks immediately after the banquet held at the German Embassy last night — where *jambon de Prague* was a notable feature of the repast ".

On September 4, 1939, Anatole de Monzie, a friend of M. Bonnet's, said to the Polish Ambassador, M. Lukasie-wicz : [1]

> What do you expect, it's always like that with Bonnet. Though a decent and honest man, he suffers from a well-nigh physical incapacity to tell the truth to the end. There are always suppressions and equivocations, and finally no one can tell how much truth there is in what he says, and how much evasion. This applies equally to his talks with diplomatists and to his reports to the Cabinet. . . .

At the end of January the need of upholding the East-European alliances, and especially that with Poland, was insisted upon in the French Chamber by speakers of all parties ; and Bonnet, exceedingly impressionable and versatile, and therefore quick to adjust his approach and technique, fell in with the prevailing mood.

> The answer was obvious [he writes]. I explained at length that the Declaration of December 6 contained an explicit recognition of our engagements towards the U.S.S.R. and Poland.

The speech was adversely commented upon in Germany, but " to prove to the German Government that the Press criticisms . . . in no way affected the attitude of the French Government ", M. Bonnet, a week later, declared in the Senate :

> France cannot limit her diplomatic action to her own territory or Empire, nor give up her position as a Great Power. To certain States she is bound by treaties which aim at maintaining the peace of Europe,

---

[1] J. Łukasiewicz, " Termin ultimatum dla Niemiec ", in the *Orzeł Biały*, September 4, 1948.

to others by age-long habits of political, economic, and intellectual co-operation. This is a precious heritage which France cannot renounce. France nowhere abdicates.

But among the captured German documents published by the Soviet Government there is a report from Welczek, dated February 18, 1939, on a talk with M. Bonnet.[1] By order from Berlin, Welczek expressed surprise at his having spoken " of cultivating and even extending French friendships in Eastern and Central Europe " — " such a relapse into the so-called Beneš policy is intolerable to us ".

> Bonnet protested loudly, and referred to the declarations he had made to me before his speech in the Chamber — see my telegram of January 24, No. 30. After all, he argued, old friendships can be maintained or extended, economically and culturally, without clashing with the German Reich, favoured as it is in the east and south-east by its geopolitical situation. . . . In foreign policy debates in Parliament things are often said for internal consumption which have no significance outside. If a French Foreign Minister has gone through fire and water to win recognition for our, in his opinion justified, claims to Sudeten German territory, and has drawn for himself conclusions from the changed position in Central Europe, surely he cannot be expected to make in Parliament an act of all-round renunciation. If he did, the warmongers would only get the upper hand . . .

It is difficult at any time to define M. Bonnet's policy: first, he would give way to pressure in a ready, complacent manner; next, he would reassert himself, and try to regain detachment and independence; and he would change colour, till he seemed to have none of his own. In January 1939 he had found it necessary to restore

[1] *Documents and Materials relating to the Eve of the Second World War*, ii. 226-32.

appearances. After December 6 a revulsion occurred in French public opinion, in the Press, and in Parliament : would it be safe for France to find herself without a single ally on the Continent ? This must have been felt even more strongly in official circles, for information that Hitler was planning an attack against the West was reaching Paris, London, and Washington from diverse reliable sources (and evidence obtained since seems to confirm it). M. Bonnet says : " The Italian demands for colonies, the anti-French campaign in the Italian Press, the fear of a Polish-German *rapprochement* against the French Empire, and the plans attributed to Hitler of an offensive against the West, dominated those first two months of 1939 ". Had Poland accepted Hitler's terms and, by entering his orbit, covered his eastern flank, his first move might well have been against the West, with colonies as prizes for Italy and Poland, both badly in need of openings for their surplus population.

> I knew . . . [writes M. Bonnet] in what danger-
> ous position France might find herself one day
> through her alliance with Poland : therefore, far
> from accepting additional obligations, I would much
> rather have been inclined to propose dissolving the
> alliance. But I was precluded from giving way to
> a feeling of resentment [at Poland's behaviour during
> the Czech crisis] . . . for we might yet need her.
> This is why the Government . . . had decided not
> to break with her, and so to avoid throwing her into
> the arms of Germany.

Indeed, Bonnet is never wholly for or against a policy : and therefore can seldom be proved to have been wrong — except in his facts. Here, for instance, he states, and repeats, that the aid of Poland's " 80 divisions " was essential to France. In reality Poland had only thirty divisions on a peace footing, with a further nine to be formed on mobilization, eleven cavalry brigades, and

some independent infantry formations; in all, slightly
more than half the army with which M. Bonnet credits
her.

Nothing tangible had resulted from M. Bonnet's wishes
to " soften " (*assouplir*) the " excessively rigid juridical
terms " of the Franco-Polish alliance, or to make it cover
the French colonies, when a radical change in Britain's
attitude was caused by Hitler's entry into Prague.
Chamberlain's guarantee to Poland on March 31, and the
provisional Anglo-Polish agreement of April 6, concluded
during Beck's visit to London, outranged the Franco-
Polish alliance of 1921 : they were free of League incantations and adjusted to Hitler's technique of " indirect
aggression ".   On April 10 the Polish Ambassador, M.
Łukasiewicz, asked that the Franco-Polish mutual obligations be brought into line with those of the Anglo-Polish
agreement, and, according to M. Bonnet, said that " M.
Beck and Lord Halifax had signed a protocol defining
the Anglo-Polish alliance ".   On the 13th M. Daladier
made a declaration in the French Chamber analogous
to Chamberlain's of March 31.   But M. Bonnet's handling of the ensuing negotiations for a political protocol
is an example both of his statecraft and of his history
writing.
    The text promising immediate aid against any direct
or indirect threat to the vital interests of either party
was, according to him, drafted at the Quai d'Orsay,
discussed with the Poles, and on May 12 accepted by the
French Cabinet.   " When . . . on May 17, I received
the Polish Ambassador . . . I expected him to bring me
an acceptance from his Government, pure and simple.
But nothing of the kind."   They now asked for a secret
article stating that the Polish Ambassador, when signing
the protocol, declared Danzig to be a vital Polish interest,
and that the French Foreign Minister took note of the

declaration. " I remarked that this article had not been discussed by the Government, and that it called for careful examination "; M. Łukasiewicz thought he knew that Britain had already accepted such an article. But on inquiry in London the French Ambassador was told that " Anglo-Polish talks had not been resumed since Beck's visit ", that the secret formula about Danzig had never come before the Cabinet, and that Chamberlain " in no way contemplated signing a text analogous to that which had been presented to me at the last moment. . . ." On May 20 M. Bonnet went to Geneva, where he learnt from Lord Halifax that the British Government would prefer not to settle the final text of the Polish agreement till after having concluded negotiations with Moscow; but as the legal advisers of the two Foreign Offices were in Geneva, they were set to work on a common text. " On my return to Paris, on May 27, I saw M. Łukasiewicz . . . and explained to him . . . that the additional point about Danzig would be examined in London, and that the French Government would anyhow sign only a text corresponding to the English text."

". . . May 18 had yet another surprise in store for us." Quite by chance the Quai d'Orsay learnt that on the previous day a military convention had been signed by General Gamelin with the Polish Minister of War, then in Paris, and that its first sentence started : " In the case of German aggression against Poland or of a threat to her vital interests in Danzig . . . the French army will . . ." Thus the military had taken upon themselves to forestall a political decision. " The General explained that he had thought that the additional protocol . . . had already been signed, and, to repair his blunder, informed the Polish Minister of War in writing that the military convention would only come into force after the new political agreement had been signed " — which was not done till September 4, 1939.

In reality the military convention was signed on the
19th, and not on the 17th (that is, after M. Bonnet had
had his " surprise ") ; and the words he cites are preceded
(as Gamelin states and I can attest) by a political reservation : " The French and Polish High Commands, acting
within the framework of decisions taken by the two
Governments . . ."[1] It is hard to believe that M. Łukasiewicz should have alleged in April that " a protocol defining the Anglo-Polish alliance " had been signed ; equally
that M. Corbin should have been told by the Foreign Office
that the British Government did not " contemplate "
assuming obligations concerning Danzig : for this was
done in the secret protocol annexed to the Anglo-Polish
treaty of August 25, 1939, of which the outlines were
settled during Beck's visit to London. The draft of the
new Franco-Polish protocol was submitted by the Poles
on April 28, and amended by the French ; the Poles
agreed to those amendments on May 12, not the 17th,
but asked for the additional article on Danzig. This,
according to M. Łukasiewicz,[2] was accepted by M. Bonnet
on the 17th, and the signing of the protocol was fixed for
the 19th, 4 P.M. On the 18th M. Bonnet sent M. Daladier
the text of the protocol, including the Danzig article without demur or reservation, and added that he expected to
sign it shortly (*à bref délai*).[3] But on the 19th he asked
M. Łukasiewicz to postpone the signing to the 20th ; on
the 20th, till after his return from Geneva ; and only in
a further talk on the telephone that day did M. Bonnet,
according to M. Łukasiewicz, for the first time mention
his inquiries in London and his doubts about Danzig.

[1] *Servir*, ii. 420. For an account of these negotiations see my book,
Diplomatic Prelude, 1938–1939, pages 456-66.
[2] The course of these negotiations is recapitulated in a letter from M.
Łukasiewicz to M. Bonnet, May 27, 1939, printed below in *Documents*, II ;
see also Łukasiewicz, " Uwagi i wspomnienia ", in the *Dziennik Polski* of
March 10 and 14, 1947.
[3] For Bonnet's letter and enclosure see *Servir*, ii. 424-5.

They met again on the 25th (not the 27th); and there followed an exchange of letters (for the first time printed below, in *Documents*, II). M. Bonnet, writing on May 26, unofficially informs M. Łukasiewicz of the text under discussion with London (it differed little from the original Franco-Polish draft); and the letter closes with an assurance that " every possible concern of the Polish Government is already covered ", seeing that " immediate and direct French aid to Poland " is pledged by M. Daladier's guarantee of April 13, which could merely be confirmed by the protocol. M. Łukasiewicz, in his reply of the 27th, reviews the course of the negotiations and concludes:

> I have informed my Government of the present state of our negotiations, and have transmitted the new formula, unofficially suggested by you and still subject to approval by the British Government. At the same time, I have not failed to inform them of the categorical assurance which you gave me on May 25, that the declaration which I propose to make about Danzig at the signing of the protocol meets with no objections on your part, and that, once the text of the protocol is fixed, you will accept my declaration . . .
> I have carefully taken note of the reference in your letter to the solemn declaration made by the Prime Minister, M. Édouard Daladier, on April 13, and to the obligations which devolve from it.

What, then, was the imbroglio about? It was reasonable for Britain to postpone fixing the terms with Poland till after the treaty with the U.S.S.R. was concluded, and for France, if she was to bring her commitments into line with those of Britain, to wait till these were fixed: therefore, after a good deal of inept handling, the matter was left in suspense. But there is a curious sequel to the story: General Gamelin and M. Noël now argue that in the absence of a political protocol the promises regarding French aid made in the military convention of May 19 were null and void (as if no obligations arose under the military treaty of 1921, or from M. Daladier's pledge of April 13, 1939). And at one time at least M. Bonnet seems to have thought likewise : according to the *Temps* of November 3, 1940, M. Bonnet, in an interview with the *Journal*, in which he pleaded strongly for Franco-German collaboration (*beachtenswert* the *Völkischer Beobachter* called it), claimed that in May 1939 he had refused to aggravate the obligations of the Franco-Polish military alliance. Was it then his purpose to torpedo the military convention when, at the last moment, he refused to sign the political protocol ? If so, his flounderings were worse than inane. But even his claim may have been an afterthought; and we may never know what, if anything, there was behind that mass of prevarications and evasions.

Perhaps best documented in M. Bonnet's book is his account of the Anglo-French-Soviet negotiations of 1939; and although it does not change the broad outlines as previously fixed, it helps to clear up some episodes. Still, documents altogether new are fewer than might seem, as a fair number of M. Bonnet's documents have been used, or even partially published, by M. Gafenco in his *Derniers Jours de l'Europe*; of some the text or gist was communicated by M. Bonnet to M. Łukasiewicz, who quotes them in his *Recollections and Remarks*; and a few appear in the memoirs of MM. Noël and Reynaud. And once more the student is up against M. Bonnet's unscholarly methods. The most interesting among his texts is the final draft of the Anglo-French-Soviet agreement, as it stood on July 24. "We were even to have initialled it," writes M. Bonnet, "for, as M. Molotov observed, there remained only a few 'unimportant differences of detail' regarding Article 1. On all others the agreement was complete." But M. Bonnet omits to specify these differences; and he leaves the reader to guess (or the student to trace) that his is

72

the Anglo-French text. Further, the transcription and dating of documents is again unreliable. Here are two examples. M. Bonnet's appeal to Lord Halifax to agree to the new Russian demand that a military convention should precede the signing of the political agreement is dated July 19 in his book, but in his own article in the *Revue de Paris* (November 1947) July 17. And this is a sentence from the crucial telegram which, on August 16, M. Bonnet sent to the French Ambassador in Warsaw, as reproduced by Gafenco: " You . . . must strongly impress on M. Beck the necessity of the Polish Government accepting Russian aid *dans les conditions nettement limitées où elle se propose* " ; the concluding words, here given in French, are omitted by M. Bonnet without any mark of deletion. Lastly, the narrative and its documents are made to serve not so much history as M. Bonnet's justification ; and this is as complex an undertaking as the course he steered. Moreover, attacked often from opposite quarters, he turns in all directions to fend and hit back. For the ultimate breakdown of the negotiations with the U.S.S.R. he blames the Poles who refused to let Russian troops pass across their territory, and he triumphantly produces anything that M. Stalin, M. Molotov or Marshal Voroshilov have said to that effect : which is to prove that it was not Munich and a loss of confidence in the Western Powers that influenced the Russians. And he rightly blames General Gamelin for not having raised the question of Russian aid in his talks with the Polish army leaders — but had not M. Bonnet himself too long shirked tackling this ticklish subject ?

On August 23, faced by the impending Russian-German agreement, M. Bonnet put the following question to the Committee of National Defence :

Must we blindly implement our alliance with Poland ? Or would it be better to press a compromise on Warsaw? This would give us time to advance our armaments, to increase our military power, and improve our diplomatic position, so as better to resist Germany if she next turned against France. But a compromise may weaken the Franco-Polish alliance, which was always deemed essential for the defence of France. Does the General Staff still hold that view?

But from the discourse M. Bonnet now adds on the advantages which were to be expected from a second Munich, it would appear that " may weaken the Franco-Polish alliance " was a euphemism. Had the line of " compromise " been adopted, " Poland," he says, " under Franco-British pressure, would have given in to Hitler's demands, and would very soon have disappeared from the map of Europe ", partitioned between Germany and Russia. But if then Hitler had attacked France,

> a new and important factor would have entered into the diplomatic situation: the Franco-Soviet Pact would have come into play. Both M. Molotov and Marshal Voroshilov were to declare on August 25, 1939, that the Franco-Soviet Pact *continued in force* (*subsistait intégralement*).

The Treaty of 1935 and Russia's instinct of self-preservation alike would have bid her render aid and assistance to France, while the question of the passage of troops across the territory of a third country would no longer have arisen. " Was it not a contingency of that kind that Marshal Voroshilov had in mind when, after the break, he said to General Doumenc: ' We shall one day resume contact. . . .' "

General Gamelin reasoned differently; if Poland were abandoned, and Germany then turned all her land and air forces, already fully mobilized, against France, it would be very difficult to effect the mobilization and concentration of the French forces; France might be unable to resist. It was decided to stand by Poland.

When next, on August 31, Mussolini offered his mediation, M. Bonnet grasped at it with both hands; a conference, he now argues, would have helped Poland to resist German demands, and also to justify to her own people concessions decided upon " in accord with her allies " (presumably the compromise which was " very soon " to wipe her off the map). But Britain and Poland, complained M. Bonnet on July 7, 1940, in a speech to a gathering of French deputies at Vichy, by insisting on a previous withdrawal of German forces from Polish territory, defeated his attempts to settle the conflict through Italian mediation.

It became obvious, even on September 2-3, 1939, that the British Government were pressing for action, while the French were hanging back. First, M. Bonnet cited constitutional reasons; a vote of the French Parliament was required for an ultimatum; and they only met in the afternoon of September 2. Next, he pleaded his promise to Ciano to wait till Sunday noon (September 3), and claimed to be bound by it even after Ciano had thrown in his hand. In between he talked about the evacuation of French women and children, still in progress. The French military, too, demanded delay in order to complete, undisturbed, their mobilization and concentration, and argued that anyhow they could not undertake any action before Monday night. The British Government proposed recalling the Ambassadors on the very day of Germany's invasion of Poland (September 1); and on September 2, at 5 p.m., informed M. Bonnet that they would give Hitler time till midnight to withdraw his troops from Poland, failing which they would open hostilities. None the less, the French Cabinet decided not to present its ultimatum before noon next day, and Chamberlain was informed to that effect by M. Corbin at 10 p.m. This was after the scene in the House of Commons. Thereupon Chamberlain telephoned to

M. Daladier, and Lord Halifax to M. Bonnet; but to no avail. At 2 A.M. M. Corbin told M. Bonnet that the British Government would refrain from opening hostilities at 6 A.M., but that their ultimatum had to be presented before the House reassembled at 10 A.M., or else they risked being overthrown.

> I still insisted with M. Corbin; our *démarches* were now to follow so close on each other that it seemed absurd not to synchronize them. Could not the sitting of the House of Commons be postponed, say till noon? " Impossible," answered M. Corbin. But he asked whether we could not reduce the expected delay.
> I once more consulted the War Office. They finally answered, as Daladier had done: " Ask London whether the British bombers could be placed tomorrow at our disposal. If so, the French General Staff could agree to reduce the delay."

This was a decision which the British General Staff could not take off-hand. M. Bonnet claims to have further pressed M. Daladier in the morning of September 3. But the military " adhered to the date of September 4, 5 A.M., for the opening of hostilities " ; and that hour was inserted in the text of the ultimatum which the French Ambassador was to deliver the same day at noon. Still, when the news came through of the British ultimatum and of the bad impression which the French delay was producing, M. Bonnet says he once more appealed to M. Daladier. And then :

> 11.30 A.M.: Daladier informed me that he had re-examined the situation with General Colson. Our General Staff had found it possible to reduce the delay by twelve hours so that hostilities would open on Sunday at 5 P.M., instead of Monday, 5 A.M. I asked immediately for Berlin. Speed was required as M. Coulondre's *démarche* was fixed for noon.
> 11.45 A.M.: the French Embassy in Berlin; M.

Coulondre, *about to start for the Wilhelmstrasse* to deliver our ultimatum, was recalled. I dictated to him the correction in my telegraphic instructions : " hostilities will begin to-day at 5 P.M." M. Coulondre, with much presence of mind, demanded to have such news confirmed by one or two of my assistants whose voices he also would recognize. I passed the telephone in turn to M. Léger and M. Bressy who were with me. And the Ambassador left to be with Ribbentrop sharp at noon.

On September 3, 1939, war was declared, *et c'est de ce jour*, says M. Bonnet, *que commence la Résistance française* ; and it was he who signed the ultimatum. One might almost conclude that he was *Résistant* No. 1. But when at night two notes from the Quai d'Orsay reached the Paris Embassies, some at least found that the notification of France having declared war on Germany was signed by M. Léger, and only that of France's pledge not to bomb open towns by M. Bonnet. And at Riom, M. Bonnet did not appear in the dock with M. Daladier and General Gamelin.

BAUDOUIN

PAUL BAUDOUIN was born in 1894; served with distinction in the First World War; then entered the State Inspectorate of Finance: a close fraternity which is the *élite* of the French Civil Service and a nursery of financiers. While thus employed he was secretary to several Ministers of Finance, including Caillaux in 1925, " with whom ", he writes in his *Diaries*,[1] " I have never ceased to be on the closest terms, seeing him frequently. He has always helped me with his advice and whole-hearted support, and there is no one to whom I owe more than I do to him." (" You are ", said Caillaux to M. Baudouin on July 12, 1940, " the one of my old assistants whom I find most like myself; that is why I have a special affection for you.") M. Baudouin left the Civil Service in 1926 and joined the Banque de l'Indochine, of which he rose to be director-general. In 1937 he and M. Charles Rist were put by M. Blum in charge of the fund for equalizing foreign exchanges; and in February 1939 he was sent by M. Daladier as semi-official intermediary to Ciano. Highly intelligent, a good organizer, persevering and ambitious, with financial interests in various parts of the French Empire besides Indo-China, and also in foreign countries, he moved a good deal in the borderlands between big finance, administration, and politics.

In February 1938 M. Baudouin published in the *Revue de Paris* an article on " The Data of the French Problem ". The task of his generation, he wrote, was to strengthen " les bases du futur en dégageant du doute et

[1] Paul Baudouin, *The Private Diaries, March 1940 to January 1941*. Translated by Sir Charles Petrie. With a Foreword by Malcolm Muggeridge. Eyre and Spottiswoode. The French title of the book is *Neuf Mois au gouvernement (avril-décembre 1940)*.

de l'incohérence actuels les données du problème français ". But as an ideological attempt in that direction the article is revealing rather than impressive. Painful truths are told about Europe's changed position in the world, and that of France in Europe, and then quickly wrapped up in unconvincing solace. Economics and finance are M. Baudouin's own province, but even there the moralizing reformer is not always above high-falutin banalities. Keen and lucid in his perceptions, he is vague in his designs : he neither seeks deep nor scans far, but is *épris* of his ideas and tends to expound even *ses petites idées* as if they were great and original thoughts. He censures both the jealousy and hatred of the needy, and " the inaction, poverty of heart, and incomprehension of the bourgeoisie which directs the home politics of France " ; speaks of " the cowardice and hypocrisy of all political régimes " ; and, with a bias towards a strong " non-party " Government, enounces that only men " free of all personal egotism and class prejudice " are fit to rule. The article reads like an advance instalment of national repentance and " regeneration " of the Vichy brand. Perhaps most explicit in it was the appeal for co-operation with Nazi Germany : M. Baudouin correctly assessed the weakness and dangers of France's actual position, but not of that which his policy would have created.

> No insurmountable barrier [he wrote] separates France from Germany. It is a crime against our country to assert that war with Germany is inevitable.
> We should understand that the youth of that great nation yearns for wider horizons, and that its disciplined and massive force is not fatally destined to oppose that of France, which is less vigorous but more subtle. We must free ourselves from the obsession of fear which has caused our country to subordinate its foreign policy to alliances that often are merely a source of weakness and are the product of dangerous

sentimentalisms. . . . The Franco-German problem should be solved peaceably without weakening the close friendship which binds us to Britain. . . . The possibility and necessity of an entente with Germany must be affirmed in spite of the incomprehension of the masses, the attraction of routine, and criticisms which, in that field, easily become abusive.

And a few pages further :

In foreign politics, let us put an end to recriminations and verbal warfare. In material strength we are no longer one of the two or three greatest Powers in the world. We should be no more than the first among the secondary Powers if the weight of armaments and the number of divisions alone counted. But do not underrate the moral and spiritual forces which richly spring forth from our ancient soil, and the power of our geographical position, both privileged and dangerous. . . . Our imperative duty is . . . to concentrate our national forces, and have the courage to make our choice and stand by our opinions. We could then, without forfeiting other nations' esteem and with increased moral authority, agree to abandon the so-called traditional policy. Such abandonment is dictated by the expanse of the new Empire, and by the supreme danger we should incur were these questions settled by sheer force. Are important concessions now necessary to avoid a conflict, or to postpone it? Perhaps; but . . . in a way, to gain time is to live.

Here then was a programme closely resembling the " new realism " and *le repli impérial* which, in that month of February 1938, M. Flandin started preaching, and which M. Reynaud stigmatized in Parliament as *la démission de la France*. Why then did he make M. Baudouin Secretary to the Cabinet in March 1940? However able and efficient, he was hardly the man to second M. Reynaud's endeavours.

While in office M. Baudouin used to dictate every

morning to his secretary a summary of the transactions of the previous day, and early in 1942, about a year after having retired, he set to work and welded his notes into the book now published. Here is M. Baudouin's own account, given to Mr. Malcolm Muggeridge who, with his permission, communicated it to me:

> In re-reading what I had dictated every morning at Vichy, I noticed that some of those notes had lost interest, while others required pruning or completing from diplomatic dispatches of which I had retained copies.
>
> I therefore, with the aid of my secretary, cut out from my daily notes all that had become unnecessary, and rendered clear [*j'ai bien précisé*] what seemed to me of historical interest.

Later on some further changes were made in the text:

> In 1942, for fear of my papers falling into German hands, I nowhere mentioned in my notes the Rougier mission to the British Government in October 1940, or the circumstances in which the Marshal decided to dismiss Laval on December 13, 1940, in order not to deviate from the terms of the agreement made with the British Government through M. Rougier and M. Dupuy, Minister of Canada.

That "agreement" having been made public by M. Flandin at his trial before the High Court, M. Baudouin added in his *Diaries* the part about those transactions. (For a British official statement concerning M. Rougier's mission see *Despatch to H.M. Ambassador in Paris*, July 13, 1945; Cmd. 6662. The concluding remark of Mr. Churchill's covering letter is that nothing in "the only accounts which H.M. Government received from M. Rougier on his mission . . . bears out his contention that Marshal Pétain regarded himself as under any commitment to H.M. Government" — in other words, there was no "agreement".)

M. Reynaud formed his Government on March 21, 1940; and the next day, in a House of 536, secured a net majority of one vote — 268 against 156, with 111 abstentions. Yet he would go on; and asked M. Baudouin to help in organizing a small War Cabinet. M. Baudouin urged him to resign; but also to improve his relations with M. Daladier, whom M. Reynaud had to retain as Minister of National Defence and of War: ". . . your administration is, and will remain, two-headed, and nothing will go right unless the two reach an understanding ".

> All the powers for directing the war [notes M. Baudouin in his *Diaries*] had from the beginning been concentrated . . . in the hands of the Minister of National Defence. All intelligence was centralized by Daladier, who objected to passing it on to his colleagues, and particularly to Paul Reynaud. The Prime Minister received nothing direct, and so exercised little effective control.

It was hoped that the Secretariat of the War Cabinet would improve matters; but a month later M. Reynaud had still to rely on Press *communiqués* for his knowledge of the military situation; and on May 15, in the thick of the German offensive, M. Baudouin writes:

> Each day, with increasing anxiety, the Premier has had to put up with the impossibility of obtaining information and exercising any influence over the High Command in which he has no confidence.

M. Daladier once said that when General Gamelin speaks " it is like sand running through one's fingers " (a sensation shared by readers of Gamelin's memoirs); and M. Albert Kammerer, a French ex-Ambassador, in his book *La Vérité sur l'armistice*, maintains that M. Daladier himself would have removed Gamelin had his Government continued. But now he stood by the man who had served several years under him, and the duel between

M. Daladier and M. Reynaud was fought over General Gamelin till, to break through the deadlock, M. Reynaud, on May 9, dissolved his Government — but was foiled once more, this time by the German offensive.[1]

M. Baudouin speaks of General Gamelin's inertia, refusal to accept responsibility, and lack of interest in the Norwegian campaign; and the description of him, though unfriendly, is not unfair. Here is Gamelin on the morning of the German invasion of Denmark and Norway, pressed by M. Reynaud for his views and plans.

> . . . quite unmoved, and merely, as was his custom, moving his hands as if he were giving a benediction, [he] quietly replied, " You are wrong to get agitated. We must wait for complete information, and must be careful not to come to any decision in the absence of it. . . ."

And on May 16, when Mr. Churchill arrived and had to be informed of the extent of the French defeat,

> General Gamelin . . . like a good lecturer, took his stand by the map and gave an admirable discourse, clear and calm, on the military situation. He showed the German thrust, and he explained the position of the French troops as well as their surprise and disorder, while our reserve divisions, capable of taking the field, were very few in number. Paul Reynaud gave me an agonized look, and Churchill asked General Gamelin to go over his explanation again. His ladylike hand marked here and there on the map the positions of our broken units and of our reserves on the move. He had no views on the future; there was not a word of to-morrow, not even a hope. While this was going on M. Daladier remained apart, red in the face, drawn. He sat in a corner like a schoolboy in disgrace.

Unruffled and reflective, and possessed of good analytical powers, General Gamelin would have made an excellent

[1] See above, page 45.

staff officer, but was neither a man of action nor a leader.
On May 20 M. Daladier was shifted to the Quai d'Orsay,
and Gamelin was replaced by General Weygand.

Early in April, when General Weygand was leaving
for Syria, M. Baudouin had said to him:

> You are the only man capable of exercising the
> supreme command, and I am convinced that before
> long you will take an aeroplane and come quickly to
> assume command of the French forces.

And he relates an anecdote about Weygand's visit to the
Northern front, on May 22, no doubt expressive of his
own feelings: a woman, in a half-deserted village near
Ypres, recognizing Weygand, exclaimed, "How can I
be frightened now you are here?" And when, on May
24, M. Reynaud said that it would be difficult to refuse
an offer of peace on moderate terms, but that then he
himself would have to resign, M. Baudouin exclaimed:

> You are not going to hand over power to a Govern-
> ment of defeatists, pledged to treat at any price! If
> you ever go, you ought to advise the President of the
> Republic to place in authority the only moral force
> which will then exist. "What is that?" M. Paul
> Reynaud asked. "General Weygand is the only
> leader worthy of the old French army."

M. Baudouin was now talking about the political government of France — but therein, too, he was General
Weygand's man rather than M. Reynaud's.

By the time Pétain entered the Government and Weygand assumed the army command, probably no one could
have saved France from military destruction; and perhaps not even at any earlier stage of the war. But Pétain,
more than anyone, was responsible for France's obsolete
army, while Weygand's responsibility in this matter still
awaits impartial scrutiny. When therefore the Riom
inquiry into the causes of the *débâcle* was precluded from

going back beyond 1936, it was clear that the father of the defeat was being screened, while Gamelin, the Republican politicians, and in particular the Popular Front (formed in 1936), were singled out for condemnation. And so they were in Pétain's and Weygand's talk as reported by M. Baudouin, and in his own contributions.

Thus, on May 23, Weygand said that he could not at first " recognize the morale of the French troops . . . so different from those I left when I gave up my command " (in 1935); but now some units were " fighting magnificently ". The next day he criticized the army leaders who had gone to war without proper equipment and organization; though he himself had, in a speech on July 4, 1939, extolled those of the French army.[1]

> I told General Weygand [writes M. Baudouin] that it was not only the material means that were lacking but also the soul. In this country the moral forces had been destroyed, and Frenchmen were no longer taught the ideas for which they were to lay down their lives. If the country was not to perish there was a great work of reconstruction to be done. I added that I was impressed by the faltering which I saw on all sides, and by the collapse of that false governing class which was at the head of the French administration. I wondered if the morale of the army and of the country was good enough to withstand a surrender on the part of the forces in the north. . . .
>
> I said to him, " We have only one object — to get France out of the ordeal which she is undergoing so as to allow her, even if defeated in the field, to rise again. Perhaps the terrible evils which she is suffering will in the end turn out to have been to her advantage. Out of evil may come good."

In 1938 M. Baudouin pleaded for concessions to Hitler, which would, in fact, have made him master of Europe; and now for peace, without asking what kind of

[1] See above, page 39.

peace and what " governing class " surrender to Hitler would earn for France : all this in the jargon of the Vichy *mystique*, of which he seemed an early adept.

When a *communiqué* was issued on May 26 stating that fifteen generals had been relieved of their commands,

> " I cannot allow," the Marshal said, " the army to be blamed for errors of policy. The real culprit is Daladier, for it was he who created the Popular Front. It is a pity that he is at the Quai d'Orsay, for if negotiations have to be undertaken with Italy or Germany how can so discredited an individual take responsibility for them ? "

Did Pétain want someone like Laval to curry favour with the Dictators ? Anyhow, to remove from the Government Daladier and Sarraut, and in time all Republican politicians, became perhaps his foremost concern.

Weygand agreed that the real culprits would not be found in the High Command.

> " What we are paying for is twenty years of blunders and of neglect. It is out of the question to punish the generals and not the teachers who have refused to develop in the children the sentiment of patriotism and sacrifice. We must not render desperate the man in the ranks who lacks everything, who has not enough anti-tank guns and who has no aeroplanes."

But was it the teachers who during those " twenty years of blunders and of neglect " had failed to provide the man in the ranks with anti-tank guns and aeroplanes ?

On the day Weygand assumed command (May 20) the Germans reached the Channel coast, cutting off the Belgian Army, almost the entire B.E.F., and the French First Army (38 divisions " in all " on page 50, but 45 on page 36). Without these only 50–65 divisions would remain to hold the Somme–Aisne front and the Maginot

line against some 140 German divisions; with no shorter
line to fall back upon, and in conditions which would not
allow of an orderly retreat. But as yet the gap between
the Somme and Arras was only 25 miles wide, and an
attempt to close it, by cutting off the German armoured
formations from the main body, seemed to offer the one
chance of retrieving the situation. It failed, for on neither
side were the allies sufficiently strong to breach the German
lines. And the irritation and pain of those tragic days
vented themselves on a new scapegoat.

> *May* 24, 10.30 A.M.—On entering, the General
> [Weygand] whispered to me, " The situation is very
> serious, for the English are falling back on the ports
> instead of attacking to the south." He told the Prime
> Minister that . . . the English had abandoned Arras
> without being compelled by the Germans to do so,
> and appeared to be retreating in the direction of the
> ports. This was contrary to the formal instructions
> given by General Weygand to the British army
> according to the plans shown on Wednesday the
> 22nd to the British Prime Minister and approved
> by him.

Weygand added that the change must have been ordered
from London; and though assured the next day by a
telegram from Mr. Churchill " that no orders contrary to
the Weygand plan had been given by London ", he is
found, on June 3, repeating the charge in a pointed and
offensive form. Throughout these weeks he would talk
of " the defection of the English " which has compelled
him " to abandon finally any offensive movement ", of
their inability " to resist the appeal of the ports ", and the
priority given to their own troops at Dunkirk. Even
during the Battle of France, when one single British
division was left in the fighting line, it was they who were
his " worry ".

In reality the two British divisions at Arras, much
under strength and hastily assembled, had fought valiantly

and suffered severely, and were withdrawn by Lord Gort only when in imminent danger of encirclement. At Dunkirk the final figures of embarkation were 225,000 British and 113,000 allied troops, although, as General Weygand himself pointed out, " the French troops were furthest from the coast ", and " in effect, of twelve French divisions only four were in a position to be evacuated ". Here, as in the vexed question of throwing in the Air Force, further effective resistance, at whatever sacrifice, was with Mr. Churchill the overruling consideration.[1] In the Supreme Council, on May 31,

> his voice broke when he told us that in order to save as many English soldiers as possible in order to form a new army he had given the order to embark the wounded last, which to all intents and purposes meant leaving them in the hands of the Germans.

General Weygand, in his recently published *Conversations with his Son*, tries to make amends :

> In the heat of action, not knowing, as I know now, the reasons for his [Lord Gort's] action, his decision gave rise in me to much sadness.

And about Dunkirk :

> The two days of May 31 and June 1 saw . . . a series of not very edifying squabbles between London and Paris as to the exact proportion of each army that was to be taken off. . . . But . . . the soldiers, who knew nothing of them, were mixing in their thousands on the beaches waiting to be taken off in a spirit of the utmost friendliness and mutual generosity.

[1] That Great Britain would have to retain the fighter squadrons charged with the defence of this island, was realized in France before the war. Thus General Gamelin said in a meeting of the French Air Council on March 15, 1938, that while one could hope that Britain will reinforce the French Air Force with bombers using French air bases, " it seems unlikely that she would agree to send to France fighter squadrons charged with the defence of her own territory" (*Servir*, ii. 321).

In a similar spirit should now be treated things said under the impact of disaster, especially after reparation has been made. But would it not have been proper also for M. Baudouin, when recording those charges, to state the facts, as now known, in notes or in the preface? Especially as he himself had injuriously retailed those charges at that time (see the *New York Times* of July 6, 1940). To blame Britain for the defeat of France was then additional justification for the armistice.

For the last fifty years Britain and France have had a joint security interest against Germany. But past experience and being limitrophe give a special turn to the attitude and policy of France : her vigilance does not relent when the Germans are down and fawn, and her risk tends to inhibit her when they grow dangerous. In the disaster of 1940 the French remembered how Britain had first befriended the Germans and next taken the lead in resisting them; but how poorly she was equipped to share in the consequent defence of France — unjust charges were often but the unconscious projection of a justified resentment. It required understanding and character to take a wider, detached view; while in certain types Britain's comparative immunity was fit to arouse even spite. Clearly it was impossible to hold France to her promise not to negotiate a separate armistice if she felt forced to do so, and all Mr. Churchill finally demanded was that France, conscious of her own interest in Britain's survival and ultimate victory, should not supply Hitler with weapons against her.

General Weygand at first declared that if the Somme–Aisne front broke, what was left of the French Army " should continue to fight where it stands until annihilated, to save the honour of the French flag " (May 24). But his second thoughts were more realistic : a useless massacre and internal anarchy had to be prevented — with the army completely destroyed "no one could say what troubles might ensue". He added: "It is necessary to sound England on all these problems". Vice-Premier Marshal Pétain most emphatically favoured an armistice: to talk of fighting to the last man was both easy and stupid, and criminal in under-populated France; and part of the army must be saved — " grouped round some leaders" it would maintain order, the basis for a "recon-struction of France". Similarly, the other Vice-Premier, M. Chautemps, wondered "if there was any point in carrying on the struggle much longer". On May 26, M. Reynaud, back from London, was asked by M. Baudouin:

> "What did you say of the necessity in which we may shortly find ourselves of breaking off the fight? In what conditions will the English free us from our promise?" "I was not able to put the question," he replied. I told him that he had done wrong; that he had not fulfilled the mission with which the War Committee had entrusted him; and that the longer this problem was postponed the more difficult it would be of solution.

But M. Reynaud was convinced that "no honourable armistice could be expected from Hitler".

During the Battle of France pressure on him increased. He was told by Weygand on June 5 that

> if the battle was lost and France overrun . . . the courageous course would be to open negotiations with the enemy. Marshal Pétain supported the Com-mander-in-Chief. M. Paul Reynaud said that he had not changed his mind: he was convinced that no peace and no armistice would be acceptable, that the armies should fight as long as possible, and that, if necessary, the Government should leave France.

The same day, he reconstructed his Cabinet. He dropped Daladier and Sarraut, but also some defeatists; and offered the Ministry of Finance to M. Baudouin, who refused as he "would rather remain at the centre of the ministry ". He became M. Reynaud's Under-Secretary at the Quai d'Orsay, as well as in the Prime Minister's department.

By June 7, the Somme–Aisne line was broken. Pétain and Baudouin pressed for an armistice. The break-up of the armies was complete, a co-ordinated defence was no longer possible, men were succumbing to fatigue, formations were disbanding — by June 10, Weygand considered that the fighting had become meaningless :

> . . . why continue to let blood flow, why hand the whole of France, in an advanced state of social decay, over to the enemy, and why deliver the army in its entirety to the Germans ?

But M. Reynaud, though anxious, was not downcast.

> He lives in the certainty of a German defeat, and everything else is a mere incident. To secure the destruction of Hitler and Nazism he would bleed France white, and would allow her complete collapse.

" In my opinion he is leading to the material ruin of France ", wrote M. Baudouin on June 12. But " why ask for an armistice ? " was M. Reynaud's argument. It would be " dishonourable and wholly futile ", as they could not trust Hitler's word.

> " France must never be separated from England and the United States. The Anglo-Saxon world will save France, and it alone can restore her."

In between the *capitulards* in the Cabinet and the irreconcilables were men who would not accept responsibility for either course, and, engaging in inconclusive discussions, tried " to find reasons for putting off a decision " ; while Mandel, himself *résistant à outrance*, sat

> silent and contemptuous to-day [June 13] as yesterday, with his stony eyes amused to record among his colleagues a fear and a mediocrity greater than even he had imagined.

Finally their scruples were assuaged by the pretence of merely exploring what terms could be obtained — as if there was a turning back from that path. On June 16, M. Reynaud resigned. At 10 P.M. he came out of the President's study,

> and confirmed that the President had asked the Marshal to form a government. " I have seen the list of the future ministers," he said, " and it is a Laval administration." He turned towards me, and remarked, " You are Minister of Foreign Affairs."

M. Baudouin claims to have accepted in order to keep out Laval,[1] whose appointment would have meant " a complete break with Britain ".

On June 16, in the early afternoon, M. Reynaud was informed that Britain would release France from her promise not to enter into separate negotiations, but on one condition only : that pending negotiations the French fleet entered British ports. The point was again emphasized in a second telegram received about two hours later ; but before there was time to communicate the telegrams to the French Cabinet they were recalled by a third and were followed by the offer of national union between the two countries : which would have automatically vested control of the French fleet in the new super-State. The offer did not appeal to the war-weary — according to Weygand it roused " indignation " — and it was they who now assumed office. Their first Cabinet meeting " lasted ten minutes ", writes M. Baudouin, " long enough to decide to ask Germany her terms for a cessation of hostilities ". He informed the British Ambassador, Sir Ronald Campbell, of it at 1 A.M. on June 17. In the afternoon Sir Ronald called again and, in M. Baudouin's absence, handed the two withdrawn telegrams of the

[1] For the way in which Laval was kept out, see also account given by Mr. Churchill, *Their Finest Hour*, page 190.

16th to the Secretary-General of the Foreign Office, M. Charles-Roux : in order to bring them " to the notice of the new French Government ". But M. Baudouin wrote :

> What is the significance of these telegrams " taken back " and then communicated afresh ? I shall clear up the mystery to-morrow.

His further account is even " curiouser " : the next day (June 18) he asked the Ambassador

> if the delivery of these documents . . . proceeded solely from a desire to clear up completely the successive phases of the Franco-British negotiation of June 16, or if it gave fresh life to these proposals on the part of the British Government?
>
> Sir Ronald Campbell . . . told me that he understood my question very well, but that before giving an answer he would like to read his instructions again. . . .

He returned and informed M. Baudouin that the handing in of these documents once more did not revive them. (Obviously the British Government had nothing to worry about at this juncture but the completeness of the French diplomatic archives.) And M. Baudouin adds in a footnote (there are only two in the whole book) : early in August, he learnt, after the return of the French Chargé d'Affaires, Marquis de Castellane, from London, that " in the view of the British Government the proposal of . . . union did not annul the two telegraphic messages of June 16 ". Does M. Baudouin even now refuse to understand that the demand contained in those two messages was merged in the proposal of union, and that it re-emerged when union was rejected? The footnote goes on to say that, according to a memorandum sent on July 12 by Lord Halifax to M. de Castellane,

> on June 18 Sir Ronald Campbell insisted to the Marshal that the French fleet should be sent into

93

British ports,[1] while on the same day I told the ambassador that a decision in this sense had been reached and that nothing was wanting but confirmation by the Council of Ministers.

This is contrary to my definite recollection of three points :

(a) The Marshal never mentioned to me any such conversation with Sir Ronald Campbell.

(b) My only conversation with the ambassador on the subject of sending the fleet into British ports, that is to say on that of the two telegrams of June 16th, was the one related above.

(c) I never acquainted the Council of Ministers with this suggestion, for I was not authorized by the English ambassador to do so.

From this resulted a misunderstanding between the two Governments, probably due to the fact that Sir Ronald misinterpreted his instructions which largely depended on the construction put by London on the progress of events.

But M. Baudouin's ignorance, amnesia, or " misunder-standings " extend much farther : throughout that week, June 17-24, messages and messengers from the British Government incessantly reminded the French of that one condition deemed essential to Britain's security or even survival (some will be found in M. Albert Kammerer's book, *La Tragédie de Mers el-Kébir*).[2] A quotation from Mr.

---

[1] The text of a personal message sent to Pétain and Weygand on the 17th, and " of which copies were to be furnished by our Ambassador to the French President and Admiral Darlan ", is printed by Mr. Churchill in *Their Finest Hour*, pages 190-91. The concluding sentence warns against " frittering away these few precious hours when the Fleet can be sailed to safety in British or American ports, carrying with it the hope of the future and the honour of France ".

[2] Even Admiral Darlan's letter to Mr. Churchill, of December 4, 1942, implicitly confirms that such a demand was made. Having mentioned the answer he gave to Mr. Alexander, Admiral Dudley Pound, and Lord Lloyd, he adds : " If I did not consent to authorize the French Fleet to proceed to British ports, it was because I knew that such a decision would bring about the total occupation of Metropolitan France as well as North Africa " (see Churchill, *op. cit.* page 203 ; for the French text of the letter see Admiral Docteur, *La Grande Énigme de la guerre, Darlan*, pages 242-4).

Churchill's speech of June 25, 1940, will suffice: when the Pétain Government was formed with a view to concluding an armistice,

> we naturally [he said] did everything in our power to secure proper arrangements for the disposition of the French Fleet. We reminded the new Government that the condition indispensable to their release had not been complied with, the condition being that it should be sent to a British port. There was plenty of time to do it. . . .

By Article 8 of the Franco-German armistice the French warships were to be disarmed and stationed in their peace-time ports (of which Cherbourg, Brest, and Lorient were in German hands); and the Germans, while promising not to seize the French warships, retained the right to use them for coast surveillance and mine-sweeping (an obviously elastic and dangerous provision). Thus Britain was to stake her existence on Hitler keeping his word, or on Laval, by far the cleverest and strongest man in the Vichy Government, failing to achieve a " reversal of alliances ". Oran, the most tragic incident in Anglo-French relations, was the result of deliberate obtuseness on the part of M. Baudouin and his colleagues. And even now, in his *Diaries*, M. Baudouin continues to misrepresent the British action; he says that " a powerful English squadron had issued an ultimatum . . . to Admiral Gensoul either to join the English fleet or to scuttle his ships ", when in reality two other alternatives were offered : to take the ships to Britain or to the French West Indies, " where they can be demilitarized to our satisfaction, or be perhaps entrusted to the U.S.A." If M. Baudouin at that time did not know the terms of the British ultimatum, here again was occasion for a footnote.

When Pétain formed his Government, on June 16, Laval refused to enter except as Foreign Minister. But a week later he joined as Deputy Premier. " I could not do anything else . . .", said Pétain to M. Baudouin. " I must have him in the Government for his intrigues will be less dangerous there than . . . outside." Thus opened the Vichy reign of virtue. On the 25th, M. Baudouin urged Pétain, in addressing the nation, to " forecast an intellectual and moral reform ", and " say that steps would be taken towards the establishment of a more stable and more pure political and social system ". He must " modify the composition of the Government ". Pétain concurred : " there were in it too many who must bear the blame for our material and moral unpreparedness ". Weygand, too, thought " that the present team contained too many Parliamentarians ". He and M. Baudouin " agreed that in the present difficult stage what was required was a benevolent despotism ". Laval wished to give the Marshal " exceptional powers " by revising the Constitution and " putting an end to the present political system ". M. Baudouin doubted whether that was feasible. But Laval was " superbly confident ". " You have no experience," he said. " Fear makes all men cowards." Pétain now tried to shelter behind the President. But

> " I will make a strong effort to obtain the full consent of Albert Lebrun to his disappearance," said Laval, and without waiting for the approval of the Marshal he immediately went off to see the President.
>   Laval came back an hour later, and gave an account to the Marshal of the way in which he had overcome the President and obtained his support for a modification of the Constitution. The Marshal looked at him with admiration and astonishment. Pierre Laval was certain of success. . . . The Marshal said . . . " All right, try."

Next, Laval started to press for a constitutional act designating him heir presumptive to Pétain. But the Marshal would not have it ; and then veered round and appointed Laval his successor.

> I asked [Laval] . . . how he had brought about
> this sudden change on the part of the Marshal who,
> only a short time before, had been opposed to his
> appointment. He told me that he had made a firm
> request to the Marshal, and this had been enough.

Pétain went on vilifying deputies and ex-Ministers —
the prosecutions of those who had gone to North Africa
and the Riom Trial were largely his own work. August
27: " The Marshal again spoke to me of his wish . . .
to get rid of all Parliamentarians . . ."; and on September 4: of all except Laval " who would remain Deputy
Prime Minister ". To M. Baudouin he said: " I know
that I can place complete confidence in you because you
identify me with the nation ".

As early as June 23, there was a scene between M.
Baudouin and Laval, " for he advocated a break with
England while I opposed it ". If Laval's view was
adopted, Baudouin said he would resign, and so would
Weygand and Darlan. Baudouin wanted France to adopt
" the attitude of a neutral country ", " defined and
limited by the armistice convention ", and preserve
" dignity in respect of Germany, and silence with regard
to England ". What Laval aimed at was a " reversal of
alliances ": close collaboration with the Germans and
war against Britain were to raise the French from the
position " of vanquished to that of associates ". And
after Oran Laval, when pressing for reprisals, had the
support of Darlan, who now " gave full rein to his dislike
of England ". They wanted to bomb Gibraltar as soon
as the British ships had returned from Oran: but M.
Baudouin made Pétain agree to postpone the operation.[1]

[1] Compare, however, Churchill, *Their Finest Hour*, pages 211-12: " On
receiving the news of Oran, they [the Vichy Government] ordered retalia-
tion by air upon Gibraltar, and a few bombs were dropped upon the harbour
from their African stations ".

Then, on July 15, Darlan prevailed once more. " I could hardly sleep for thinking what a first-class blunder it will be. . . ." But again he persuaded Pétain to abandon the operation, this time for good. Meantime, Laval started his journeys to Paris, waiting for, or on, Abetz.

> Is it proper [writes M. Baudouin] that the Deputy Prime Minister of France should make a journey just to meet M. Abetz? When I asked Laval this, he replied, " If it had been necessary I would have waited all night in the gutter for Abetz." General Weygand and I were very worried, and we were also concerned by the silence of the Marshal, who did not dare to express an opinion in front of Pierre Laval. . . . We feel him [Laval] to be open to anything, ready for anything, or rather opposed to nothing. He knows neither physical nor moral shocks.

Laval declared " that only by the complete victory of Germany would a lasting reconstruction of Europe be possible ". Even Pétain thought " that his Deputy Prime Minister and heir presumptive was going a little far ", or rather " advancing into a vacuum " : for there was no response from the Germans, and no concessions either with regard to prisoners of war, or reparation payments, or the demarcation line, or a return of the French Government to Paris, or the provisioning of unoccupied France. Next followed measures in Alsace-Lorraine which amounted to *de facto* annexation. There was no fixed policy towards France; " do not let us think ", said Laval's henchman, Marquet, on August 24, " that France occupies an important place in German thoughts ". In consequence friendship for Britain was reviving in the country, this being " the natural form of French reaction against the Germans ". " The Germans ", wrote M. Baudouin on August 23, " are systematically destroying . . . the chances of reconciliation which existed after the armistice." By September there was a " wide gulf between the [French] Government and the country ".

The strong, authoritarian Government which Vichy was to have given France was dissolving into sheer incoherence.

> . . . unity of control in the ministry [writes M. Baudouin on August 30] is more lacking than ever. Everybody is going his own way without a thought for the whole. There is a complete lack of driving force, and of a leader.

Darlan and Laval were pursuing their anglophobe activities, while M. Baudouin was trying to establish secret contacts with London, across the Madrid Embassies and M. Rougier. On August 6, M. Baudouin was told by General Huntziger that Darlan had communicated to the Germans " secret information concerning the British Navy which he had learnt at the beginning of the war " ; and that he had the movements of English ships watched, and passed on the information to the Germans. " Obsessed by Gibraltar ", at the end of September, after Dakar, he finally obtained Pétain's consent to bombing it. On another occasion, without telling anyone, not even Laval, he sent a cruiser squadron on an operation which might easily have led to an armed encounter with the British Navy. Laval, for his part, calmly told the Cabinet on August 30,

> as if he was quite unconscious of the enormity he was relating, that he had offered the Field-Marshal [von Brauchitsch] the entry of France into the war against England. Von Brauchitsch had received this offer with contempt. " We have no need of your assistance, which would in any case be of little account." Pierre Laval was not at all rebuffed by the German refusal, and he recommended the opening of hostilities with England.

That " insensate overture . . . stresses the terrible danger in which we find ourselves in the absence of all knowledge of what Laval is doing ". On October 22 the Cabinet learnt that Laval had met Hitler and Ribbentrop. " The immediate effect will be to bring to an abrupt end the negotiations which for three weeks I have been carrying on with England through Madrid." Next, the Marshal was to meet Hitler, and seemed greatly pleased with the prospect; while M. Baudouin told him that " a declaration of war by France on England would be criminal ".

> What we can do [wrote M. Baudouin on October 23] is to work out a *modus vivendi* in the economic field for the period of the armistice; also, if the Germans so desire, to try, with the feeble means at our disposal, to bridge the gulf between the German and Anglo-Saxon worlds in order to arrive at peace. As the weeks go by I become the more convinced that Western civilization is in a fair way to commit suicide.

And on the 24th, M. Rougier told Lord Halifax in London that

> M. Baudouin . . . had come to the conclusion that although Germany would not be able successfully to invade this country, Great Britain would not be able to conquer Germany. He therefore foresaw a long and costly struggle which would result in the spread of bolshevism throughout Europe.

M. Baudouin was Foreign Minister, but Laval threatened to resign if he accompanied Pétain to the meeting with Hitler at Montoire; and the Marshal gave way. This decided M. Baudouin: he was " not going to be mixed up in any doubtful business ", and was determined " to have done with a policy and with manœuvres which seemed to me to be fatal to the country ". " New policies are inaugurated in the dark "; " some form of collaboration was promised, but of what nature we are ignorant ". He resigned; but Pétain, " as father and as chief ", ordered M. Baudouin " to remain near him ". " The Marshal . . . was frightened of the policy which Laval was forcing on him " — " I had to obey the Marshal's order." He stayed on as Minister Secretary to Pétain.

Consequently M. Baudouin is able to throw some light on perhaps the most mysterious transaction at Vichy — the dismissal and arrest of Laval on December 13, 1940. Not that this is clear even now; the cross-currents and motives cannot be easily disentangled. Laval had over-reached himself. Opinion throughout France, occupied and unoccupied, was hardening against collaboration; there was unrest in the army and a reaction in the Cabinet; even the Marshal was worried by the policy of collabora-tion being " directed by a man who does not enjoy the confidence of the country ". On December 2, in Laval's absence, the Cabinet learnt that he had agreed to military co-operation with the Germans in Africa; they were upset at a policy of " giving, without any recompense, ad-vantages to Germany by way of preparing for negotia-tions ". " This was not a meeting of the Council of Ministers, but rather a trial of Pierre Laval and his policy." And, M. Baudouin adds : " If he had been there, nobody would have said anything ".

> After the meeting of the Council [writes M. Baudouin] I had a talk with the Marshal, and I stressed the pace at which Laval was leading us to disaster. England would never forgive us if we went back on the under-taking given by Rougier, and it would be a crime to do so. We must get rid of Laval. The Marshal, who was leaving in a few minutes for Marseilles, agreed.

A group of Ministers now decided to extract Laval's dismissal from the Marshal. Darlan, jealous of Laval, joined them. M. Flandin, Laval's " personal enemy ", was summoned. Laval thought of making himself " Head of the Government with the Marshal remaining merely Head of the State ". " I have had enough of Pierre Laval's policy ", said the Marshal on December 8. " Montoire represented a reverse which we cannot hide."

And on the 11th : " I have made up my mind to get rid of
Laval ". But Laval staged a new stunt : the ashes of the
Duke of Reichstadt were being brought from Vienna to
Paris, and Hitler asked Pétain to receive them at the
Invalides. Was this to get him to Paris? Suspicious by
nature, he at first refused to go, but then gave in to Laval.
The situation was fraught with dangers. " The dismissal
must take. place to-night ", wrote M. Baudouin on
December 13. The Council of Ministers met at 8 P.M.
Pétain said he meant to make some changes, and asked
them all to sign a letter of collective resignation. Next
he revealed that only two resignations would be accepted,
of which Laval's was one. " You do not possess the confidence of the French people, and . . . you no longer
possess mine." Laval was put under arrest.

The *coup* brought on German intervention. Abetz
came down to Vichy. Laval was freed but not reinstated.
" Germany has chosen Darlan," writes Baudouin, on
December 17, " who has been making a great effort to
gain her confidence for a long time past." And on the
22nd : ". . . the skilful manipulation of the events of
December 13 had resulted in a much greater servility to
Germany. . . ." " Nothing will any longer stop me from
leaving the Government, and the sooner the better." He
wanted to have done with " this game of marionettes ",
and its " sordid intrigues ".

> I am alone in wishing to escape from this poisonous
> atmosphere : the others are eyeing one another with
> suspicion, and only think of staying where they are.

M. Baudouin left on January 2, 1941 ; the Marshal
remained. He said : " The Germans would appoint
Darlan in my place, for they love Darlan up to the point
of embracing him and his ironclads ".

There was a credit side to M. Baudouin's political
balance-sheet which, whatever his mistakes, deserves
attention.

THE END OF VICHY

M. STUCKI was Swiss Minister in Vichy during the four years of the régime. As representative of a country neutral *par excellence*, and therefore entrusted by both sides with the guardianship of their interests when required, he envisaged his task in a wide humanitarian spirit, and gave neutrality, however scrupulously preserved, an active character: disregarding personal danger, he laboured to save human lives and to avert unnecessary suffering, without distinction of nationality or party. In his account of the work done,[1] there is quiet pride in his country's rôle and satisfaction with his own performance, artlessly displayed. He disclaims literary merit for his book, and speaks of its " sober, almost office-like narrative ", and of his pursuit of truth; which includes testimony on behalf of " a man who once was Head of the French State ". The book is both honest and naive.

Its story centres in the arrest and deportation of Marshal Pétain by the Germans and M. Stucki's subsequent quest for an orderly transfer of power at Vichy to the French resistance forces; these transactions are related largely in extracts from his diary, which cover August 12-20 and 22-27, 1944, and form almost half the book. Accredited to the Vichyites, he witnessed their daily sufferings and humiliations at the hands of the Germans, and the endeavours of the more decent among them to lighten the burdens of their countrymen. The moral loss which their policy inflicted on France, though perhaps perceived, was not brought home to him with the same force. But he is not uncritical; he writes, for instance:

It was the tragedy of French leadership since 1940

[1] Walter Stucki, *Von Pétain zur Vierten Republik*. Herbert Lang and Cie, Bern.

that, devoid of all psychological understanding of German mentality, they too often thought themselves bound to give in, and did not dare sufficiently to play out their one but powerful trump, the great interest which the Germans had in the preservation of peace and order in France.

Still, M. Stucki fails to ask himself how a Government of Vichy's complexion could have played that trump.

For Laval M. Stucki had a hearty dislike, but for Pétain he expresses pity, as " his age and character deprived him of the necessary strength and determination " ; but he admits that there was also vanity and the desire to retain power. And yet M. Stucki shows a sentimental devotion to the Marshal, frankly expressed also on occasions when it exposed him to difficulties and criticism. He said at the headquarters of the F.F.I. (Forces Françaises de l'Intérieur) : " I come from Vichy, whose name grates on your ears. I have spent there four years with Marshal Pétain, whom you have been taught to hate, but whom I respect as a good Frenchman, and whom I now pity in his bitter fate. . . ." And when receiving the freedom of liberated Vichy, M. Stucki considered it " a matter of decency and loyalty ", after having spoken of " the brave F.F.I. ", to commemorate " also the old Marshal of whose brutal arrest I had been a witness ". For this " undiplomatic and misplaced remark " he incurred severe, and perhaps not unjustified, criticism in the Swiss Press.

When, by the summer of 1944, Germany's defeat was merely a question of time, Pétain's, and even Laval's, attitude stiffened. For instance, Pétain refused to congratulate Hitler on his escape from the attempt on July 20 (two years earlier, Pétain had congratulated him in fulsome terms on the British failure at Dieppe). By the middle of August Laval, having gone to Paris, was beating about for a way to rehabilitate himself and save his neck ;

while Pétain's entourage thought of rigging up the old Marshal as " Résistant No. 1 " (some even wished him to get into touch with the *Armée secrète* and place himself in their hands). Naturally neither Pétain nor Laval felt like following the defeated Germans as a " Government in exile ", and each, separately, took M. Stucki for witness that he would never do so voluntarily. They hung on to that last peculiar scrap of respectability : not to collaborate with the Germans any longer when the doom of the Germans was sealed.

Then followed Pétain's arrest, which M. Stucki relates with sincere emotion, and apparently without perceiving certain farcical aspects. Perhaps the final touch of unconscious comedy was put on it by M. Stucki's own sensible and well-meaning concern for human life : the gates of Pétain's residence were closed, the doors were barred, the guards were posted, and there was to be no surrender ; but not any fighting either, for M. Stucki had persuaded both sides not to load, nor use any lethal weapons. So it all finished in an attack with butts, boots, or crow-bars, against iron and wood ; a beautifully prearranged assault against Vichy's inert redoubt. When at last the German commander, a regular soldier who in the (invisible and immaterial) depth of his heart was anti-Nazi, reached Pétain's bed-chamber, he found the Marshal only in shirt and trousers, tying up his shoes. Pétain raised his head and said : " Ah, c'est vous." General von Neubronn bowed deep and announced : " You know, Herr Marschall, what painful duty brings me here." Pétain nodded : " En effet, je sais que je suis votre prisonnier " ; and with faint irony : " Vous me permettez quand même de m'habiller ? " Whereupon Neubronn withdrew and waited with the others in profound silence.

CIANO'S EARLY DIARY

In a secluded room of the Italian Foreign Office, the Palazzo Chigi, Ciano kept his diary, making in it his daily entries. Married to Mussolini's daughter Edda, an ambitious woman, he was appointed Foreign Minister in 1936, at the age of 33, and retained the post till February 1943. The diary, which starts on August 23, 1937, covers practically his entire term of office. He greatly cherished these records, and would show them, or read passages from them, even to strangers; and in his last entry, written in Verona jail on December 23, 1943, shortly before his execution, he refers regretfully to the " excellent material " which they would have made for his autobiography, while in a letter addressed the same day to Mr. Churchill he speaks of them as evidence against the Nazis, " this loathsome clique of bandits . . . with whom later that tragic puppet Mussolini associated himself through his vanity and disregard of moral values ". How much must Ciano have forgotten of his own thoughts and actions! especially of those recorded in the diary for 1937–1938, now published for the first time. The five books covering the years 1939–1943, Edda Ciano managed to carry away when in 1944 she left the Parma clinic and in disguise escaped across the Swiss frontier; published in America in 1946, they have gone through various editions and translations. Those for 1937–1938 she had to leave behind, and the doctor at the clinic, under threat of death, handed them over to the Gestapo. Recovered in 1947, they were published in Italy the year after,[1] but so far have not appeared in English.

The transactions of which they treat may seem less momentous than those dealt with in the later volumes;

[1] Galeazzo Ciano, *Diario*, 1937–38. Capelli. Bologna.

but as a picture of the author and his master they are perhaps of even greater value: not yet overwhelmed by irrefragable reality, these men are still free to revel in the pretence of their imagined rôles and idealized selves. But photographs for which people pose, autobiographies, and diaries are mediums of self-expression which easily lend themselves to self-exposure; and autoportraits fondly delineated in the hey-day of success even more so than apologias drawn up in adversity: there is greater scope for vanity, poor taste, and wrong values.

Ciano's early *Diary* should be read at least twice. The first time to accompany him through the passing show: immature even for his age both in looks and mind, he lives hand-to-mouth, enjoying rank, wealth, and power in an almost childish manner. Charming and plausible, sharp and intelligent, he can be amusing. He talks with apparent frankness: he lacks moral standards and relishes it. But his enthusiasms seem excessive; they serve a purpose, of which he himself is perhaps not fully conscious, and are expressed in *clichés* such as suggest a deliberate cutting out of critical faculties. Business is transacted not without ability or shrewdness, but at short range. On that level the *Diary* contains many an important historical fact or detail, and many a good anecdote, and by and large there is no reason to doubt its veracity.

But then let the reader sit back, and go through the book once more: these are the memoirs of the Italian Foreign Minister and perhaps the only man who at that time had intimate access to Italy's dictator; and though in fear of him, Ciano, himself highly impressionable and unsteady, had considerable influence with Mussolini, who was far more easily swayed than most people would have supposed. Does a clear pattern emerge of Italian foreign policy? Did these men calculate the results of their actions? The reader becomes aware of Ciano's concepts having lacked depth and shape; they were two-dimensional; all was surface. He strutted about the stage playing a set part in an unreal setting. It would have been well for Mussolini and Ciano if, having said their piece, they could each time have walked off the stage to the applause of their public. Thus the Duce had carried on for ten years to his own satisfaction, and without upsetting Europe. But now a different troupe had invaded the stage, intermingling with his own in a joint play which he had originally conceived: even more fantastic in their evil fancies than himself, and dead serious about them — what had been verbiage was to change into large-scale action. And Mussolini was forced to translate into life what had hitherto been elaborate make-belief. Reality beset with anxieties, difficult to hide yet not to be avowed, breaks through the brightly coloured surface: a comic and a gruesome scene.

Duce-worship was the first rule of the game. In Ciano it was too absolute to be altogether genuine; it suited the pattern of his life and his derivative greatness; but, entwined with fear, it would easily topple over into resentment. "The Duce is pleased"; "the Duce is in good humour": "the Duce has expressed his approval"; "one works solely to please him . . . this is the greatest satisfaction". "The sacred person of the Duce." When a Minister complained — "even if right he should not worry the Chief". On receiving expressions of love and loyalty from an opponent, Ciano wrote with perhaps too conscious virtue: "What do such declarations mean? Oaths of fealty are sworn to the Chief: between comrades they savour of plotting. And that I flee with all my strength." And when, in February 1938, Grandi tried to play the peace-maker with Britain: "Nothing doing. Peace and war are in Mussolini's hand, and in his alone. No one else should claim a personal rôle." But less than a week later, Ciano wrote in his *Diary*:

> *Choc* [a French paper] attacks me saying that I
> am a real danger to peace, as I have no feeling for
> Latinity, and that I desire to profit from tragedy.
> There is much exaggeration in it, but also some truth.
> My conception of the Fascist Empire is not static.
> We must go ahead. And it is right that the sated
> should worry.

" The Duce's conversation is delightful. No one is
richer in imagery or more colourful." " The Duce,
crystal-clear in exposition and most strictly logical. . . ."
" The Duce is invariably right." And during the Czech
crisis of September 1938 :

> The Duce speaks. A grand, serene speech.
> Rarely do words equal deeds. This time, yes. Even
> if nothing more happens, the Duce has written a
> page of history wrought of courage, loyalty, and
> honour.

In another crisis : " Mussolini is calm. Very calm. . . .
He awaits events with his monumental imperturbability."
And on February 2, 1938 :

> I told the Duce of the impression which his
> military oratory produced yesterday. He is pleased.
> He loves and adopts more and more the steel-like
> style of the soldier.

The Duce is " heroic ". When told that the French
considered Italy " Enemy No. 1 " : " A great honour.
I want to be feared and hated rather than helped and
patronized ". When he heard of reactions to Italian air-
raids on Spanish towns, " he rejoiced at the Italians spread-
ing horror by their aggression rather than causing pleasure
as mandolinists ". And on another occasion : " They
must learn to be less *simpatici*, and become hard, im-
placable, odious. That is : masters." And here is the
heroic concept of house-training :

April 20, 1938. The Duce rightly flew into a violent rage against some Bari peasants who, on a visit to the Brown House at Munich, misbehaved and relieved themselves in the staircase. . . . The Chief said that our people must be given a higher racial concept, indispensable also in the task of Imperial colonization. He inveighed against the " sons of slaves ", and added that if they bore a distinctive somatic mark, he would exterminate them all; convinced that he was rendering a great service to Italy and to humanity.

Ciano would ape Mussolini's militarist theatricals. " I envy the French *Les Invalides*," he wrote on August 27, 1937, " and the Germans the Military Museum. No painting is worth a banner taken from the enemy." The same day, about the Duce's retinue on his journey to Germany : " Take care of their uniforms. We must look more Prussian than the Prussians." (And Mussolini himself on June 18, 1938 : " Italy will never be sufficiently Prussianized ".) On seeing widows and invalids of the Spanish war, Ciano ponders and concludes : " Sacrifice is necessary to create the bold and strong spirit of nations ". On December 19, 1937, thinking of European war : " Sometimes I ask myself whether it is not for us ourselves to force the pace and fire the fuse ". Pariani, Chief of the Italian General Staff, thought the early spring of 1939 possibly the most suitable time for such a war.

February 14, 1938. Pariani believes in a lightning war and initial surprise. Attack on Egypt, attack on the fleets, invasion of France. The war will be won at Suez and in Paris. I suggested to him that it might be useful to set up immediately a secret Italian-German War Committee. He agrees and thinks it possible, now that Blomberg has been dismissed. . . . I suggested studying a plan of attack against France across Switzerland.

But to Mr. Churchill he wrote in 1943 about the Nazis:
" I was the only foreigner to see at close quarters this
loathsome clique of bandits preparing to plunge the world
into a bloody war ".[1] There was a difference — Mussolini and Ciano would talk of fighting the world, but pounce
only on the weak: Abyssinia, Spain, Albania, Greece, or,
to please the Nazis, on the Jews.

Mussolini said in the Grand Council on October 7,
1938, thinking of Albania: " I was born never to leave
the Italians in peace. First Africa, to-day Spain, to-
morrow something else." The Council applauded.
Occasionally he would spin bold day-dreams. Thus on
December 21, 1937:

> " Indeed, I prepare for the Italians the greatest
> surprise. As soon as Spain is finished, I shall publish
> a communiqué which will remain classical."   I
> remember [writes Ciano] that in August 1935 he
> planned a surprise attack against the British Home
> Fleet at Alexandria and Malta. He then said to
> me: " In one night one can change the course of
> history." Afterwards he did not do it as the reports
> on the preparedness of the British fleet were not
> sufficiently accurate and because our own fleet hung
> back. But he meditates on such a plan and matures
> it ever since.

On December 31, 1937, Mussolini inquired about the
strength of his air force; and, satisfied, said that " if the
British don't conclude the agreement, the day of that
famous communiqué is drawing near! "

Ciano's foreign policy was ultra-Fascist, and so long
as he could think of Italy and Germany as equal partners,
blatantly pro-German and pro-Nazi. He boasted of
having " started " the pro-German policy, and was
pleased when, on September 4, 1937, the crowd " for the

[1] Winston S. Churchill, *Their Finest Hour*, page 115.

first time loudly applauded the Germans ". " The solid unity of the Axis must always be felt." When the Polish Foreign Minister, Beck, proposed to visit Rome, " there is nothing against it ", wrote Ciano, " provided the Germans are agreeable ". When Japan asked for recognition of Manchukuo : " it will be necessary to concert it with Berlin ". In 1937 he regretted that the German Foreign Office, " representatives of the Diplomatic International " and supporters of " the *ancien régime* ", had still "too much influence over the Führer". In October he told Hess, then in Rome, that in Italy " the most Fascist Ministry is that of Foreign Affairs ". He asked for Hassel's recall and desired for successor " a partyman ", the alliance being based mainly on " the identity of the political régimes ". " You cannot change the heads of these old men. The men have to be changed." Therefore, on February 5, 1938 : " The changes in the German Government are good. They move rapidly towards integral Nazification, which is useful to the Axis. . . . The Duce, too, is very pleased. . . . Ribbentrop at the Foreign Office is excellent . . . he is hostile to the English who treated him badly." " In Italy too," wrote Ciano on another occasion, " fifteen years were required to conquer the Palazzo Chigi. And I alone know the labour I have to undergo to make these goats keep step with the Fascist march. . . ." They jittered " at the time of the Abyssinian affair, and do so now every time the heroic *élan* of Mussolini cuts across the traditional lines of professional diplomacy ". Indeed, a new tone and new methods were introduced by Fascist *dinamismo*.

Abstracting of documents and breaking of ciphers is done in diplomacy but not talked about. The Fascist Government were well served by their information service. A spy in the British Embassy regularly supplied them with photographs of its secret documents ; and the copies in the Italian archives bear marks of having been carefully studied by Mussolini, otherwise not a great reader. Smaller, or less regular, scoops from other sources can be traced in the *Diary* (only the Russian and German ciphers and archives apparently proved immune). What is unusual is the brazen and extensive use made of material thus acquired. In September 1936 Grandi managed to obtain a copy of a dossier circulated by Mr. Eden to the Cabinet: it was entitled " The German Peril " and consisted of 32 documents and a covering note. Mussolini mentioned it to the Nazi Minister Hans Frank on September 23, 1936 : " a document from which Ribbentrop . . . will be able to gauge what are likely to be the results of his mission ". And when in October Ciano went to Berchtesgaden, he showed the dossier to Hitler, who " reacted violently ".[1] Further numerous examples can be culled from the *Diary*. Thus on August 28, 1937 :

> . . . I have sent Stoyadinovič [Yugoslav Prime Minister] photographic proof of the Franco-Czech conspiracy against him. . . . The stroke has gone home.

And on March 1, 1938 :

> I have given Christič [Yugoslav Minister in Rome] a copy of the Prague telegrams [deciphered wires of the French Minister]. It appears that Beneš called Yugoslavia and Rumania " vile ". I believe that there will be a lively reaction in Belgrade.

On November 11, 1937, he sent Schuschnigg two purloined British documents " compromising " for Guido Schmidt, the Austrian Foreign Minister. And on November 25 :

> Anfuso [*chef de cabinet* to Ciano] . . . will take to Schuschnigg a Czech document containing serious

---

[1] See *L' Europa verso la catastrofe*, pages 78 and 94 ; or its English translation, *Ciano's Diplomatic Papers*, pages 46 and 56-7.

statements by Hornbostel (Schmidt?) hostile to the Axis and friendly to the Western democracies. . . . I have also sent a copy of the document to Göring.

November 29: Schuschnigg "was much impressed by the quality of our information service". And on December 16:

> I mean to demand the head of Guido Schmidt. He talked to the British about the interceptions which I had communicated to Schuschnigg. This, of course, appears from a further interception.

These entries in Ciano's *Diary* tally with evidence given in March 1947 at the trial of Guido Schmidt in Vienna. Hornbostel, at the time of the *Anschluss* Director-General of the Austrian Foreign Office, spoke in the witness-box of a meeting which Schmidt and he had in September 1937, during a League of Nations meeting, with Sir Robert Vansittart at a restaurant outside Geneva; Vansittart's report of the talk was apparently one of the "intercepted" documents with which Ciano tried to blackmail Schuschnigg. And Berger-Waldenegg, late Austrian Minister in Rome: "Toward the end of November, Ciano told me of a diary he kept, showed it to me, and read out a few passages: he had recently sent Anfuso on a special mission to Schuschnigg to warn him against Schmidt". Ciano added that he had documentary evidence of Schmidt "plotting (*er pakelt*) with certain people in England".[1]

> December 1, 1937. I gave the Japanese Military Attaché the plans of Singapore [obtained through the Italian Consul]. He was much impressed by the gesture. We must assiduously cultivate the Japanese General Staff to attain the military agreement that shall settle the game with England.
> December 23, 1937. I was sharp with the Greek

[1] See *Der Hochverratsprozess gegen Dr. Guido Schmidt vor dem Wiener Volksgericht*, 1947, pages 186 and 288.

Minister. We have received a minute of the talk between Eden and the King of Greece. After the visit to Rome, he went to London to incite the British against us. He spoke badly about me: he called me ironically the super-Metternich. However, the Greeks of the Dodecanese *shall pay dear for it*.[1]

Probably nothing was done to them: but even without a bite the bark is significant.

Mussolini and Ciano were hatching a *coup* against Albania, and the date of it was fixed a year ahead. King Zog tried to placate them; invited Ciano to be witness at his wedding; contrary to the protocol, called on him at Durazzo; and in October 1938 sent an A.D.C. to him with the following message: " Albania is already in the hands of Italy which controls every sphere of her national life. The King is devoted. The people is grateful. Why should you want more? " " I turned amiable and genial ", writes Ciano. " This cheered him up. And he appreciated it most when, emphasizing every syllable, I told him how well-disposed I was to him, and that, whatever happened, I would consider him our man." A fortnight later, on October 27:

> The preparations in Albania are rapidly going ahead. . . . The action begins to take shape; the murder of the King (apparently —— will undertake it for 10 million [lire]), street disturbances, a descent from the hills of bands faithful to us. . . . Italy is asked to intervene. . . .

On December 3 Ciano records having seen —— " the man who prepares the stroke against the King of Albania ". And on the 5th: " The disappearance of the King will remove every centre of resistance ". Zog is still alive in 1949.

But there is also evidence of crimes which were committed. Thus on September 17, 1937:

[1] Italics in the original.

The Duce apprehends that the French police may be on the track of the authors of the Paris outrages [*attentati*]. Em.[Emanuele, chief of the Italian secret service] tells me that this is impossible. Anyhow, we are not in it. These are Frenchmen in the service of Met. . . .

Even the lowest tactics would be employed by Mussolini and avowed by Ciano. Under date of November 12, 1938, two anonymous letters are mentioned in the *Diary* sent by Mussolini to the Belgian Ambassador when in an intercepted dispatch he was found saying that the Italian people did not want war. And on December 16 : " Some time ago [November 1937] Percy Loraine spoke badly of Italy, and the Duce had anonymous letters sent to him containing choice insults and equally well selected newspaper cuttings with photographs of our armed forces ".

In writing to Mr. Churchill from Verona jail, Ciano spoke of " the cause of liberty and justice, in the triumph of which I fanatically believe " (" fanatically " echoes Hitler). But in 1937 Ciano felt much more certain of the triumph of an efficient police :

> October 18. A review of the Police. . . . Very beautiful. A perfect small army equipped with all the most modern weapons. With such a police, if faithful, no movement of the street is possible ; in a few minutes any riot would be crushed. Truly the modern State has always the means of self-defence, provided the man in authority is determined to use them. Himmler, who was present, expressed great admiration.

Mussolini hated the middle classes whose ideas of a good life ran counter to his heroics : Christian morality, respect for human rights, mercy or pity, peaceful enjoyment of property, a free growth of the arts and of knowledge, civic liberty — these were repellent to him both in his " proletarian " and in his totalitarian moods, which continually intermingled in a joint concept of " revolution ". And of that class and mentality France and England were the home and the cherished exponents. He hated them too, France even more than England, and professed to despise them; believed them decadent; and yearned to despoil them. Ciano aped him, though himself less consistently anti-British and less bitterly anti-French. September 14, 1937: " The Duce is in great form: aggressive and anti-British ". November 2: " The Tripartite Pact, so called anti-Communist, [is] in reality clearly anti-British ". December 23: Talk with Falange leaders: " Anglophobe. Spoke of retaking Gibraltar . . . I did not fail to encourage them." January 4, 1938: Saw O'Kelly, Vice-President of Eire: " Very anti-British ". January 20: Told Bose that India should look to Italy and Japan, " the two countries which have shaken Britain's prestige ". On December 25, 1937, instructed by the Duce, Ciano said to the Japanese Ambassador:

> " Moderate your attitude toward Washington: sharpen it toward London. For two reasons: first, to divide the two. Secondly, because in a conflict with the United States, we can do nothing concrete for you, whereas in a war against Great Britain we undertake to give you the maximum of support." The Ambassador, *diplomate de carrière*, and therefore prudent, reserved, and godfearing, was somewhat perturbed by my declarations.

And on the very eve of signing the new agreement with Britain, April 15, 1938:

> The Egyptians claim parity of rights with regard to the waters of the Tana River. Our officials raise many objections. I think we should agree. First, because it is meaningless, and next, because we should do a thing which helps to draw Cairo away from London.

An analysis of British policy toward Italy and her Abyssinian and Spanish adventures had better be deferred till the time when the British diplomatic documents bearing on the Agreement of April 16, 1938, are available — which cannot be far distant. But Ciano's *Diary*, to say the least, makes one doubt the premises and methods of Chamberlain's policy. A friendly Mussolini was, in the schemes of the appeasers, to restrain Hitler and his encroachments : seldom has a more inappropriate part been assigned to a jackal. Hitler had feelings of comradeship for Mussolini but no political regard, and the Axis partner was no better informed about his schemes and intentions than were his opponents. Nor would Mussolini, if he could, have tried to put the brake on Hitler unless he saw more danger than loot resulting from his undertakings. But the more *empressement* the British Government showed to gain Mussolini's friendship, the more he was convinced of their timorous weakness and the more he despised them. A firm attitude and a strictly correct approach, such as are of the tradition of British diplomacy, might have disconcerted Mussolini : [1] courting him swelled his self-important conceit. Reading British wires and dispatches, Mussolini and Ciano knew where they stood. October 15, 1937 : Lord Perth (the Ambassador) " is staking on the card of an agreement with us and wants to win ". February 12, 1938 : The British " hold out the possibility of an understanding. Towards which we remain colder than the British would think." March 8 : " Chamberlain is more interested than ourselves in bringing about an agreement : on this he has staked his political future, and perhaps even that of the entire Conservative party ".

[1] When on one occasion Mussolini bombastically addressed Lord Curzon : " My principle in politics is nothing for nothing ", Curzon replied : " That's very interesting, Mr. Mussolini. And pray, what has Italy to offer ? "

In London, Chamberlain was in constant touch with Grandi through unofficial intermediaries, behind Mr. Eden's back. But even in Rome, where Perth was a convinced adherent of Chamberlain's Italian policy, he thought fit to transact business of State through his sister-in-law. On December 22, 1937, Ciano sat at lunch next to Lady Chamberlain who talked " understanding, agreement, and friendship ". He notes: " Lady Chamberlain wears a Fascist badge. I am too much a patriot to appreciate such a gesture in an Englishwoman at such a time." On January 1, another talk; and she showed him a letter from the Prime Minister with little to it. So far, the business, though ill-advised, was unimportant. But then on February 1 :

> I went with Lady Chamberlain to the Duce, to whom she showed an important letter from Neville Chamberlain. Two points: Great Britain is inclined formally to acknowledge the Empire [of Italy in Abyssinia]; conversations can start about the end of the month. Mussolini approved and agreed. Lady Chamberlain will write to her relative to give the Duce's reaction which was clearly favourable. . . . He dictated to Lady Chamberlain the terms of the letter.
>
> February 17. A short casual talk with Perth to whom I spoke more or less on the lines of my letter to Grandi. Similarly to Lady Chamberlain who has, however, so far received no reply to her letter of February 1.

Eden resigned on February 20 — and perhaps the Prime Minister no longer required unofficial intermediaries. Perth's personal relations with Ciano were excellent. April 16, 1938: " Perth is a friend. Scores of his reports in our hands testify to it." December 16: " He is a man who has laboured hard and has come to understand Fascismo and even to love it. There is sincere affection between us." Such a friendly relation might perhaps have influenced Ciano who, in October 1938, when Ribbentrop proposed an alliance, thought that Italy should not close the door on Britain. But Ciano did not count for much — nor did Mussolini himself.

The *Anschluss* was the first occasion for secret searchings of heart and doubts. Its prospect was envisaged with calm ; the event was accepted with feigned indifference ; but occasional remarks betoken different feelings. On November 24, 1937, Ciano wrote :

> I have given Ghigi instructions for his mission to Vienna. . . . I thus defined to him the task of the Italian Minister at the Ballplatz : a doctor who gives oxygen to the dying patient without the heir noticing it. If in doubt : the heir matters more than the patient.

Mussolini, irritated at the Austrians, said on January 2, 1938, " that when the Spanish question is settled, he will invite Göring to Nazify Austria ". And Ciano on February 13 : " The *Anschluss* is inevitable, but should be put off as long as possible ". On February 17 he starts yarns about a " horizontal Axis " composed of Italy, Yugoslavia, Hungary, and Poland, as a necessary complement to the " vertical Axis ". It was seriously discussed with Beck during his visits to Rome (March 7-10 and 14), and remained until the summer of 1939 one of those clever paper calculations devoid of substance. Meantime the Duce himself started fretting at the way the Germans, without a word of warning, confronted him with a rapidly changing situation. But what was he to do ? He could not go to war over Austria. At first he highly approved of Schuschnigg's " strong speech " of February 24, its " imagination and stage management ". But Nazi reactions turned praise into criticism : Schuschnigg had talked big without possessing the means. And on March 11 Ciano wrote : " We cannot assume from here

the responsibility of advising him in one sense or another ".
That night the Prince of Hesse, son-in-law of King Victor-
Emmanuel and Hitler's liaison-officer with Mussolini,
arrived with a letter, acknowledging the Brenner as Italy's
frontier. " We ask Berlin's permission . . . to publish
the letter. The Führer agrees but asks for suppression of
two passages directed against Czechoslovakia."

> March 13. To-day calm is restored. What
> happened is no pleasure for us : certainly not. But
> some day it will be seen that it was all inevitable.
> The Duce says that an *équivoque* has been removed
> from the map of Europe. He noted the three which
> continue, and should, he thinks, meet the same fate
> in this order : Czechoslovakia, Switzerland, and
> Belgium.

On March 16 the Duce addressed the Chamber on the
Austrian problem :

> A magnificent speech. Made a deep and con-
> crete impression. Incalculable reverberations . . .
> Seldom have I " lived " a speech of his as to-day.
> The country has received a cut with the whip, and
> the melancholics are isolated and lost from sight.

But on March 7 Ciano spoke of Beck's lack of interest in
the *Anschluss* as " disproportionate to the importance
which the problem may assume for Poland " — perhaps
a deflected criticism ; and on April 21 : " The Germans
should not forget that the *Anschluss* has shaken many
Italians ".

Mussolini hated Czechoslovakia for being loyal to
France and democratic. When the Czechs mobilized on
May 21, he expressed to the German Ambassador his
" *désintéressement* in the future of Prague, and his complete
solidarity with Germany ". But he would have wished
to know her real intentions, and was told nothing. On
August 19 the Italian Military Attaché reported from

Berlin that a conflict was expected for the end of September, and everything was ready for action. August 20 :

> I send written instructions to Attolico to go to Ribbentrop [writes Ciano] and ask exactly what the Reich intends to do about Czechoslovakia, and this in order that " we should be able to take timely measures on our Western frontier." This communication will greatly appeal to the Germans as it shows how far we are prepared to go with them.

Should France intervene, the Duce is determined to place himself " with all his forces at the side of Germany. . . . Hence the need to know things fully and in good time." August 26: "Attolico has spoken to Ribbentrop in accordance with my instructions of the 20th. The reply is by no means clear . . . no final decision seems to have been taken." September 2 : " The Duce is anxious because the Germans tell us precious little about their programme regarding Czechoslovakia. . . . He wants to know how far Germany means to push things, and how and where she expects to be helped by us." September 3 :

> Attolico had a talk with Ribbentrop. Nothing new. If there is provocation, the Germans will attack. . . . It is fitting for us not to ask any further questions. It is clear that the Germans don't want to draw us into the game. This leaves us the fullest freedom of action in all circumstances.

On September 7, Hesse arrived with a memorandum from the Führer : " He will attack if Czechoslovakia provokes : to-day he is not yet in a position to fix a precise programme." On the 8th, the French Chargé d'Affaires tried to find out what had been settled between the Duce and the Führer : " I put on an air of mystery. In reality : nothing fixed." On the 12th, Hitler proposed to Mussolini a secret meeting on the Brenner, not later than the 25th. The same day Chamberlain appealed to him to intervene with Hitler who, Chamberlain thought, was kept in the dark concerning the steps undertaken by Britain (in favour of the Germans). " Such nonsense proves that the English have gone hysterical ", said Mussolini; and ordered Ciano to offer the Germans further support. And when he heard of Chamberlain's flight to Berchtesgaden, he exclaimed: " There will be no war. But this is the end of British prestige." And on September 17:

> I reached a decision. If war breaks out between Germany, Prague, Paris, and Moscow, I remain neutral. If Great Britain intervenes, extending the war and giving it an ideological character, then we shall go into the fire. Italy and Fascismo could not remain neutral.

So not even Soviet Russia, but only Britain, would have given the war an ideological character — strange indeed! But perhaps there was a different reason why the Duce would pair with this country. He said on August 29: " The British will do anything to avert a conflict, which they fear more than any other country in the world ". And Ciano, later, on September 25: " In England people kneel in the streets and pray for peace. In Italy they wait with calmness, aware and strong."

In March 1940, when it became clear that a German offensive in the West was imminent and Hitler suggested a meeting on the Brenner, Mussolini said to Ciano:

> " I shall do as Bertoldo did. He accepted the death sentence on condition that he chose the tree on which he was to be hanged. Needless to say, he never found that tree. I shall agree to enter the war, but reserve for myself the choice of the moment."

On September 28, 1938, on the point of starting for Munich, the Duce said: " As you see, I am moderately happy, for, be it at a high price, we could have finished off France and Great Britain for good. Of this we now

have overwhelming evidence." At Kufstein they met
Hitler, who explained that he meant " to put an end to
Czechoslovakia in her present shape, as she immobilises
forty divisions and ties up his hands with regard to France.
With Czechoslovakia properly deflated, twelve divisions
will suffice. . . ." At the Führerhaus in Munich, Hitler
cordially welcomed the Italians, but was stiff towards
Chamberlain and Daladier.

> There is a vague feeling of embarrassment,
> especially among the French. I speak to Daladier,
> and next to François-Poncet, about trifling matters.
> Then to Chamberlain who asks to speak to the Duce.
> He thanks the Duce for what he has done so far.
> But the Duce is cold and does not respond, and the
> conversation flags.

After Hitler, Chamberlain, and Daladier had spoken,[1]
Mussolini proposed as a basis for the further discussion a
document which, says Ciano, " was in reality sent the
previous night by our Embassy as giving the wishes of
the German Government ". (Erich Kordt, at that time
chef de cabinet to Ribbentrop, states that it was drafted by
Göring, Neurath, and Weizsäcker; approved by Hitler;
and given, without Ribbentrop's knowledge, to Attolico
for transmission to Rome.)[2] It was accepted, and the
discussion turned to details.

> The Duce, slightly annoyed by the vaguely
> Parliamentary atmosphere which always develops in
> such conferences, walks about the room, his hands
> in his pockets, somewhat *distrait*. Occasionally he
> helps to find a formula. His great mind, always
> ahead of events and men, has dismissed the agree-
> ment. . . . He has gone beyond and thinks of other
> things.

[1] According to the German minute, Mussolini spoke before Daladier;
see *Documents and Materials relating to the Eve of the Second World War*, publ. by
the Ministry of Foreign Affairs of the U.S.S.R., i. 236-7.
[2] *Wahn und Wirklichkeit*, page 131.

He speaks again when the problem of the Magyar and Polish minorities comes up for discussion. The others, all of them, would have liked to drop it. . . . But as always happens when there is a strong will, it prevails and others rally to it. . . .

. . . It is suggested that the Duce should postpone his departure and meet Chamberlain. But the Duce dismisses the idea in order not to hurt German susceptibilities.

Yet there was to be an Anglo-German postscript to Munich; and on October 2, the Prince of Hesse explained it to Ciano: Chamberlain asked for an interview with Hitler; and started by talking about a conference on Spain, and about abolishing bombers.

Finally he pulled a piece of paper from his pocket with the draft communiqué, and declared that he needed it for his position in Parliament. The Führer did not think he could refuse it. The Duce, to whom I repeated it [writes Ciano], said: "The explanations were unnecessary. You don't refuse a thirsty man a glass of lemonade."

The shams of Munich soon died upon their authors. For a while they could still strut about in fancy-dress, applauded for their make-belief. But the livid light of day was bound to break on them — how long would the game be allowed to continue? Hitler had no interest in the trappings and tinsel of Munich. The terrifying preponderance which Germany achieved in that night was all too real: rendered more ghastly by the characters and minds of her rulers and the inhumanity of her people. The Duce returned home in triumph: the card-sharping helpmate of the winner, the mediator honoured by self-interested " friends " of the victim. " From the Brenner to Rome," wrote Ciano, " from the King to the peasants, the Duce had a reception such as I had never seen." But even his tawdry glory could not last. He, too, had to readjust himself to a new, oppressive reality. Ciano's paean on the Duce's rôle at Munich seems as yet undisturbed even by the admission that the arbitrator had received his formula from Berlin. But four weeks later a jarring, faintly ironic, note creeps, perhaps for the first time, into the Valhalla *motif* sounded by Ciano for the heroic Duce :

> October 24. The Duce . . . talks to me about . . . a reduction of armaments : he wants to restore war to a more heroic plane by eliminating all that is too complex in its mechanism. In practice, to place restrictions on weapons which are too expensive for us.

The Italians now busied themselves about their " horizontal Axis ", and suffered humiliation. They tried to satisfy Poland's aspiration to a place among the Great Powers, Hungary's claims to Czechoslovak territory, and the wishes of both for a common frontier across Carpatho-Russia. But Hitler thought, for a short while, that he could make the Czechs into his janissary vanguard in the East ; and he anyhow disliked the Magyars : his politics were mostly those of pre-1914 Vienna. The Magyars were growing impatient and approached Rome with a request for the Four Power conference foreshadowed at Munich, to determine their gains at the expense of Czechoslovakia. Mussolini transmitted it to London, Paris, and Berlin, and informed Warsaw and Belgrade. But Hitler would have none of it. " This is our first climb down," wrote Ciano, " and it greatly vexes me." Others followed, and Mussolini grew wary :

> Having read the Polish reports, he made me inform Berlin that we did not insist on a common Polish-Magyar frontier. He thinks it of no practical use, while any attempt at encircling the Germans he considers worse than stupid — absolutely absurd.

He was too much of a realist seriously to engage in the game of the " horizontal Axis " once the Germans were aware of it.

But Ciano, the Magyars, and the Poles continued to spin such fancies. On October 21, Hungary suggested frontier arbitration by the Axis in Slovakia, by the Axis plus Poland in Carpatho-Russia. Mussolini told Ciano " to feel Germany's pulse before inviting Poland ". Ribbentrop " turned up his nose at the idea ". It was therefore dropped. On the 24th, Mussolini instructed Ciano " to take a clear stand against the Magyar claim to Carpatho-Russia, as the French Press gives an anti-German turn to the attempt to establish a common Polish-Magyar frontier ". Finally Germany agreed to Axis arbitration on the Hungarian-Czechoslovak frontier. On October 28, Ribbentrop arrived in Rome.

> He had not grasped the political significance of the Axis arbitration [writes Ciano]. I told him, it sets the seal on the fact that Franco-British influence in Danubian and Balkanic Europe has collapsed for good and all. A gigantic event: of no less import than Munich. Perhaps I convinced him. But he continues hostile to the Magyars, and defends the Czech cause with a zeal which I would describe as shameless.

They met again in Vienna on November 2. Ribbentrop still

> means to plead the cause of Prague. But he is poorly, very poorly prepared for the discussion. He is not properly briefed, nor is his staff familiar with the problems. This plays into my hand.

The next day, in a private sitting,

> I take the lead and, meeting with few objections, trace in red pencil the line of the new frontier. Ribbentrop's unpreparedness allows me to carve out

for Hungary territory which could have indeed been the subject of much heated argument.

(Equally unprepared appeared Ribbentrop at the Nuremberg Trial.)

On October 28, Ribbentrop had offered Mussolini a Triple Alliance with Germany and Japan. The Duce hesitated, while Ciano was averse to such an irrevocable step. But had they still freedom of choice? On December 23, 1938, Mussolini ordered Ciano to notify Ribbentrop of Italy's acceptance. And thus Ciano's early *Diary* closes with a new chapter in Italo-German relations.

" THE PACT OF STEEL ":
A STUDY IN LEVITY

THE Nazi-Fascist Alliance, known as " the Pact of Steel ", was inherent in the affinities of the two systems, the personal relationship of the two dictators, and the parallelism of their policies; and it seems doubtful whether it seriously influenced the course of events; the Molotov-Ribbentrop treaty of August 23, 1939, and not the Pact of Steel, made Hitler believe, first, that the Western Powers would not dare to succour Poland, and next, that he could take them on anyhow. Nor did the pact hasten Italy's entry into the war: it merely caused Mussolini some qualms when in September 1939 his own conduct seemed to reproduce the part played by Italy in 1914: he was haunted by her consequent reputation among the Germans and had wished her to live it down. But no pact was needed to bring him in when France had collapsed and Britain seemed doomed. The Abyssinian war had broken the Stresa front and, followed by the unopposed remilitarization of the Rhineland and Mussolini's Spanish adventure, paved the way for the *Anschluss*. After that, he could hardly try to realize his ambitions except as Hitler's jackal: and for him alone Hitler seems to have felt loyal comradeship — more indeed than Mussolini, gnawed by envy, was able to reciprocate.

But though the Pact of Steel was a symptom rather than a factor in the history of 1939, the moves and methods of the Powers concerned are revealing; and the story of those negotiations is told with meticulous care and thorough knowledge by Professor Mario Toscano,[1] now Historical Adviser to the Italian Foreign Office and vice-

[1] Mario Toscano, *Le origini del patto d' acciaio*. Sansoni. Firenze. 1948.

president of the commission entrusted with the publication of the Italian diplomatic documents, 1861–1943. He has been able to supplement the material contained in Ciano's *Diary* and the published Ciano *Papers*, in the Nuremberg documents and those of the International Military Tribunal for the Far East, with unpublished Italian diplomatic telegrams and dispatches (among which those from Attolico, Ambassador in Berlin, are of outstanding interest), and with information derived from Italian survivors of those years. The book forms an excellent introduction to the forthcoming volume of Italian documents covering the period May 22 to September 3, 1939, which, in the absence of an Italian Green Book on the origins of the war, will receive priority in the publication of more recent documents.

In 1937 a military alliance was suggested to Berlin by the Japanese General Staff (not the Government): its spokesman was the military attaché, General Oshima, who next became Ambassador, and even as such continued to represent the Army rather than the Government. But Germany was not ready for a move which would have affected London and Washington no less than Moscow. Similarly hints at a Triple Alliance dropped at the signing of the Tripartite Anti-Comintern Treaty in November 1937, were not taken up by Germany. In May 1938, during Hitler's visit to Italy, Mussolini, who had just concluded an agreement with Great Britain and was negotiating one with France, thought of a pact which would give new contents to the Axis; or else people might start talking of its demise and of a return to Stresa. But the Italians were not prepared as yet to go the whole length of " a pact of military assistance, public or secret ", as proposed by Ribbentrop. Ciano wrote in his *Diary* on May 6 :

Ribbentrop . . . is exuberant and sometimes shows levity. The Duce says he is of the type of Germans that disgrace Germany. He talks right and left of war, without fixing either opponent or objective. Sometimes he wants, jointly with Japan, to destroy Russia. Or again his bolts strike France and England. Occasionally he threatens the United States. This puts me on my guard against his schemes.

When next, on June 19, Ribbentrop gave Attolico " confidentially " his " personal notions " on a German-Italian military alliance (the Führer " generally agrees with me in these matters "), he protested that Germany did not mean to drag Italy into a war over Czechoslovakia. The breach was widening between the democracies and the authoritarian States, and it was time for these to form a *bloc*; and results were expected from the meeting of Hitler and Mussolini, " who are among the greatest personalities known to history ". Attolico replied that Mussolini, in his recent speech at Genoa, had declared that in an ideological war " the totalitarian States would immediately form a *bloc* "; and, in accordance with instructions previously received, Attolico suggested the following points to be dealt with in an agreement: frontiers (the Alto Adige and the removal of its German population); " consultation "; political and diplomatic support, possibly accompanied by secret military clauses. But, retorted Ribbentrop, why thus hide the element which has given the Axis its deterrent strength? What he wanted was " a plain, open military alliance " (*ipsissima verba*: Attolico did not speak German, and their talks were in English). Such an alliance alone would enable the two Powers to retain their gains and to realize their further aims. Italy would find them in the Mediterranean and Germany " for instance " in Czechoslovakia. He mentioned that he was sounding Tokyo about a " military triangle ".

Ciano found Attolico's report " very important and interesting ", and suggested a personal meeting (by now Mussolini was disappointed in Italy's agreement with Britain, and was turning against one with France). In another talk at the end of July Attolico argued that the problems of the Danube Basin required clarification : as an object of discord it had replaced the *Anschluss* in the calculations of their opponents. The next move occurred on September 30, at Munich, when Ribbentrop produced the draft of a tripartite German-Italian-Japanese alliance (" the greatest thing in the world ") : it stipulated for consultation in diplomatic difficulties ; political and diplomatic support should one of the contracting parties be threatened ; and aid and assistance against unprovoked aggression. After signature the application of the treaty to particular cases was to be settled, and only when " the mode and extent of political, military, and economic assistance " were fixed would it come into force. (The political *éclat* would thus be secured, while heeding Japanese reluctance to assume ill-defined commitments.)

The precise nature of the Italian answer is not known (and probably it was not precise). Then, on October 23, Ribbentrop, having received a reply from the Japanese military and naval attachés, telephoned to Ciano : he was coming to Rome with a personal message from Hitler.

> What does he want ? [wrote Ciano in his *Diary*].
> I mistrust Ribbentrop's initiatives. He is vain,
> frivolous, and loquacious. The Duce says that it is
> enough to look at his head to see that he lacks brains.
> Still more tact. I don't quite like the way those
> telephone calls of the last days were made. For the
> present we have to put up with it. But some time
> it will be necessary to call a halt to such making of
> policy by *coups de téléphone*.

Before Ribbentrop arrived in Rome, on October 27 Lord Perth informed Ciano that Britain was prepared to

have the April agreement come into force as from the
middle of November. " We must keep both doors open ",
noted Ciano in his *Diary*. " An alliance concluded now
would close one of them, and not the less important,
perhaps for ever." The same day the Japanese attachés
communicated to him their counter-draft, which emphasized in its preamble the anti-Communist character of
the treaty, but otherwise, with some minor additions,
reproduced the three articles of the German draft. After
a first talk with Ribbentrop Ciano wrote :

> Ribbentrop has really come for a tripartite mili-
> tary alliance. . . . He has got into his head the idea
> of war, he wants war, his war . . . He does not name
> either enemies or objectives, but wants war in three
> or four years.

Ciano was more intelligent and subtle than Ribbentrop ;
yet the reader of his *Diary* feels that he judged the other
man *en connaissance de cause* ; though his critical sense did
not extend to his own person.

The next day Ribbentrop expounded to Mussolini the
Führer's reasons for wishing to see the triple military
alliance concluded. War with the Western democracies
was unavoidable within three or four years; and the present
position of the Axis was " exceptionally favourable ".
Previously he had hesitated for fear of making England
and France rearm, or causing the downfall of the
appeasers, or provoking an Anglo-American alliance ;
now they were anyhow rearming as fast as they could,
Chamberlain and Daladier were safe, and danger of war
would render America merely more isolationist. Japan's
power was formidable, but to refuse the pact might play
into the hands of her pacifist " financiers".

> The Czechoslovak crisis has proved our strength.
> We have the advantage of the initiative and are
> masters of the situation. We cannot be attacked.
> . . . Since September we can face war with the

> great' democracies. . . . Czechoslovakia is practically finished. . . . Toward Poland the Reich means to pursue a policy of friendship respecting her vital needs, especially her access to the sea. . . . Russia is weak and will remain so for years to come : all our dynamic strength [*dinamismo*] can be directed against the democracies.

The Duce agreed that the alliance had to come, but doubted whether this was the time for it. An alliance was " a sacred pledge ", to be observed in full. But while Italian public opinion accepted the Axis, it was not quite ripe for a military alliance.

> When the time comes to conclude a German-Italian alliance, it will be necessary to fix objectives. We must not form a purely defensive alliance. There is no need for it, as no one thinks of attacking the totalitarian States. What we want is an alliance to redraw the map of the world. For this objectives and conquests will have to be fixed ; we, for our part, know where we must go.

Mussolini envisaged a dual alliance only ; whereas Japan entered into Hitler's *Weltpolitik* as a check on the United States and Russia, an alliance with her might have hindered rather than helped Mussolini at that juncture in his pursuit of Mediterranean objectives. Ribbentrop spoke of friendship with Poland : to Professor Toscano an example of Nazi " insincerity *erga omnes* ". While that insincerity can hardly be doubted, Ribbentrop's discourse exhibits one facet of Nazi policy at that juncture : the claims which he had raised against Poland in his talk with M. Lipski, Polish Ambassador in Berlin, on October 24 — and these were kept secret both from the Western Powers and from Italy — were not nearly as formidable as the offer he had made of German friendship. The formal inclusion in the Reich of an anyhow Nazified Danzig, and an extra-territorial *autostrade* across the Corridor, would not have cut off Poland's access to the sea, especially if she entered Germany's orbit; but her doing so would have severed her ties with the West and destroyed her independence. Although the direction suggested by Ribbentrop for Axis *dinamismo* followed that of Mussolini's interests, there was little response. Possibly Mussolini had learnt not to take Ribbentrop's schemes seriously; moreover, with all his braggadocio, he would not face a major war. Lastly an ephemeral personal factor influenced his attitude (a human proclivity unchecked in dictators) :

> At Munich [writes Professor Toscano] Mussolini, in appearance more than in reality (for his proposals had been supplied by the Germans) came out as arbitrator and mediator, though as one decidedly partial to the Germans; who in the end aimed at obtaining even more. An alliance with Hitler, concluded so soon after, would obviously have made Mussolini lose the position he had acquired toward Britain and France, which he could not desire; nor could he wish to encourage new Nazi enterprises: he feared their bearing and repercussions on Italian interests, especially in the Danube Basin.

On November 23-24 Chamberlain and Lord Halifax visited Paris; meantime Germany was negotiating with France the Declaration of December 6. No great significance attached to either move (moreover, as appears from Ciano's *Diary*, the Germans had obtained a previous *nihil obstat* from Mussolini for their negotiations). None the less these developments grated on the Duce's excitable, unsteady disposition: on November 24 he telegraphed to Attolico that if the Anglo-French Entente was being transformed into " a true and proper military alliance ", he would be prepared to conclude one with Germany immediately; and on the 30th the scene was staged in the Italian Parliament of shouted revendications against France. On January 2, 1939, Ciano informed

Ribbentrop, both over the telephone and by a personal letter, that the Duce waived his previous reservations regarding the time for concluding the military alliance, and offered to have it signed towards the end of the month. In June Ribbentrop had affirmed that German preoccupations in Czechoslovakia did not enter into his proposal; now the Italians denied any connexion between their claims against France and their offer : they were prompted by " the proved existence of a Franco-British military pact ", by " warlike tendencies in responsible French circles ", and by " the military preparations of the United States ". The treaty was " to be presented to the world as a peace pact ". Thus within two months, and for no cogent reasons, everything was turned topsy-turvy. In 1917–1918 it used to be said in light-hearted Vienna that the situation in Austria was desperate but not serious. Hitler, too, and Mussolini, Ribbentrop and Ciano were desperately dangerous, but not serious; as is seen in the negotiations which lead up to the conclusion of the Pact of Steel.

Ribbentrop thought that by the end of January a tripartite treaty, including Japan, could be ready for signature; and he described it to Attolico as " one of the greatest events in history ". Attolico put to him two *desiderata*, to be treated not as conditions but as " essential requests " (Ciano thought that he made too much of them) : the one concerned " greater correctness in economic relations ", and the other the Alto Adige (an announcement of population transfer was to put an end to all doubts). On January 6 Attolico was given a new draft of the pact, approved by the Führer. The overt treaty reproduced the Japanese draft of October 1938, with its reference in the preamble to " the strengthening of the defences against the Communist corrosion " ; while the secret annexe set up an elaborate (and obscure) system of joint commissions. The only amendment to this draft suggested by Mussolini was to delete the phrase about " Communist corrosion ".

Delays ensued; the Japanese Foreign Minister and the Admiralty were opposed to the alliance urged by the Army and its representatives in Berlin and Rome: Japan might have accepted the treaty if enabled to restrict its application to Russia, but would not engage simultaneously on a second front against the Anglo-Saxon Powers. Shiratori, Japanese Ambassador to Rome, explained to Attolico

> that no Japanese Government could ever accept so vague a treaty of alliance. . . . A military strengthening of the Anti-Comintern Pact would be interpreted as referring foremost, if not exclusively, to war against the U.S.S.R. But this was naturally of limited interest to the European totalitarian Powers; hence a detailed definition was required of the cases covered by the treaty; what would Germany and Italy have to do in case of a conflict between Japan and Russia, or Japan of one between England and Germany or between Italy and France? What would Germany and Italy have to do in case of war between Japan and America? etc., etc. All this would have to be foreseen and exactly stated in the treaty. But for this — and he did not doubt the final result — time was required, and the European Powers, accustomed to correspond or negotiate over the telephone, should understand that the same methods could not be applied to Japan.

Ciano, after reading these remarks, noted in his *Diary*, on March 6, apparently oblivious of his own previous strictures on diplomacy by telephone:

> . . . is it really possible to bring distant Japan so deeply into European life, which is becoming more and more convulsed and nervous and liable to be changed from hour to hour by a telephone call?

And two days later, with the same lack of self-critical humour:

The delays and procedure of the Japanese make me doubt the possibility of effective collaboration between Fascist and Nazi *dinamismo* and the phlegmatic slowness of Japan.

A few days later Hitler entered Prague, and started to redraw the map of Europe without any reference to his partner in " dynamics ". What had become of Mussolini's presumed ascendancy at Munich? It was not the Czechoslovakia of the Paris Peace Treaties, but of the Munich settlement and of the Vienna Award of which Mussolini claimed paternity, that Hitler was destroying. Moreover, developments in Slovakia reacted on Croatia, and German activities were reported from Zagreb. Ciano made serious representations to the German Ambassador, and on March 18 Attolico wrote to Rome about the need of " a fundamental clarification " : was there equality of rights and obligations between the Axis Powers, and what did the Germans make of the elementary duty of informing and consulting their partner? Was Italy to be excluded from the Balkans, with " only *the waters of the Mediterranean* reserved to her " ? Ciano deeply resented Hitler's action, and so at first did Mussolini; who next concluded that German hegemony was henceforth established in Europe, and, moreover, that Italy could not play " the prostitute " by changing her policy. On March 20 Ribbentrop, in a personal letter to Ciano, thanked Italy for her attitude, " full of understanding and friendship ", and offered lame excuses for Germany's sudden, " unpremeditated " decisions; he repeated the Führer's assurance that in all Mediterranean questions " the policy of the Axis shall be determined by Rome, and that Germany will therefore never pursue in Mediterranean countries a policy independent of Italy ". Ciano replied by a short and dry letter — and this was all there was of Italian ill-humour. The mere fact that London reacted to Hitler's entry into Prague by attempts to build up a

defensive front against aggression based on the " democratic Powers ", drew Mussolini nearer to Hitler, while
Ciano, who had long panted for his very own adventure
in Albania, knew that he needed German support;
dinamismo forced Italy into a position of dependency on
Germany, and Ciano himself bears a heavy responsibility
for Spain, Albania, and the attack on Greece. There was
never to be " a true and proper clarification " of Axis
relations, writes Professor Toscano.

> No problem was thoroughly discussed. No precise
> obligations were formulated or assumed, and, barring
> Ribbentrop's letter, things were committed to un-
> certain memory, and not to paper. The ambiguity
> of Italo-German relations . . . was more than ever
> incurable. Hitler was not interested in clarifying
> them, while Mussolini feared the consequences of a
> thorough clarification.

On April 7 Italy invaded Albania. On the 13th the
Western Powers announced their guarantees to Rumania
and Greece; and they were negotiating with Russia and
Turkey: these were developments that affected the
sphere of interests claimed by Italy in the Balkans. On
April 28 Hitler delivered a speech directed against
Britain and Poland, but without a single hostile reference
to Soviet Russia. Japan, however, insisted on giving the
tripartite military alliance an exclusively anti-Russian
character. This might have made Russia join the Western
Powers, which would not have suited Germany's book.
Hence, in spite of Ribbentrop's reluctance to shelve his
Weltpolitik, by the end of April serious negotiations were
confined to the two Axis Powers.

On April 14 Göring arrived in Rome. The upshot of
several windy and verbose talks was to emphasize German-
Italian solidarity; the inevitability of a conflict with the
Western Powers; the need of both Axis Powers for an
interval in which to complete their armaments; and

Germany's determination to solve the Polish problem.
There was an obvious and disquieting contradiction
between the last two propositions; this made the Italians
urgently seek direct contact with Ribbentrop, who in reply
suggested a meeting with Ciano at Como between May 6
and 8; he would bring with him a draft of the German-
Italian pact. Attolico telegraphed on May 2 a warning
against negotiating such a pact " in a hurry and, as it
were, *stante pede* ".

> A pact limited to Italy and Germany could not
> be a vague document, such as that prepared by Japan.
> It needs to be more precise, take account of certain
> indispensable premises (the Brenner frontier: solu-
> tion of the German problem in the Alto Adige),
> acknowledge the right of either side to its own
> *Lebensraum*, and define the limits and modes of inter-
> pretation of interests in mixed zones, confirming our
> right to an equal share in trade and expansion in the
> Balkans and the Danube Basin, etc., etc.
> Further, in view of past experience, a treaty of
> alliance with Germany would have to fix clearly the
> extent of obligatory mutual consultation in all matters
> of common interest. . . .
> Similarly, an Italo-German pact would have to
> enter much more thoroughly into military details
> than a vague tripartite pact reinforcing the anti-
> Comintern agreement. But all this cannot be
> improvised and would have to be quietly pre-
> pared. . . .

Attolico knew only too well the two men to whom he
was preaching, and preaching in vain.

On May 4 Attolico reported that the Legal Department of the German Foreign Office had been instructed
to prepare the draft of a dual alliance; and the same day
Mussolini gave Ciano instructions for his talks with
Ribbentrop. " It is my firm conviction ", he wrote,
" that the two European Powers of the Axis require a
period of peace of at least three years. It is only after

1943 that a war effort will have the best prospects of victory." Italy had to organize Libya and Albania for war, and pacify Abyssinia which would be able to raise an army of half a million men; reconstruct her navy and re-equip her artillery; develop economic autarchy, cash in the foreign money which the Exhibition of 1942 was expected to attract, repatriate the Italians from France, and transfer many of her war industries from the Po Valley to the south; lastly, strengthen the ties between the two Axis nations, which would be greatly helped by a *détente* between the Church and Nazism, " much desired by the Vatican ". " For all these reasons Fascist Italy does not desire to hasten a European war, though convinced of its being unavoidable." In a further *tour d'horizon*, Mussolini spoke of his agreement with Britain as formal rather than substantial, and as " of negative rather than of positive application ". " In case of a war limited to Italy and France, the Italian Government does not ask for German help in men but merely in *matériel*." He admitted an understanding with Russia to the extent of keeping her out of a hostile *bloc*, but beyond that it would be misunderstood within the Axis countries and would weaken their connexion. (What Mussolini really apprehended was that an understanding between Germany and Russia would reduce still farther Italy's rôle in the alliance.)

On May 5 the French Press published reports of bloody anti-German demonstrations in Milan: whereupon Mussolini had the Ciano-Ribbentrop meeting transferred from Como to Milan. When the two met the next day Ribbentrop's talk was obliging and inconclusive (and even what he said was never fixed in an agreed minute): in Poland, time is working for Germany; the Poles are megalomaniacs, with no sense of reality; France and England are getting tired of them, and soon no one will be prepared to go to war over Poland; Germany does

not mean " to take the first step ", but of course if provoked " will react in the sharpest manner " ; Germany,
too, is convinced of the need for peace for a period of
" not less than four or five years ", but if war is forced on
her, etc. He promised to send the draft for a treaty of
alliance to be signed with great solemnity in Berlin.

At night Mussolini had the truly original idea of
having the pact announced before its terms were settled,
and telephoned accordingly to Ciano. Ribbentrop, who
still hankered after the inclusion of Japan, demurred, but
telephoned to Hitler who agreed; whereupon an official
announcement was prepared and published : the relations
of the two Axis States were to be fixed definitely and form-
ally by means of a political and military pact. That
announcement, writes Professor Toscano, " could serve
as an excellent means of diplomatic pressure on France.
They were playing with fire, but this had become a
habit. . . ."

On May 12, the draft treaty was given to Attolico with
the suggestion of signing some time between May 21
and 24.

> The German and the Italian peoples, closely
> bound to each other by the deep affinity of their ways
> of life and the complete solidarity of their interests,
> have determined in future to stand guard side by side
> and with united forces over their eternal rights to
> life and over the maintenance of peace.

.   .   .   .   .   .

> Should it happen that, contrary to the wishes and
> hopes of the Contracting Parties, one of them was
> involved in war . . . the other will place itself
> immediately as ally at its side, and support it with all
> its forces by land, on sea, and in the air.

No time-limit was set to the duration of that treaty,
between " National-Socialist Germany and Fascist Italy ",
although revisions were foreseen without indication of

date. In a secret annexe special provisions were made for co-operation in matters of Press and propaganda.

Attolico pointed out in his comments that the Brenner frontier was nowhere mentioned; that the customary formula about " unprovoked aggression " was dropped, enjoining the completest solidarity, offensive no less than defensive; and that the expression " eternal rights to life " lent itself " to the most varied alarmist interpretations ". He suggested that at least in the title a defensive character should be ascribed to the treaty; and that quinquennial periods of revision should be fixed. (As Professor Toscano points out, the automatism of support to a high degree stultified the consultation clause, and, given Germany's superiority, was bound " in its improvident latitude " to work against Italy.)

" I have never read such a pact ", Ciano wrote in his *Diary*. " It is real and proper dynamite." Attolico was authorized to put forward amendments concerning the Alto Adige and periods of revision — otherwise that extraordinary draft was accepted without demur : after having talked of the need of peace for at least three years, Mussolini left it to Hitler to start war whenever he chose, with Italy bound to range herself immediately by his side, no matter how or why the war had been started. And only after the " Pact of Steel " had been signed in Berlin with much flourish on May 22 did he bethink himself of establishing its exact bearing.

On May 21 Mussolini sent General Cavallero to Hitler with a memorandum putting his own interpretation on the pact. The document reproduces in full Ciano's instructions shown to Ribbentrop at Milan, which gave at great length Mussolini's reasons for wishing to see peace preserved for at least three years. The rest (including a paragraph about weakening the internal unity of enemy States by means of anti-Semitic, pacifist, or regionalist movements, or by revolts in their colonies) was window-dressing :

what Mussolini sought was the Führer's official approval for his time-table, which would have made it the basis for directives to be prepared by the two General Staffs. But Hitler merely thanked him in a verbal message for his note, declared " in principle " his agreement with its argument, and expressed the wish to talk over matters personally with Mussolini. On May 23, the day after the Pact of Steel had been signed, Hitler had decided " at the first suitable opportunity to attack Poland " ; and on August 11 Ciano was informed by Ribbentrop at Salzburg that war was imminent. The Italians now wanted to protest (some even to cancel the pact) ; but when Ciano, on August 21, tried to arrange a further meeting with Ribbentrop, in order to clarify matters that should have been clarified before the pact was signed, he learnt that Ribbentrop was going to Moscow " to sign a political pact with the Soviet Government ". " There is no doubt," wrote Ciano in his *Diary*, " the Germans have struck a master blow. The European situation is upset."

THE DEATH OF A TYRANT

On May 5, 1943, Mussolini appeared for the last time on the balcony of the Palazzo Venezia from which he used to harangue enthusiastic or obsequious crowds; on July 11 the allies landed in Sicily, and on July 24 a meeting of the Fascist Grand Council resulted in Mussolini's downfall and arrest. Rescued two months later by German airborne troops from imprisonment in the hotel on the Gran Sasso, he had his last fling in the " Fascist Republic ", remembered for atrocities which, under German patronage, it committed on other Italians, and for the Verona trial of members of the Grand Council who, after having voted against Mussolini, had the ill luck to fall into his hands. But by November 1944 Mussolini's Fascist army had vanished, and on April 27, 1945, he himself, while trying to make his escape to Germany, was caught by Italian partisans, and shot the next day.

The story of the two years between Mussolini's deposition and his death is told in Signor Saporiti's book,[1] which has the merit of presenting a good deal of material that is new, or at least not easily accessible to English readers, and the demerit of doing so in an unscholarly manner. Some of the documents are known from other sources: for instance, Grandi's Order of the Day voted by the Fascist Grand Council, or the letter addressed to Mussolini at the time of the Verona trial by Ciano's mother. In both cases Signor Saporiti omits sentences, or even whole paragraphs, for no apparent reason except that he is unaware of the importance of textual accuracy; similarly he sometimes prints a mere summary in inverted commas as if it were the full text. Nor is it always clear from which of several documents he is quoting. Many of the docu-

---

[1] Pietro Saporiti, *Empty Balcony*. Gollancz.

ments are not easy to come by — *e.g.* Bottai's minute of the Grand Council of July 24, 1943 (previously quoted by Signor Saporiti in *Le Monde* in July 1946), or the report which Mainetti, the priest in whose parish Mussolini was arrested, wrote about it to his bishop.

To these the author, who is a journalist, adds interviews he had with participants in the transactions ; the most important among them is Count Dino Grandi, " the man who brought Fascism tumbling to the ground in hopes of getting his country out of the war ", but a few days later, realizing that " there was no place for him in Italy ", left for Portugal. There, " living in extremely modest circumstances in a small white villa at Estoril, the smart seaside suburb of Lisbon ", he gave the author an account, vivid and self-satisfied, of his performance, and Signor Saporiti reproduces it in the manner of a journalist telling his story, rather than of a historian critically examining it.

Various accounts of the same events are not always collated in the book, even when previously given by the author himself : thus in *Empty Balcony* it is " land-surveyor Mottarella, partisan, re-examining lorry, plate number W.H. 529,507 ", who discovers Mussolini under a heap of old blankets, while in an article published by Signor Saporiti in the *Chicago Daily News* of April 24, 1946, it is Giuseppe Negri whose discovery of Mussolini is circumstantially related. Some other accounts of the arrest, even when given by men who took part in it, seem to have been neglected — for instance, that published in July 1946, in the *Corriere Lombardo*, by Lazzaro Urbano and Bellini delle Stelle. While, therefore, Signor Saporiti's book can hardly be treated as authoritative, in broad outlines the picture it gives is probably a true one. How puny and mean these votaries and exponents of force appear when overtaken by disaster ! Sycophants who owed their rank and standing to Mussolini turned against him when he himself had to admit : " To-day I certainly am the best hated man in Italy ". Grandi had drawn up an Order of the Day to be moved in the Council; it called for the resumption by the King of his constitutional powers including the command of the armed forces, and thus " under the veil of clever words " challenged the dictatorship. For two days before the meeting Grandi and Bottai canvassed and gained the adherence of ten others, out of a total of twenty-eight members; among the ten were Ciano, for some time past a covert critic of Mussolini, and also Marshal de Bono and Count de Vecchi, the two surviving Quadrumviri of the March on Rome; but most of the members " would not accept the responsibility of taking definite action during the session unless the debate took a favourable turn ".

With one short interval the meeting lasted from 5.15 P.M. on July 24 till 2.42 the next morning. It was opened by Mussolini with an *exposé* which Signor Saporiti seems to reproduce from Mussolini's own book, *Storia di un anno* (*Il tempo del bastone e della carota*) — *The History of One Year* (*The Time of the Stick and the Carrot*). The dictator was both depressed and petulant. Bottai — " according to his own report " not fully confirmed by others — from the outset adopted a bold line, and Grandi is reported to have addressed Mussolini in severe, even aggressive, terms (apparently the following passages are quoted by the author from Bottai and not from Grandi) :

> Take from your cap that ridiculous Marshal's badge that you so inelegantly awarded yourself. Try to become again the Mussolini of olden days. But you cannot. It is too late. By your folly and by your weakness we have come to see the destinies of a great people treated like private affairs.

Mussolini seemed to quaver and lose his arrogance; then heartened by support, he turned on his opponents, taunted them with the "fabulous" wealth some of them were known to have acquired, and told them that he had enough evidence to send them all to the gallows.[1] "You more than anyone", he said, pointing to Ciano. And later on : "If the King accepts the restoration of military powers that means my execution". But if not, "what will your position be, gentlemen. . .?" "The Duce is blackmailing us", cried Grandi, and various members in turn threatened their opponents with execution. Then, in the course of a confused debate, Suardo, President of the Senate, "rose in tears to declare that he withdrew his signature from the Grandi resolution "; and Ciano began to waver. Still, on a division it was carried by nineteen votes to six; next day Mussolini himself would have to carry it to the King. "You have brought about a crisis in the régime", he said, closing the session.

There is something incongruous and bizarre in that gathering of Mussolini's puppets which, by working the hollow forms of a sham constitution, enabled the discredited representative of monarchy to overthrow the dictator. After the meeting Grandi went straight to the King's Chamberlain, Count Acquarone, who was expecting him. "With Mussolini," he said, "the whole totalitarian régime will crash ", but "an immediate German reaction " must be expected; Grandi claims to have advised immediate peace, or even collaboration with the Allies. As for his own future, this was the end of his political life : "I have played the part of Tallien to the Italian Robespierre. I have finished." Next day, at 5 P.M., Mussolini waited on the King, and was told that his person would be protected but that he had to leave the Government. When he stepped outside, his car was gone :

[1] Mussolini kept a private archive of material for use against both friends and opponents ; see Emilio Re, *Storia di un archivio. Le carte di Mussolini.* Many of those precious files he carried away from Rome, and some came subsequently into Anglo-American hands.

a military ambulance drew up and he was arrested. He turned docile — " a very frightened and humble man ".

Between the close of the Council meeting and the interview with the King he had taken no counter-measures or precautions. Signor Saporiti ascribes it to megalomania : he did not believe that he could be over-thrown. On the conscious plane, contempt of his opponents may have accounted in part for the listless pursuit of routine activities during the intervening hours ; but deep down there must have been the paralysing weariness of the man who has run his course, has lost, and cannot face his further responsibilities. This would not preclude a subsequent violent reaction to the results of such brief, half-conscious self-abandonment. When the Germans enabled Mussolini partially to recover power, revenge on his treacherous henchmen became his domi-nant passion. Six of them, including Ciano and De Bono, were rounded up and tried. Their defence was unim-pressive and often abject, for there had been neither a policy nor principles behind their revolt. They now pleaded that they might have committed an error but had not planned the overthrow of the régime nor of the Duce : there was shuffling and shambling, feigned naivety or ignorance, but none of the strength or courage which springs from moral convictions. Five were executed, and in their death they are of no greater interest than any other victims of gang-warfare. Then the wheel turned once more. Mussolini reached his sordid end.

" THE UNNECESSARY WAR "

THE first of probably five volumes on *The Second World War*, by Mr. Winston Churchill,[1] covers in its two books the inter-war period, 1919–1939, and his tenure of the Admiralty, September 3, 1939–May 10, 1940. The " Theme of the Volume " (or rather of Book One) is : " How the English-speaking peoples through their unwisdom, carelessness, and good nature allowed the wicked to rearm."

> One day President Roosevelt told me that he was asking publicly for suggestions about what the war should be called. I said at once " The Unnecessary War." There never was a war more easy to stop than that which has just wrecked what was left of the world from the previous struggle.

" Up till 1934 at least, German rearmament could have been prevented without the loss of a single life. It was not time that was lacking." " Looking back, I am astonished at the length of time that was granted to us." Even in 1934, years had yet to run " before we were to be confronted with the supreme ordeal. Had we acted even now with reasonable prudence and healthy energy, it might never have come to pass." Year after year Mr. Churchill protested against a policy that " lacked both magnitude and urgency " — " the bold path is the path of safety ", he wrote on October 9, 1937.

> All the words and actions for which I am accountable between the wars had as their object only the prevention of a second World War ; and, of course, of making sure that if the worst happened we won, or at least survived.

[1] Winston S. Churchill, *The Second World War. The Gathering Storm.* London : Cassell and Co., Ltd.

His speeches " commanded attention, but did not, un-happily, wake to action the crowded, puzzled Houses which heard them " — " nothing that one could say made the slightest difference ".   " I felt a sensation of despair.   To be so entirely convinced . . . and not to be able to make Parliament and the nation heed the warning . . . was an experience most painful."   In Britain " life flowed placidly downstream ", with every-one agreed " to keep things quiet " ; in France the whirl-pool of internal politics kept affairs " in constant flux and in motion without particular significance " ; and the Governments of both countries " were equally incapable of any drastic or clear-cut action ".   " Nor can the United States escape the censure of history " for " the improvident aloofness " of its foreign policy.   There was " paralysis of thought and action among the leaders of the former and future Allies ".   It seems almost incredible, and certainly incomprehensible, that with danger so patent and the chances of escape so many, the nations should have meandered into the abyss, drawn into it one by one, most of them lacking on the brink the strength to resist, and, while more remote, the will to succour.

Mr. Churchill had long stood in the forefront of politics when Baldwin, Ramsay MacDonald, and Neville Chamber-lain, each older than he, were hardly known.   Yet these three were to hold the Premiership for eighteen years and keep him out of office for ten.   The political breach with Baldwin occurred over India, in January 1931 ; Mr. Churchill withdrew from his shadow cabinet and was not invited to take part in the Coalition Govern-ment.   " I can truthfully affirm that I never felt resent-ment, still less pain, at being so decisively discarded in a moment of national stress."   He did not desire office, " having had so much of it, and being opposed to the Government on their Indian policy ".   But by 1935, with the passage of the India Bill,

> this barrier had fallen away. The growing German
> menace made me anxious to lay my hands upon our
> military machine. . . . It was understood that the
> Admiralty would be vacant, and I wished very much
> to go there should the Conservatives be returned to
> power.

But he knew that if the Government could do without
him " they would certainly be very glad. To some extent
this depended upon their majority." When its size
became known " Mr. Baldwin lost no time in announcing
through the Central Office that there was no intention to
include me in the Government ".

Another chance offered when in March 1936 a Ministry
for the Co-ordination of Defence was about to be created.
Mr. Churchill's appointment was urged by some, opposed
by others; and for a whole month was canvassed and
considered. But on March 9, following on Hitler's
Rhineland *coup*, Baldwin selected Sir Thomas Inskip. "To
me this definite, and as it seemed final, exclusion from
all share in our preparations for defence was a heavy
blow." In May 1937 Neville Chamberlain succeeded
Baldwin.

> In these closing years before the war, I should
> have found it easier to work with Baldwin, as I knew
> him, than with Chamberlain; but neither of them
> had any wish to work with me except in the last
> resort.

In the summer of 1939 there was widespread demand for
an " All-in-Government ". " I should certainly have
joined the Government had I been invited." But it was
the opinion of the then ruling circles that Mr. Churchill
would make a suitable Minister in war-time only: and
they refused to admit that war had long ago been started
by Hitler.

The Government of 1931 " was in appearance one of the strongest, and in fact one of the weakest, in British records " ; and while Mr. MacDonald " reigned in increasing decrepitude at the summit of the British system ", the European situation was reversed to Britain's peril. None the less, at the general election of 1935, Mr. Baldwin, now Premier, obtained a great majority ; the administration saw " its errors and shortcomings acclaimed by the nation ", and " the Conservative Party lay tranquil in his hand". He retired in 1937 ; by then Germany had remilitarized the Rhineland, attained ascendancy in the air, and won Italy over ; the prestige of the Western Powers was sinking.

In the 'twenties Mr. Churchill coined the maxim : " the redress of the grievances of the vanquished should precede the disarmament of the victors " ; and at no time did he close his mind " to an attempt to give Germany greater satisfaction on her eastern frontier ". Where and how this should, or could, have been done, fairly and safely, is not stated ; nor does Mr. Churchill examine what likelihood there was of ever exhausting German " grievances ". A more practical policy was contained in his argument on the two-way guarantee of Locarno : it would work so long as France remained armed and Germany disarmed, for Germany could not, and France would not, attack — " I was therefore always equally opposed to the disarmament of France and to the rearmament of Germany ". As early as May 1932 he declared in the House of Commons, that to put " Germany and France on an equal footing in armaments . . . would bring us within practical distance of almost measureless calamity ". But this was what the " MacDonald Plan " of March 1933 meant to accomplish ; and far into 1934, Mr. MacDonald, " armed with Mr. Baldwin's political power ", continued to preach disarmament to France, and practise it upon the British,

" flocculently supported " by public opinion.   When on March 23, 1933, Mr. Churchill exclaimed, " Thank God for the French Army ", there was a " look of pain and aversion . . . on the faces of Members in all parts of the House ".   " We go on perpetually asking the French to weaken themselves ", he said on March 14, 1934.   " And . . . we always hold out the hope that if they do it and get into trouble, we will then in some way or other go to their aid, although we have nothing with which to go to their aid."   All this was present in Mr. Churchill's mind when in June 1940, at Tours, he witnessed the agony of France :   " and that is why, even when proposals for a separate peace were mentioned, I spoke only words of comfort and reassurance. . . ."

It takes several years to raise and equip an army and to train its reserves ; even longer to build a navy ; " the air, and the air alone, offered Hitler a chance of a short cut, first to equality and next to predominance in a vital military arm over France and Britain ".   Preparations for a German air force had been made under the Weimar Republic : Hitler and Göring had merely to extend and accelerate the work which the " good Germans " had so well started.   Mr. Churchill was aware of the danger. He said in the House of Commons on March 14, 1933 : " We should be well advised to concentrate upon our air defences " ; on February 7, 1934 : " We are vulnerable as we have never been before " ; and in March 1934 he warned against the day, " not perhaps distant ", when the German air force could be used to blackmail this country.   In July 1934 he declared : " If the Government have to admit at any time in the next few years that the German air forces are stronger than our own, then they will be held . . . to have failed in their prime duty to the country ".   In March 1935 Sir John Simon and Mr. Eden were told by Hitler in Berlin that the German air force had already reached parity with that of Britain (which was said with a purpose, and was, as yet, hardly true) ; and on May 22 Mr. Baldwin had to admit to have been wrong in his estimate of the future. " There I was completely wrong. We were completely misled on that subject." Even then no measures were taken by the Government proportionate to the need, while the Opposition merely continued repeating Geneva incantations uncorrelated to reality. Disarmament " became a link between the two Front Benches ".

" There is no record in our history of any Government asking Parliament and the people for the necessary measures of defence and being refused." But before the general election of 1935 Mr. Baldwin promised " there will be no great armaments " ; and a year later explained in the House, with an "appalling frankness" which "carried naked truth about his motives into indecency ", that had he demanded armaments to match those of Germany, it would have lost him the election. In June 1937 " he laid down the wide authority he had gathered and carefully maintained, but had used as little as possible ". Compared with his successor, Baldwin was

> the wiser, more comprehending personality, but without detailed executive capacity. He was largely detached from foreign and military affairs. He knew little of Europe, and disliked what he knew. He had a deep knowledge of British party politics, and represented in a broad way some of the strengths and many of the infirmities of our island race. . . . He had a genius for waiting upon events and an imperturbability under adverse criticism. He was singularly adroit in letting events work for him, and capable of seizing the ripe moment when it came. He seemed to me to revive the impressions history gives us of Sir Robert Walpole. . . .

Even severer strictures in the narrative seem well founded : Mr. Churchill's picture of Baldwin will be found in substantial agreement with that given of him by a close collaborator and friend in the Memoir printed by *The Times* after his death in December 1947.

On March 9, 1935, Germany announced the formation of an air force, forbidden by the Treaty of Versailles, and on the 16th introduced compulsory military service; while battleships of far larger size than allowed under the Treaty were known to be building. Then "a most surprising act was committed by the British Government": without consulting the French or informing the League, to whom they themselves were appealing at that time against Hitler's violation of the military clauses of the Treaty, they proceeded by a private agreement to sweep away its naval clauses. Germany was conceded the right to build submarines, denied to her under the Treaty, and allowed a programme of new construction which would set her yards to work at maximum activity for a number of years. Thus the Anglo-German Naval Agreement imposed "no practical limitation or restraint . . . upon German naval expansion".

Mr. Churchill is equally critical of the Government's handling of the Abyssinian problem. At the Stresa Conference Mr. MacDonald and Sir John Simon avoided the subject, even when given pointedly an opening by Mussolini. But by July the Government were prepared "to lead opinion in Europe against Italy's Abyssinian designs". Consulted in August by the Foreign Secretary, Mr. Churchill, with the German menace uppermost in mind, warned him not to go farther than he could carry France with him, and generally "advised the Ministers not to try to take a leading part". "France had much to worry about, and only very silly people, of whom there are extremely large numbers in every country, could ignore all this." Anyhow it was all idle parade. "The Prime Minister had declared that sanctions meant war; secondly, he was resolved there must be no war; and thirdly, he

decided upon sanctions." Had Britain gone to the bitter
end and knocked out Mussolini, this might have put a
restraint on " the greater dictator ". As it was she emerged
from the crisis " thoroughly weakened ".

Book One is a history of the years preceding the Second
World War by a statesman who, though not in office,
was at all times a powerful factor in national work and
politics. In June 1935, at the Government's invitation,
he joined the newly formed Committee on Air Defence
Research, and thus came into close touch with the
development of scientific methods and devices, foremost
among them radar.

When in 1940, the chief responsibility fell upon me
and our national survival depended upon victory in
the air, I had the advantage of a layman's insight
into the problems of air warfare resulting from four
years of study and thought based upon the fullest
official and technical information.

He would also at various times exchange with Ministers
confidential information on matters of national importance; or they would apply for his advice or opinion,
without this in any way interfering with the freedom of
either side in public controversy. Even foreign statesmen
and Ambassadors would resort to him, especially those of
allied or friendly nations. But he declined to visit Hitler.

I would gladly have met Hitler with the authority
of Britain behind me. But as a private individual I
should have placed myself and my country at a
disadvantage. If I had agreed with the Dictator-
host, I should have misled him. If I had disagreed,
he would have been offended, and I should have
been accused of spoiling Anglo-German relations.
. . . All those Englishmen who visited the German
Fuehrer in these years were embarrassed or compromised . . . Hitler had a power of fascinating
men, and the sense of force and authority is apt to

assert itself unduly upon the tourist. Unless the terms
are equal, it is better to keep away.

Unlike Baldwin, Neville Chamberlain " conceived himself able to comprehend the whole field of Europe, and
indeed the world. . . . He had formed decided judgments about all the political figures of the day, both at
home and abroad, and felt himself capable of dealing with
them." " Imbued with a sense of a special and personal
mission to come to friendly terms with the Dictators of
Italy and Germany ", he considered that the Foreign
Office was obstructing his attempts, and from the outset
asserted his right to discuss foreign affairs with foreign
ambassadors. During such a conversation with Count
Grandi, he wrote a personal letter to Mussolini and dis-
patched it without consulting Mr. Eden. " I did not
show my letter to the Foreign Secretary," noted Chamberlain in his *Diary*,[1] " for I had the feeling that he would
object to it." He went even farther, and, as appears from
Grandi's dispatch of February 19, 1938 — published in
L' Europa verso la Catastrofe[2] with the wrong date of February
13 — he kept up " a direct and ' secret ' connexion "
with the Italian Ambassador through an intermediary,
" with whom ", wrote Grandi, " I am since January 15,
as it were, in daily touch. . . ."

In the autumn of 1937 Lord Halifax accepted Göring's
invitation to come to Germany " on a sports visit ".
Chamberlain " thought it would be a very good thing ".
" I had the impression ", writes Mr. Churchill, " that
Eden was surprised and did not like it." On November 5
the secret conference held by Hitler at the Reich Chan-
cellery, and minuted in the so-called Hossbach notes,
marks the transition to planned aggression ; and on the

[1] Keith Feiling, *The Life of Neville Chamberlain*, page 330.
[2] An English translation, edited by Malcolm Muggeridge, has been
published by Odhams Press under the title *Ciano's Diplomatic Papers*.

19th Lord Halifax had a talk with Hitler.[1] " Nothing came of all this ", writes Mr. Churchill, " but chatter and bewilderment."

During these November days, Eden became increasingly concerned about our slow rearmament. On the eleventh, he had an interview with the Prime Minister and tried to convey his misgivings. Mr. Neville Chamberlain after a while refused to listen to him. He advised him to " go home and take an aspirin ". When Halifax returned from Berlin, he reported that Hitler had told him the colonial question was the only outstanding issue between Britain and Germany.

Mr. Eden felt " almost isolated in the Cabinet ". " But the actual breach came over a new and separate issue." On January 11, 1938, President Roosevelt, anxious about the international difficulties, proposed to call a conference to Washington to discuss the underlying causes : but only if his suggestion met with " the cordial approval and wholehearted support " of the British Government. The British Ambassador strongly urged acceptance in the interest of Anglo-American co-operation. Eden was in France, and Chamberlain replied by telling the President about his attempts to reach a friendly settlement with Italy, and asking him to consider whether his proposal might not cut across the British efforts. Eden returned on the 15th. " He had been urged to come back, not by his chief, who was content to act without him, but by his devoted officials at the Foreign Office." The reply was modified in certain respects. But the rebuff to the President's overture stood.

We must regard its rejection — for such it was — as the loss of the last frail chance to save the world

[1] The German minute of the conversation appears in the Soviet publication, *Documents and Materials relating to the Eve of the Second World War*, i. 14-45, see below, pages 207-9 ; also in the Anglo-American publication, *Documents on German Foreign Policy, 1918–1945*, Series D (1937–1945), vol. i. 55-67.

from tyranny otherwise than by war. That Mr. Chamberlain, with his limited outlook and inexperience of the European scene, should have possessed the self-sufficiency to wave away the proffered hand stretched out across the Atlantic leaves one, even at this date, breathless with amazement.

About the interview which Chamberlain and Eden had with Grandi on February 18, the Italian report supplies further information. Grandi calls it " one of the most paradoxical and extraordinary " in his experience. " Chamberlain and Eden were not a Prime Minister and a Foreign Secretary discussing a delicate international situation with a foreign ambassador ; there were before me . . . two enemies facing each other, like two cocks in truly proper fighting posture." Grandi felt that Chamberlain was trying to elicit from him replies to be used against Eden in the Cabinet.[1] Two days later Eden resigned ; and Mussolini " did not repulse the British repentance ".

The day after Hitler had entered Vienna Mr. Churchill spoke of the calculated programme of aggression, unfolding stage by stage.

> If we go on waiting upon events, how much shall we throw away of resources now available for our security and the maintenance of peace ? How many friends will be alienated, how many potential allies shall we see go one by one down the grisly gulf? How many times will bluff succeed until behind bluff ever-gathering forces have accumulated reality ?

He spoke about the position of Czechoslovakia, " a small democratic State ", with an army " only two or three times as large as ours ", and a munition supply " only three times as great as that of Italy ", but still with a will to live.

[1] See *L' Europa verso la catastrofe*, page 276; and *Ciano's Diplomatic Papers*, pages 182-3.

Mr. Churchill's considered judgment on Munich is
summed up in two sentences: " There is no merit in
putting off a war for a year if, when it comes, it is a far
worse war or one harder to win " and " I remain convinced . . . that it would have been better . . . to fight
Hitler in 1938 than it was when we finally had to do so
in September, 1939." Mr. Churchill touches upon the
question " whether decisive action by Britain and France
would have forced Hitler to recede or have led to his overthrow by a military conspiracy ", and further quotes some
of the opinions of German generals about the military
chances at the time. But while German " conspiracies "
had a peculiar way of not coming off, and German
military opinions repeatedly proved wrong, there are
indisputable facts to support Mr. Churchill's thesis. The
Czechs had thirty-five divisions, better equipped than any
other allied army ; an excellent defensive system covering
most of their frontier ; and a powerful armaments
industry. The Skoda works was " the second most important arsenal in Central Europe ", and its production
alone was in 1938–1939 nearly equal to the output of
the British arms factories: Munich made it " change
sides adversely ". Lastly, Czechoslovakia was a potential
Russian air base wedged between Berlin, Vienna, and
Munich. The liquidation of Czechoslovakia was a
disastrous loss to the allies.

Further, the as yet unripened German army had a
great deal to gain by the additional year. Had the Germans attacked Czechoslovakia in September 1938, only
five effective and eight reserve divisions would have been
available to hold their western front against a hundred
French divisions. In armaments, the advance of the
Western Powers was " petty " during the year compared
with that of the Germans. " Munition production on a
nation-wide plan is a four years' task. The first year
yields nothing ; the second very little ; the third a lot,

and the fourth a flood." In 1938 Germany had reached the third or fourth year of most intense preparation, while Britain was merely starting, with a much weaker impulse. In the air alone Britain began to improve her position. But though in 1938 there might have been air raids on London, " for which we were lamentably unprepared ", there could have been no " decisive Air Battle of Britain " until the Germans obtained the necessary bases in France and the Low Countries : and in 1938 the Germans had not the tanks with which they broke the French front. " For all the above reasons, the year's breathing-space said to be ' gained ' by Munich left Britain and France in a much worse position . . . than they had been at the Munich crisis."

One more argument could be adduced in support of Mr. Churchill's thesis. He uses some harsh expressions about the men who then ruled Poland ; and few would choose to defend their very mean action in Teschen. There was a streak of the gangster in Colonel Beck, and a passion for power-display and booty. But even he would have preferred to practise these against, rather than in the company of, the Germans. In March and October 1933 Pilsudski had proposed preventive military action against Hitler ; and when Hitler entered the Rhineland, on March 7, 1936, no one urged an immediate armed riposte as strongly as Beck. Had the Western Powers shown firmness in the summer of 1938, they might have had Poland with them ; but Beck was not to be impressed or convinced by a Runciman mission or by propitiatory flights to Berchtesgaden and Godesberg.

About the moral side of Munich Mr. Churchill's judgment is equally clear. Responsible French statesmen had repeatedly declared that France's engagements toward Czechoslovakia " are sacred and cannot be evaded ". Here was a solemn obligation. " For the French Government to leave her faithful ally, Czechoslovakia, to her

fate was a melancholy lapse . . . and it must be recorded
with regret that the British Government not only ac-
quiesced but encouraged the French Government in a
fatal course." " The British and French Cabinets at this
time presented a front of two overripe melons crushed
together ; whereas what was needed was a gleam of steel."

When, on Hitler's entry into Vienna, Russia proposed
a conference on the situation, Mr. Churchill urged an
alliance with her as " the only hope of checking the Nazi
onrush " ; and he was not impressed by Chamberlain's
argument about the evils of " exclusive groups of nations "
when the alternative was being mopped up one by one by
the aggressor. On August 31, 1938, in a letter to Lord
Halifax, he again pressed for joint action with Russia.
On September 2, M. Maisky came to see him at Chartwell
" upon a matter of urgency " and told him " in precise
and formal terms " about a conversation between Litvinov
and the French Chargé d'Affaires in Moscow. Litvinov
had declared that the Soviet Union was resolved to fulfil
its obligations to Czechoslovakia ; had proposed an appeal
to the League Council under Article 11, expecting its
verdict to influence Rumania's attitude ; and had
suggested immediate staff conversations between Russia,
France, and Czechoslovakia, and consultation between
Russia and the Western Powers. Mr. Churchill, realizing
that he was being resorted to because the Soviet Government feared a rebuff from the Foreign Office, immediately
transmitted the communication to Lord Halifax, but
received a " guarded " reply. On September 26 he saw
Chamberlain and Halifax, and the outcome was the
Foreign Office *communiqué* that " Great Britain and Russia
will certainly stand by France " if she has to come to the
assistance of Czechoslovakia. (The significance of this
communiqué is still questioned in M. Bonnet's memoirs.)[1]

[1] See *Défense de la paix. De Washington au Quai d'Orsay*, pages 272-3.

" We must get in Russia," was the slogan of the Conservatives grouped around Mr. Churchill; and he does not
doubt Russia's willingness at that time " to join the
Western Powers and go all lengths to save Czechoslovakia ".

Of Russia in 1939, Mr. Churchill writes under the
heading " The Soviet Enigma ". He still thinks that an
alliance of the Western Powers with Russia offered the
only chance of averting the Second World War; that her
offer should therefore have been accepted, leaving " the
method by which it could be made effective in the case of
war to be adjusted between allies engaged against a common enemy " ; and the fact that the Nazi-Soviet agreement could be made marks to him " the culminating
failure of British and French foreign policy and diplomacy
over several years ". Even now it is not possible to fix
the moment when Stalin abandoned all intention of working with the Western Powers and decided to come to
terms with Hitler. " Indeed, it seems probable that there
never was such a moment " ; and " a veil of deceit "
covers that " transmogrification of which only totalitarian
States are capable ".

On September 1 Mr. Churchill was asked by the Prime
Minister to join " a small War Cabinet of Ministers with-
out departments ". But when the War Cabinet was
formed, the Service Ministers were included, and Mr.
Churchill accepted the Admiralty, preferring a definite
task to " exalted brooding over the work done by others ".
On the 14th he went on a visit to Scapa and met the
Commander-in-Chief. On the 17th, in the evening,

> we anchored in Loch Ewe. . . . On every side rose
> the purple hills of Scotland in all their splendour.
> My thoughts went back a quarter of a century to
> that other September when I had last visited Sir
> John Jellicoe and his captains in this very bay, and

had found them with their long lines of battleships
and cruisers drawn out at anchor, a prey to the same
uncertainties as now afflicted us. Most of the
captains and admirals of those days were dead, or
had long passed into retirement . . . an entirely
different generation filled the uniforms and posts.
Only the ships had most of them been laid down in
my tenure. None of them was new. It was a strange
experience, like suddenly resuming a previous incarna-
tion. It seemed that I was all that survived in the
same position I had held so long ago.

But no; the dangers from submarine and aircraft had
survived, and grown much more serious.

No one had ever been over the same terrible
course twice with such an interval between. No one
had felt its dangers and responsibilities from the
summit as I had or . . . understood how First
Lords of the Admiralty are treated when great
ships are sunk and things go wrong. If we were
in fact going over the same cycle a second time,
should I have once again to endure the pangs of
dismissal ? . . .

And what of the supreme measureless ordeal in
which we were again irrevocably plunged ? Poland
in its agony; France but a pale reflection of her
former warlike ardour; the Russian Colossus no
longer an ally, not even neutral, possibly to become a
foe. Italy no friend. Japan no ally. Would America
ever come in again ? The British Empire remained
intact and gloriously united, but ill-prepared, un-
ready. We still had command of the sea. We were
woefully outmatched in numbers in the new mortal
weapon of the air. Somehow the light faded out of
the landscape.

The British Navy, overwhelmingly superior to the
German, " had to face enormous and innumerable duties,
rather than an antagonist ". Asserting its command over
the seas, it offered immense targets to the enemy; and
work on securing its bases, on building anti-submarine

fleets, on arming a thousand merchant ships with at least one anti-submarine gun each, was pressed with the utmost speed. Next, the magnetic mine had to be overcome. But the First Lord, not to let the Navy be driven, or subside, into a defensive strategy, was searching for forms of counter-offensive. The greatest then contemplated, "Operation Catherine", to wrest from the Germans the command of the Baltic, could not be carried out in the circumstances of the period; others, feasible and necessary, were delayed and frustrated by conflicting views; and all the while in the vastness of the seas the Navy was making exertions of which knowledge reached the public but occasionally through actions such as that off the River Plate.

A double interest attaches to the book; it lies in the great drama, and in the man who counted for so much in it. Mr. Churchill is now seen in action, and his personality breaks through his factual account. Below stubborn pugnacity and a brilliant, imaginative versatility appear great emotional intensity, intuitive insight, and warm human feelings: factors in his greatness. (He seems to treasure human contacts — see his account of the one occasion on which he got "a natural, human reaction" from Mr. Molotov, and of "the only intimate social conversation" which over a period of twenty years he had with Neville Chamberlain.) But, sensitive and impressionable, he steps back to gain perspective: and wide horizons open, with more vision than analysis in their delineation. Next, there is his amazing capacity for work and absence of fixed doctrine; and where the personal element appears, there is modesty, admitting uneasy thoughts and doubts, chagrin and relief (a curious contrast to Neville Chamberlain's rigid, narrow, doctrinaire self-certainty). There is also intense impatience, which Mr. Churchill does not conceal, and which was severely tried while he had to work in an uncongenial team, often kept out or kept under.

Two naval operations Mr. Churchill pressed on the Cabinet and on the French; and he failed to carry either till it was too late. At the end of November the Gulf of Bothnia normally freezes, but the Germans could continue their essential imports of Swedish iron ore through Norwegian territorial waters. These Mr. Churchill wanted to mine — " Operation Wilfred ", so called " because by itself it was so small and innocent "; yet such was " the array of negative arguments and forces " that, having first raised the matter on September 29, he could not obtain a favourable decision till the beginning of April: " the sense of extreme emergency seemed lacking ". But the Germans, too, appreciated the importance of bases in Norway. " The two Admiralties thought . . . along the same lines . . . and the one had obtained decisions from its Government." The other operation, " Royal Marine ", was a plan for launching or dropping fluvial mines in the Rhine. But the French objected to aggressive action which might draw reprisals upon them; and maintained that attitude till the German offensive opened in the Low Countries. " The prolonged and oppressive pause " which followed on the destruction of Poland continued through months of " pretended war ": " endless discussions about trivial points, no decisions taken, or if taken rescinded, and the rule ' Don't be unkind to the enemy, you will only make him angry ' ".

Mr. Churchill shared the belief in the superiority of the defensive on land; but at least he tried to see it carried through consistently, and in a letter to Chamberlain on September 15, 1939, urged that " the French frontier behind Belgium should be fortified night and day by every conceivable resource." And he seems to have agreed with the British Chiefs of Staff that unless the Belgians arranged in time for concerted action against a German advance, this " should be met in prepared positions on the French frontier ". But at the meeting o the Allied Supreme Council in Paris, on November 17, at which it was decided to advance to the Meuse–Antwerp line, Mr. Churchill was not present — " I had not at that time reached the position where I should be invited to accompany the Prime Minister to these meetings ". It was not till February that he was asked to do so. The story of how that Council developed plans to relieve Finland by way of Scandinavia, without ever facing " the issue of what to do if Norway and Sweden refused [transit for the troops], as seemed probable ", makes peculiar reading; and so does that of the Norwegian campaign: " one stroke of misfortune after another, the results of want of means or of indifferent management, fell upon us, almost daily ", while " surprise, ruthlessness, and precision " were characteristics of the German onslaught. The epic of Narvik fiord, the hesitations over Trondheim, the failure of the pincer movement from Namsos and Andalsnes, the dispersion of resources, and the deadlock between the military and naval chiefs in the expedition against Narvik, are discussed in detail and with great frankness.

When on April 22 the Prime Minister and Mr. Churchill arrived in Paris for a meeting of the Allied Supreme Council, M. Reynaud made " a statement on the general military position which by its gravity dwarfed our Scandinavian excursions ". On the western front the allies were facing a large and growing German numerical superiority " which was already three to two and would presently rise to two to one ".

> To this point, then, had we come from the days of the Rhineland occupation in 1936, when a mere operation of police would have sufficed; or since Munich, when Germany, occupied with Czecho-slovakia, could spare but thirteen divisions for the Western front; or even since September, 1939, when,

while the Polish resistance lasted, there were but forty-two German divisions in the West.

On May 7-8 followed the debate in which Mr. Amery, amid ringing cheers, also from Conservatives, addressed Chamberlain in Cromwell's words to the Long Parliament : " You have sat too long here for any good you have been doing. Depart, I say, and let us have done with you. In the name of God, go ! " Shaken by the debate and the division which followed, Chamberlain decided to try to form a National Government, but found that Labour would not serve under him. In the early morning of May 10 the Germans opened their offensive in the west, which made Chamberlain feel that it was necessary for him to remain at his post ; but others felt that it made it the more necessary to have a National Government. At 11 A.M. Mr. Churchill was summoned to Downing Street, where he found Lord Halifax. " We took our seats at the table opposite Mr. Chamberlain." He said that it was beyond his power to form a National Government — whom should he advise the King to send for ?

I have had many important interviews in my public life, and this was certainly the most important. Usually I talk a great deal, but on this occasion I was silent.

There was a long pause after Chamberlain had spoken. " Then at length Halifax spoke," and explained that as a peer he could hardly discharge the duties of Prime Minister in a war like this.

He spoke for some minutes . . . and by the time he had finished, it was clear that the duty would fall upon me — had in fact fallen upon me. Then, for the first time, I spoke. I said I would have no communications with either of the Opposition parties until I had the King's commission to form a Government. On this the momentous conversation came to an end, and we reverted to our ordinary easy and familiar manners of men who had worked for years together and whose lives in and out of office had been spent in all the friendliness of British politics. I then went back to the Admiralty, where, as may well be imagined, much awaited me.

At 6 P.M. Mr. Churchill was summoned to the Palace, and was asked by the King to form a Government. By 10 P.M. its nucleus was formed.

I cannot conceal from the reader of this truthful account that as I went to bed at about 3 A.M. I was conscious of a profound sense of relief. At last I had authority to give directions over the whole scene. . . . I was sure I should not fail. Therefore, although impatient for the morning, I slept soundly and had no need for cheering dreams. Facts are better than dreams.

THE ROAD TO MUNICH

" STATESMEN are not called upon only to settle easy questions," writes Mr. Churchill. " These often settle themselves. It is where the balance quivers and the proportions are veiled in mist that the opportunity for world-saving decisions presents itself." No critic of the statesmen responsible for the policy of Britain and France during the Munich period can deny that the situation was one of exceptional difficulty, nor any apologist assert that theirs were "world-saving decisions". Their own pronouncements, set against the course of events, carry judgment on their reasonings and actions. Yet a policy does not emerge full-grown from the thoughts of its authors; a suggestion or idea, as it travels along, undergoes transformations, sometimes bizarre like those in a dream; and every situation has its peculiar slant; but one of the tests of statesmanship is the degree of control, retained over developments. To judge of that, very full evidence is required by the historian. The prolegomena to the Second World War still hold public attention; numerous books and memoirs appear on the subject; it was therefore right to advance the publication of the British documents " most relevant to the origins of the war ". While the previous two series, beginning with 1919 and 1930, will be continued, a third has been started to cover the eighteen months preceding September, 1939; its first volume,[1] now published, opens with the German annexation of Austria and closes with the decision to send the Runciman mission to Czechoslovakia.

The editors state that

[1] E. L. Woodward and Rohan Butler (Editors); *Documents on British Foreign Policy, 1919–1939.* Third Series, vol. i. 1938. H.M. Stationery Office.

their purpose is to provide from the Foreign Office archives a full documentation of the course and execution of policy . . . and also to give, within reasonable limits of space, the information received from Missions abroad upon which from time to time decisions of policy were taken.

They do not aim " at a complete record of the processes of formulation of policy as distinct from its execution ", for this would "have to include an account of discussions and divergences of view in the Cabinet and between Departments or individuals ".

Full publication of recent diplomatic documents, as practised since 1919, is bound to have a certain inhibiting influence on the writers; but while the consequent restraint need not be prejudicial in the drafting of maturely considered statements and opinions, it must not be allowed to affect intimate discussions of a policy in the making. On the other hand, selection governed by political considerations would throw an intolerable responsibility on the editor, and yield a distorted picture. As it is, whoever reads the truly painful story told in this volume will recognize that nothing has been withheld; and in the documents emanating from the Foreign Office the " intramural " element can at times be (profitably) distinguished from political and extra-departmental influences. For within the Foreign Office even in this period, one of the saddest and most depressed in its history, there was no lack of sound knowledge of European affairs, or of sane insight into them. And the willingness which they have shown to allow all their material to see daylight does them honour now.

From the fall of Austria there is an immediate transition to the Czech drama : things to come are projected with ghastly clarity. The story opens on March 9, 1938, with Schuschnigg's decision to hold a plebiscite, against protests from Seyss-Inquart, his Minister of the Interior, imposed on him by Hitler under the Berchtesgaden agreement; if he is backed by Hitler, reported the British Minister from Vienna, " the situation may at any moment become dangerous". On March 10, Lord Halifax told Ribbentrop, then in London, that the British Government recognized " the reality of the problems from the German point of view, connected with Austria and Czechoslovakia ", and had consistently striven for a peaceful solution; but the German attitude suggested that " something more than fair treatment of minorities was involved "; and if war should start " it was quite impossible to say . . . who might not become involved ". Lord Halifax hoped the German Government would restrain its followers from interfering " with the smooth and free holding of the plebiscite "; Ribbentrop, that the British Government would use their influence with Schuschnigg to cancel it.

> I answered [Lord Halifax telegraphed to Sir Nevile Henderson in Berlin] that whatever might be his view or mine about the plebiscite, it seemed a tall order to say that the Head of a State could not have a plebiscite if he wanted to. I did not happen to believe in plebiscites much, but I thought it scarcely possible to deny the right to the Head of a State to resort to a plebiscite if he so desired.

The next day, March 11, Schuschnigg, under threat of German invasion, agreed to cancel the plebiscite, only to be told that he must resign. He asked " for *immediate* advice of His Majesty's Government "; but they declined the responsibility

> of advising the Chancellor to take any course of action which might expose his country to dangers against which His Majesty's Government are unable to guarantee protection.

Still, Ribbentrop was talked to and warned of the

" deplorable effect " which the latest developments must exercise on Anglo-German relations. He replied that surely it was necessary to seek peaceful solutions of obstinate problems ; one was now " got out of the way " : and British public opinion " might, without much difficulty, be guided to take a realist view of what had passed ". Lord Halifax answered that " what we were witnessing was an exhibition of naked force ", and public opinion would inevitably ask

> what there was to prevent the German Government from seeking to apply in similar fashion naked force to the solution of their problems in Czechoslovakia or to any other in which they thought it might be useful. The conclusion must be that the German leaders were people who had no use for negotiation, but relied solely on the strong hand.

On March 12 Ciano noted in his *Diary*: " I am convinced that Great Britain will accept what has happened with indignant resignation ". The three forecasts proved singularly accurate.

Meantime Henderson expatiated on the failure of his efforts " to save Austria from the consequences of Dr. Schuschnigg's ill-conceived and ill-prepared folly ". And even to Göring, on March 12, he " reluctantly " admitted " that Dr. Schuschnigg had acted with precipitate folly ". This " may well be your personal view. . . ." Lord Halifax telegraphed back

> and you are, of course, entitled to express that view in your communications with me. But I cannot help feeling that by the admission to General Göring quoted above you cannot but have diminished the force of the protest you were instructed to make. . . .
> There was not, I think, any doubt as to my own views on the subject of the plebiscite . . . and it is of first importance that any communications you make to German Government should conform to the instructions you receive from me and to the attitude I

myself adopt in my communications to German representatives here.

Henderson replied :

> My telegram . . . was somewhat hurriedly
> drafted in the middle of the night and I fear did not
> accurately reproduce my long passage of arms with
> Field-Marshal Göring. . . . I did not actually use
> the words " precipitate folly."

On April 14 Henderson was asked to refrain from discussing the Sudeten question in any detail with German
Ministers — " and you will no doubt feel the wisdom of
prudent reserve on the matter even in private conversation with individuals ". But on May 7 he, " speaking
quite confidentially ", conveyed to the Political Director
of the German Foreign Office information which was to
have been withheld from them ; and when asked not to do
so again, " even personally and confidentially ", he
replied :

> I submit that the effect of any representation
> which I may make to German Government will be
> greatly diminished if I am not authorized to have a
> certain latitude in the expression of personal opinion.

And on May 19, in a private letter to Lord Halifax :

> Believe me or not, and anyway your department
> seems to have some doubts, I have not prejudiced the
> issue in any way with the German Government. . . .
> I have kept the discussion on the broadest possible
> lines.

Such performances continued. From the outset the
choice of Henderson for Berlin was unfortunate ; but it
was more than unfortunate that the Secretary of State
should have retained him there till September 1939.

On March 12 Göring gave his word to Henderson that
the German troops would be withdrawn from Austria " as
soon as situation was stable ", and that a " free election

would be held without any intimidation whatsoever ".
He said that Hitler was going to Bavaria (" I gathered
he wishes to cross the frontier himself and visit grave of
his mother "). " He also told me he had given his word
to Czechoslovak Minister that no action was contemplated against his country." [1]

But all were agreed (until Munich) that " German
assurances are of uncertain value ". By March 24 Henderson considered that Hitler had given " full warning with
regard to Czechoslovakia ", and no time must be lost if a
peaceable solution was to be reached ; that German hegemony east of the Rhine was a fact, and " Central and
Eastern Europe will in general have to dance as Hitler
pipes ". And on April 13 :

> I was always convinced that Austria was bound to
> become part of Germany in some form sooner or
> later. Austria is now eliminated — and without
> bloodshed. . . . But there remains the kindred pro-

---

[1] For the full story of these promises see report of the Czechoslovak
Minister in Berlin, M. Mastný, of March 12, 1938, in F. Berber, *Europäische
Politik, 1933–1938, im Spiegel der Prager Akten* (1942), 3rd edition, pages 94-5.
These are gleanings from captured Czech documents published for purposes
of German propaganda ; but as Germans very seldom realize that anything they have done may be wrong, and as, moreover, they could not at
that time expect an early disclosure of their schemings from their own
corresponding documents, some things are included in the book which now
tell against them. On March 11, at 11 P.M., Mastný attended a reception
at Göring's, who expressed pleasure at Mastný having come, " for he wanted
to declare to me on his word of honour that there was not the least reason
for Czechoslovakia to feel any anxiety. . . . Germany had no hostile intentions of any kind towards her, but, on the contrary, wished to continue
advancing towards a *rapprochement*." Göring mentioned news having
reached them of a Czechoslovak mobilization. Mastný went back to his
Legation, telephoned to Prague the gist of the talk, and was told that no
mobilization had been ordered. After 1 A.M. he returned to Göring, who
now repeated his assurances on behalf of Hitler. In the morning of March
12, Göring repeated them for the third time over the telephone. The same
day, at 5.30 P.M., Mastný saw Neurath who, during Ribbentrop's absence
in London, was once more in charge of the Foreign Office, and who now in
turn repeated those assurances to Mastný ; see a further dispatch of March
12 from Mastný, Berber, pages 95-8.

blem of the Sudetendeutschen and after that Danzig,
a settlement with Poland and Memel.

Others viewed that programme with less perky resignation.
France, perturbed at the prospect of one country after
another succumbing to German aggression, with a growing reluctance in them to resist, declared that she would
stand by Czechoslovakia if attacked; and, fearing that
silence " might have disastrous effects ", urged Britain to
announce her support in advance. But Mr. Chamberlain,
in the House of Commons on March 24, declined to give
a " prior guarantee ", though a war, he said, would hardly
" be confined to those who have assumed such obligations ".

The British attitude was explained in a series of earlier
communications to the French Government. Britain's
obligations to Czechoslovakia were " those of one member
of the League to another "; and while she fully maintained her Locarno promise to France, of assistance against
unprovoked German aggression, she would not add to it
by " entering in advance into new and more extensive
commitments " on the European Continent (with public
opinion here and in the Dominions averse to it), nor
address a warning to Germany which could not be
effectively enforced. The French themselves hardly knew
how they could render assistance to Czechoslovakia,[1] and
British reflections on the subject were not encouraging.
France and Russia could not stop the Germans from over-
running Czechoslovakia; to restore her would require a
long war ; and if Britain became engaged, her contribution at first could merely be an economic blockade.

His Majesty's Government feel, therefore, that
every possible step should be taken both by the

---

[1] For a discussion on the subject, provoked by British inquiries, see
minutes of the meeting of the French Committee of National Defence on
March 15, 1938; printed in full in Gamelin, *Servir*, ii. 322-8.

French Government and by his Majesty's Government to help remove the causes of friction or even of conflict by using their good offices with the Government of Czechoslovakia to bring about a settlement of questions affecting the position of the German minority. His Majesty's Government believe that it is possible to find such a solution of German minority questions as would be compatible with ensuring the integrity of the Czechoslovak State, while retaining that minority within the frontiers of Czechoslovakia.

Such optimism was but half-sincere : it had to be professed and persisted in if pressure was to be exerted on the Czechs " to go to the limit of concession " in an attempt to attain " a comprehensive and lasting settlement ". Still, the information which was reaching London seemed to indicate that nothing short of complete territorial autonomy would satisfy the Sudetens (or Hitler, who financed and directed them) ; and that this was to enable them to vote themselves into the Reich (but without the Sudetenland Czechoslovakia would hardly be a viable State). Further, that minority questions were but one aspect of the problem, and that a reversal of Czechoslovakia's foreign policy was demanded by both Hitler and the Sudetens, who would not be satisfied even by her abandoning her alliances with France and Russia, and assuming neutrality, but meant to force her into the German orbit, a truncated vassal State. Thus, to avert war at an inauspicious time, the Czechs were being driven into the abyss, and they were blamed for not moving faster. Possibly Czechoslovakia was doomed either way ; but, except for M. Daladier, no one seems to have given sufficient thought to the worse situation which would arise when Hitler took up the next point on his programme.

Mr. (now Sir Basil) Newton expected an early German move against Czechoslovakia, and in three communications, of March 15 and April 11 and 12, reviewed the situation. Czechoslovakia would "welcome some definite promise of support from His Majesty's Government ", to enable her " to preserve her complete independence ". He himself thought her political position essentially unsound and " not permanently tenable " ; it would therefore be no kindness to try to maintain it. Germany would " never rest content with a potentially hostile Czechoslovakia thrust into her flank " : the internal and external aspects of the Czechoslovak problem were inter-related, and the sting would be taken out of minority questions by a change in her international orientation. He named the alternatives of neutrality or inclusion in the German orbit, but admitted that neutrality might be no more tenable than the existing position. If France in her own interest tried to maintain it, Britain should refuse to incur the risk of war ; and the Czechs themselves doubted whether France " would give them effective support unless backed up by Great Britain ". A neutralization of Czechoslovakia " might well be a blow to the prestige of the democratic Powers and a corresponding access " to Germany's, whose ambitions were limited only by her power to achieve them ; still, " a glance at the map suggests " that the least favourable place for resisting her was in Czechoslovakia (as if Poland, hostile to Russia, had offered better ground). He further admitted that the process of adjusting the position of Czechoslovakia might " turn into a landslide ", and result in her dismemberment ; and that the fear that every concession would be made into a step in that direction stiffened Czech resistance to such a policy.

About the internal problem Mr. Newton could hardly have had any illusions. He himself reported on March 19 that the thoughts of the Henlein party were " moving to actual incorporation in the Reich ". This was confirmed by his Military Attaché who, after visiting the Sudetenland, wrote on April 3 that they would not be content " with

anything the Czechs have it in their power to concede ".
Talking to the German Minister in Prague, Dr. Eisenlohr,
on April 5, Mr. Newton spoke of an impression

> that those concerned did not honestly desire a final
> settlement but merely a loosening of the Sudeten
> German connexion with Prague in order to facilitate
> the eventual detachment of these areas and their
> incorporation in the Germanic Reich.

But, as Newton explained on May 16, this would soon
raise the question " whether the Czech centre of Bohemia
should or should not follow the German fringe into the
Reich ". The Paris Peace Conference considered the
Czech provinces an indivisible natural region, and their
reasons were valid also from the reverse point of view. The
Czech and German districts were inter-dependent economically. Czech Bohemia and Moravia intervene
between Berlin and Vienna, Silesia and Austria. Having
gained the Sudetenland, the Reich, for military even more
than for commercial reasons, would next reach out for the
rest. The Nazi refusal to include " inferior races " in the
Reich

> brings little comfort to the Czechs. Those who have
> studied *Mein Kampf* in detail assert that it also pro-
> vides for vassal States of alien population, and they
> believe that may well be what the Reich has in mind
> for them.

On May 10, when Newton spoke to Eisenlohr about the
need of reaching " an equitable, comprehensive and final
settlement ",

> Dr. Eisenlohr . . . smiled at the word final (*end-
> gültig*), saying that nothing was ever final. . . . I
> observed that it would be difficult to encourage the
> Czechs to make great efforts . . . if there loomed in
> the background the shadow of the eventual disruption
> of the State. I am sorry to say, however, that my

intuitive impression from his general attitude was that the Sudeten German party might continue indefinitely to extract from the Czechoslovak Government the maximum concessions obtainable under whatsoever pressure could be applied, and that then, however favourable the position achieved might be, they would feel perfectly free to secede and break up the Czechoslovak Republic if it suited their purpose or that of the German Reich to do so. . . .

Towards the end of the talks Newton asked Eisenlohr what he thought of a policy of neutrality for Czechoslovakia.

Dr. Eisenlohr was contemplating a map on my wall at the time and said that, while neutrality might be suitable for a country like Switzerland, it was not possible for a State with the geographical situation and peculiar shape of Czechoslovakia. Czechoslovakia was surrounded on three sides by the Reich and had in the past only prospered through the protection of the Reich.

Thus even the " Protectorate " was adumbrated.

It is now known from documents presented at the Nuremberg Trial that military plans against Czechoslovakia were drafted in June 1937; that at the conference of November 5, 1937, when Hitler spoke of Germany's need for more territory in Europe, Austria and Czechoslovakia were specifically envisaged;[1] and that on April 21, 1938, he discussed with Keitel three possible modes of proceeding against Czechoslovakia:[2]

(1) Strategic surprise attack out of clear sky without cause or justification, has been declined. As resulting hostile world opinion might produce serious situation. Such a measure is justified only for the elimination of the last opponent on the Continent.

[1] *International Military Tribunal Document*, 386-PS (Hossbach notes).
[2] 388-PS (Schmundt file), item 2.

(2) Action after a time of diplomatic clashes, which gradually become more acute and lead to war.

(3) Lightning-swift action as the result of an incident (*e.g.* assassination of German Minister in connexion with an anti-German demonstration).

(Dr. Eisenlohr, who was not a Nazi, was obviously considered a suitable object for a Nazi-instigated " incident ".) A draft directive of May 20 prescribed : " The *Propaganda War* must . . . intimidate Czechoslovakia by threats and reduce her power of resistance ".[1]   On May 28 Hitler declared : " It is my unalterable decision to smash Czechoslovakia by military action in the near future ". But on June 18 :[2]

> I will decide to take action against Czechoslovakia only if I am firmly convinced, as in the case of the demilitarized zone and the entry into Austria, that France will not march and therefore England will not intervene.

The final directive was signed by Hitler on June 24.

It is further proved that Henlein and his Sudeten party had drawn money from the German Government since 1935 ;[3] and on March 16, 1938, Eisenlohr wrote to the Berlin Foreign Office :[4]

> The line of German foreign policy as transmitted by the German Legation is exclusively decisive for the policy of the Sudeten German Party. My directives are to be complied with implicitly. . . . I now hope to have the Sudeten German Party under firm control.

On March 17 Henlein asked Ribbentrop for " a very early personal talk " to review the situation — he had for that reason postponed for four weeks the congress of his party, scheduled for March 26–27.[5] On March 28 he saw Hitler and received directives ; and the next day, at a

---

[1] 388-PS, item 12.   [2] *Ibid.* item 30.   [3] 3059-PS.
    [4] 3060-PS.   [5] 2789-PS.

conference with Ribbentrop, it was decided, that the Sudetens should avoid " prematurely accepting " the concessions which the Czechoslovak Government might make to them, or entering that Government, but should gradually raise and amplify their demands.[1]

Meantime Göring, the " swashbuckling conversationalist " whose rantings were more serious than his solemn assurances, on April 16 talked to Henderson about " dividing the appendix (which is his favourite term for Czechoslovakia) between Poland, Hungary and Germany " ; on June 23, about " the incorporation of the Sudetens in the Reich being sooner or later inevitable " ; and to the King of Sweden he talked at the end of April " of pushing the Czechs back to Russia, where they belong " (there was a Nazi scheme for such a population transfer). And on July 18 members of Göring's entourage were reported by Henderson to have alluded, in talking to press correspondents, to the " possibility of serious developments at the end of August ".

When the Sudeten congress met at Carlsbad on April 24 complete territorial autonomy was demanded for the Sudetenland, and, besides, " recognition of the Germans throughout Czechoslovakia as a corporate body " — *i.e.* non-territorial autonomy for the *Volksdeutsche*, free to "form their lives " on Nazi principles. Henderson was an immediate convert to that programme, convinced of " the necessity of federalism in Czechoslovakia ". It would be difficult, he admitted on May 3, to press such an arrangement on the Czechs unless it had

> the prospect of acceptance by Germany or of permanency. I have little confidence that it will have such a permanent prospect. It is much more probable that in the end the Sudeten will vote themselves out of all union with Prague and into the German Reich.

[1] 2788-PS.

Yet his attitude during the months to come was what it had been towards Austria and was to be towards Poland : the Germans are right, only their methods are wrong, and they must have their way. " We are on a weak moral basis " ; " the Germans are convinced of the justice of their cause " (May 6) ; the Sudetens " fail to see why they should be sacrificed in order to preserve the balance of power in Europe " ; " a war for the Sudeten would be quite the most senseless of undertakings " (May 19). The Germans claim " the sacred right of self-determination " for the Sudetens, but are willing to hold their hand provided such a measure of autonomy is conceded " as will enable them . . . to vote themselves . . . into the Reich at a later date " (May 19). " All depends now on M. Beneš' reactions, or rather action " (May 13) ; the key to a peaceful solution lies at Prague " and not at Berlin " (May 22) ; " I am profoundly convinced we should use firmest language at Prague and insist on really comprehensive scheme of settlement " (May 24) ; " I honestly believe that the moment has come for Prague to get a real twist of the screw. And something that the Czech nation as a whole will appreciate. It is the French job, but if they won't face it I believe we shall have to " (July 18).

Between 1933 and 1938 Czechoslovakia, not wishing to dissociate herself from France, repeatedly declined German offers of a bilateral treaty, such as was signed with Poland in January 1934.[1] The offer was renewed by Hitler on February 16, 1938 ; but Austria's experience over her treaty of July 1936 was, wrote Newton on March 20,

a grim warning against conclusion of an agreement

[1] The earliest approach, in the autumn of 1933, is mentioned in President Beneš' letter to me, of April 20, 1944, printed below in *Documents*, I, pages 281-5. For a detailed account of another in 1936, see E. Beneš, *Paměti*. 1947, pages 24-34.

by a weak country with Germany in isolation . . . later on, however innocent and apparently clear its terms, the Reich will protest that they have not been faithfully observed and proceed to demand either acceptance of more compromising commitments, or acting as judge in their own case immediately execute whatever sentence they please against their victim.

A few days later the Czechs were informed that His Majesty's Government were prepared to exchange views with them on their minority problem; and on March 25 Sir Samuel Hoare suggested to Jan Masaryk, Czechoslovak Minister in London, that they should ask for the good offices of the Western Powers to reach a satisfactory arrangement. The Czechs thereupon offered to submit their scheme to the British and French Governments, hoping that, if approved, it would have their support in Berlin. Lord Halifax replied on April 9:

> His Majesty's Government do not possess enough knowledge of the complexities of the Sudeten German problem . . . to adjudicate on the merits of any solution that the Czechoslovak Government may propose. To do so would require his Majesty's Government to send out a special investigator to take evidence on the spot — a course which in present circumstances I do not favour. . . . If, however, the Czechoslovak Government wish to take us into their confidence, we should certainly endeavour to formulate our views frankly, within the limits of our ability to do so, but our ability will necessarily be restricted if we are not at the same time in possession of the views and wishes of the Henlein party.
>
> I cannot at this stage say whether his Majesty's Government would be prepared to give support in Berlin to any specific proposals.

And on April 12:

> It is . . . essential that the Czechoslovak Government should be brought to face the realities of the present situation and to realize the necessity of making

wide concessions to the German minority rather than superficial measures which will no longer meet the case.

Lord Halifax proposed that Britain and France should "use their influence in Prague, preferably in concert, in furtherance of such a settlement", and ask the Czechs

> to keep us informed of developments; and that we should thereafter continue to watch the situation very closely and be ready at any appropriate moment and in any appropriate manner to use our influence to assist to secure a settlement.

He added a warning against "too broad an interpretation" of the Prime Minister's statement that Britain might become involved in war over Czechoslovakia; a probability should not be treated as a certainty; nor should the Czechs feel encouraged to seek "some less radical solution of the German minority problem" than was called for by the situation.

When MM. Daladier and Bonnet came to London on April 28, the first day was spent in discussing the military position. The main effort of each country, said Lord Halifax, must be directed to home defence; British assistance to France would be chiefly by sea and in the air; while on land it would not exceed two divisions. Chamberlain added that even this was not an absolute undertaking. M. Daladier said that France was able to "confront the German army victoriously", but her weakness lay in her aircraft industry not having passed sufficiently from "an artisan basis" to mass production.

The next day was devoted to the Czech problem. Lord Halifax spoke of its "urgent gravity", of the "great exaltation" of German opinion on both sides of the frontier, and of the "perpetually growing" demands of the Sudetens. The military situation was disquieting, and everything must be done to avoid war, which "might carry considerable risk for both France and Great

Britain ". And while the Germans must not be encouraged to think that they could force on Czechoslovakia any settlement they chose, the Czechs should be induced to attempt " a comprehensive settlement ". Czechoslovakia would have to cease being a national State including minorities and become a State of different nationalities. It might be difficult to pronounce upon the merits of any Czech scheme, or assume responsibility for it; but it might not " be possible, or . . . even right, to avoid expressing our views ", which would have to be based on its "intrinsic merits" and on its "settlement value" — *i.e.* how far Henlein would be prepared to accept it.

M. Daladier said that nowhere had minorities been treated as well as in Czechoslovakia. He himself was convinced that Henlein did not seek concessions but the destruction of the Czechoslovak State. To demand further concessions from the Czechs would only be admissible if, in case they were rejected by the Germans, " we should be prepared to support the Czechoslovak Government and prevent the dismemberment of Czechoslovakia "; but not " if we were determined not to accept the responsibilities implicit in the action we had taken ". " It was not really at Prague that it was necessary to bring pressure to bear." The Germans were tearing up treaties and destroying the equilibrium of Europe. Austria was destroyed, "and all we had done was to offer our condolences ". To-day it was Czechoslovakia, to-morrow it may be Rumania, where the Iron Guard worked for the Nazis. Another capitulation would prepare the way " for the very war we wished to avoid ". The Czechoslovak army was not to be despised; Russia's army had suffered through the " purges ", but she " still possessed the strongest air force in Europe "; and the military situation was governed by the political situation, " and could be decided by determination shown by statesmen ".

Chamberlain replied that Beneš would not be pressed

" to accept terms which, in effect, meant the destruction of his country ", but must not be led to expect greater support than could be given. Nor should bluff be tried on Germany. " For his part he doubted very much whether Herr Hitler really desired to destroy the Czechoslovak State or rather a Czechoslovak State." If so, he " did not see how this could be prevented. But . . . he did not believe that such a decision had been reached." As for German intrigues in Rumania, these " might merely represent preparations against the encirclement which Germany undoubtedly thought she had to guard against. . . ." He thought " that a less menacing interpretation might be placed upon the facts " than M. Daladier had suggested. Some time " we might be compelled to go to war " ; but " only dire necessity would ever persuade him to wage a preventive war."

The Berlin telegrams of the Quai d'Orsay, said M. Bonnet, pointed not to Hitler wishing to preserve " a Czechoslovakia transformed into a neutral State on a federal basis ", but to his wanting to wipe her off the map — to annex the German districts and let Poland have Teschen, Hungary Slovakia, and the Czechs a small State in the German orbit. France will stand by her obligations to Czechoslovakia ; but the efficacy of her action will largely depend on the support received from Britain.

M. Daladier, answering Chamberlain, repudiated the suggestion that to protect " an independent people against unprovoked aggression " meant to favour preventive war or an encirclement of Germany. " Where was there any question of encirclement in this ? " Nor did he mean to bluff : Germany was bluffing, or at least had done so in the past. She could still be stopped now, but not after she had seized all the resources of central and eastern Europe.

If the common policy of France and Great Britain was inspired by sentiments of weakness . . . the only result would be to precipitate renewed violence. . . . If . . . inspired by firmness . . . a European war might be avoided.

But Chamberlain demurred against their committing themselves " to a particular Czechoslovak plan of concessions which might not prove acceptable to the German Government ". Concerted representations should be made in Prague, while His Majesty's Government would " try to ascertain from the German Government what was their idea of a peaceful settlement ". If the Germans proved unreasonable, they would be warned that France would stand by her treaty obligations to Czechoslovakia, and the British Government would repeat the declaration of March 24 — that Britain might be drawn into a war.

The meeting was adjourned ; M. Daladier consulted his colleagues ; and finished by accepting Chamberlain's proposals — an ominous conclusion to the Franco-British conversations. On May 5 Lord Halifax told the Soviet Ambassador that both sides h'ad found them " of great value " and " had been able to reach complete agreement ". Indeed, a week later at Geneva, M. Bonnet explained to Lord Halifax that he

> wanted H.M.G. to put as much pressure as possible on Dr. Beneš to reach a settlement with the Sudeten Deutsch in order to save France from the cruel dilemma of dishonouring her Agreements or becoming involved in war.

When on April 10 M. Daladier had, in forming his Government, substituted M. Bonnet for M. Paul-Boncour, it was known that he meant to keep France out of a war over Czechoslovakia :[1] there was an inexplicable contradiction between his own thinking and his choice of his Foreign Minister.

[1] For Paul-Boncour's account of his talks with Daladier on April 10, see his memoirs, *Entre les deux guerres*, iii. 96-103. See also Beneš, *Paměti*, pages 61-2.

On May 4 Lord Halifax, when sending Mr. Newton instructions for the concerted *démarche*, remarked that " a great gulf " seemed still to divide Henlein from the Czechs, who " have, therefore, I feel a good way to go yet before they can hope to find the basis of a reasonable compromise ". The Czechs begged that Britain should do nothing " to raise pretensions of Henlein party ", nor press for a public admission that Czechoslovakia was a State of nationalities; and that Berlin should not be asked what they wanted, for this would encourage unreasonable demands. But Lord Halifax found these reactions " disappointing ", and Mr. Newton was instructed to impress Beneš and the Prime Minister, Dr. Hodža, with " the responsibility which rests upon them ". Beneš replied by " most categorical, formal and sincere assurances that Czechoslovak Government are convinced of necessity of coming to an agreement without delay ". He spoke of Czechoslovakia's Western orientation, and when reminded of Britain's limited interest in Czechoslovakia said he was satisfied that she understood the menace which German dominion over Central Europe implied to her. The next day, May 17, Mr. Newton suggested that uneasiness should be expressed to Masaryk " lest Czechoslovak Government might yet fail to go either as far or . . . as fast as was necessary to take advantage of an opportunity likely to be vital for future of Czechoslovakia ".

Henderson was instructed to tell the Germans about the *démarche* without disclosing the nature of the settlement urged in Prague (which he promptly disclosed); he was to add that there was no desire to interfere in what the Germans might regard as their own domestic sphere (the Sudetenland — nothing of that kind was said to the Czechs). On May 12 Ribbentrop declared that it was entirely for Henlein to decide what would be " a satisfactory settlement ", but he repeated several times with evident sincerity that German Government earnestly desired a peaceful and friendly solution. . . . It was . . . clear throughout my interview that while German Government are inclined to put faith in sincerity of yourself and Prime Minister, they have less in French Government, and none in M. Beneš.

Minister for Foreign Affairs begged that I would keep him informed of result of our *démarche* at Prague, and I said that I would do so if I were authorized to. . . .

Finally Herr von Ribbentrop said, and I agreed, that we must now wait to see result of advice which we are giving at Prague. . . . His request to be kept informed and in touch with me indicates very clearly that far from resenting our interference Herr von Ribbentrop not only welcomed it, but regards it as the only hope of . . . peaceful solution.

And on May 18 Henderson wrote :

There is some hope of my being able to exercise moderating influence here if I keep in touch with the German Government as continuously and closely as possible. . . .

Official at Ministry . . . stated that German Government genuinely appreciated British step at Prague and would welcome rather than repel further British efforts to secure an agreed settlement on German lines.

Meantime, on May 14, Henlein had arrived in London (expenses paid by Berlin) ; affirmed he had never received orders or even recommendations from Berlin ;[1] was " very reasonable ", took what " was said in very good part ", and seemed " genuinely anxious for a speedy settlement ". Sir Robert (now Lord) Vansittart wrote on May 16 :

Before leaving for England, Henlein saw Ribbentrop and was instructed to place the blame on the Czechs. Weizsäcker wrote on May 12 : " In London, Herr Henlein will deny that he acts on orders of Berlin. . . ." (See Military Tribunal IV, U.S.A. *v.* Weizsäcker, Pros. Exh. 63, NG-3555, D.B. 3-A, page 38.)

> . . . I found Herr Henlein far more reasonable
> and amenable than I had dared to hope. . . . We
> parted on as friendly terms as ever. . . . This visit
> opens up distinct possibilities, but no more than
> possibilities. . . .

On May 20 German troop movements were reported
toward the Czech frontiers; and the Czechs called up
one class of reservists. The alarm may have been premature; Germans do not go into action without a full
directive, and this was only being drafted. Berlin now
indulged in rage and threatening language. But as Mr.
Newton pointed out on May 24, with sense and fairness
(and this was acknowledged by Lord Halifax),

> the German Government cannot seriously maintain
> that the enrolment of one class of Czech reservists was
> an act of aggression against Germany. Their real
> complaint of Czech wickedness can only be that the
> Czechs showed the intention to defend themselves if
> attacked. . . . Field-Marshal Göring has lately been
> making no secret of his intention to liquidate Czecho-
> slovakia this summer. . . . With the Austrian ex-
> ample before them the Czechoslovak Government
> . . . were surely not only within their rights in
> taking some counter measures, but they owed it to
> their population to do so.

On May 21 Lord Halifax warned the German Government that in case of a conflict France would be compelled
to intervene, and His Majesty's Government could not
guarantee that they would not " become involved also ".
M. Bonnet declared at a Press conference that France
would observe her treaty obligations to Czechoslovakia.
But to the British Ambassador, Sir Eric Phipps, he spoke
about the hasty and unfortunate action of the Czechs,
who had mobilized without consulting the French; said
that their action " might well cause Germans to maintain
that Czechs had violated terms of their arbitration treaty

with Germany"; [1] and gave Phipps the impression of being only too anxious to follow any lead Britain might give at Prague with a view to averting war. [2] (The next day Henderson, " speaking confidentially ", told Herr von Weizsäcker " that the French Government had taken grave exception to the calling up of Czech reserves. . . . I did in fact the best I could to convince him of French good faith as well as our own.") On the 22nd, to offset the warnings given to Berlin, Lord Halifax warned the French not to assume that " His Majesty's Government would at once take joint military action with them to preserve Czechoslovakia against German aggression ", and begged them not to act without ample previous consultation. M. Bonnet, wrote Phipps, replied that he " would not dream " of doing so, and repeated

> that he would readily put any pressure on Czecho-slovak Government that you might think at any moment desirable in order to ensure a peaceful solu-tion of Sudeten question. I pointed out that it behoved the Czechs to be more than reasonable, for alternative for them would be total annihilation. His Excellency heartily agreed. Moreover, he said, if Czechoslovakia were really unreasonable the French Government might well declare that France con-sidered herself released from her bond.
>
> M. Bonnet remarked that all that the French Government desired was not to be placed before the

[1] A violation of that treaty by the Czechs would have freed France from her obligations.

[2] An account of that conversation, stated to have been given the same night by M. Bonnet to M. Osusky, Czechoslovak Minister in Paris, appears in Osusky's report of May 22, 1938, printed by Berber, *op. cit.* pages 110-11 : " The British Ambassador . . . asked whether the French Government had been informed beforehand about the Czechoslovak mobilization. He added that that mobilization might justify one by Germany. Bonnet replied that this was not a mobilization against Germany, but measures for the maintenance of order during the elections " [local elections were being held in Czechoslovakia].

dreadful alternative of breaking their pledge or of beginning another world war.

Next, Bonnet spoke to the Czech Minister " with the utmost severity "; urged the Czechs to demobilize and make a " very generous " offer to Henlein; and, talking to Phipps, " paid tribute to reasonable attitude of German Government ", to which the Czechs must respond by " a large and generous contribution to the cause of peace ". Meanwhile Henderson argued that if German confidence in British sincerity was to be maintained, it was essential for the Czechs " to give concrete evidence of a change of heart ".

Beneš and Hodža in public announcements had promised equality and self-administration to the Sudetens. But these, who, in Mr. Newton's words, " have been demanding satisfaction of undefined, and in fact undefinable, conditions before they would even consent to negotiate for a settlement ", now refused to do so until the military measures were revoked: a demand " affecting the sovereignty and authority of the State "; indeed the failure of the German Government to stop " the shufflings of the Sudeten German Party " made Mr. Newton rightly doubt their own good faith. But Lord Halifax thought that Henlein " should, if possible, get some satisfaction regarding Czechoslovak military measures "; and that " although the Czechs may have some reason to distrust the good faith of the German Government ", also the German doubt of Beneš's good faith " is not wholly unjustified ".

The crisis of May 20–22, coupled with a shooting incident in the Sudetenland, produced a new sense of anxious urgency in the British Government: local safeguards were sought against further incidents, and speedy solutions for the major problems. Great Britain had been slow to rearm, and the Government, impressed by Germany's superiority, especially in the air, were firmly con-

vinced that Britain and France could not stand up to her
(little attention was paid to the numerous — and accurate
— reports that Germany was as yet unprepared for a major
war). They were determined to avoid war at any cost,
willing to throw Czechoslovakia to the wolves, and therefore careful not to tie themselves up with her. Threats
and promptings with which she was hustled along were
hedged in with reservations disowning all responsibility of
His Majesty's Government; and France, lest she dragged
in Britain, was gently encouraged to disembarrass herself
of her treaty obligations.

On May 22 His Majesty's Government offered to send
an observer to the Sudetenland to report on the situation;
and next suggested an international commission to
investigate frontier incidents; but the Germans replied
that this should be purely British, and its activities " confined to Czechoslovak territory and internal disorder —
i.e. not frontier incidents ". Lastly, His Majesty's Government, not wishing " to be manœuvred into the position
of arbitrator ", meant, in case of a deadlock between
the Czechs and the Sudetens, to propose an international
commission to investigate its cause and devise means for
overcoming it. But Henderson warned them that
international mediation would not be acceptable to the
German Government.

> The intervention of His Majesty's Government in
> the dispute is welcome only in so far as it serves to
> bring pressure to bear on Czechoslovak Government
> to meet Sudeten demands and thus to preserve peace.

On May 25 Lord Halifax, " in a purely personal
capacity ", spoke to Masaryk about Czechoslovakia's external problem: there was no protecting her against a
German attack; France had accepted her obligations
" under conditions very different from those which prevailed to-day "; Czechoslovakia could not abandon " her

foreign connexions at German dictation " ; but could she not adopt " a position of neutrality " ? Though there was no guarantee of permanence in such a solution, she would, by renouncing guarantees which were no longer effective, remove " the principal elements of provocation to Germany ".

An even more drastic step was canvassed when, at the end of the month, Mr. (now Sir William) Strang was sent to Prague and Berlin for personal talks with His Majesty's Representatives.

> We did not want [he said] to get into the position of endorsing Dr. Beneš' plan (however good it might be) and then having to run away from it because the Germans rejected it and became violent again. . . . In these circumstances the best standing ground for Dr. Beneš and for ourselves might be the early offer of a plebiscite [for the Sudetens] . . . on the two questions : (1) acceptance of the plan ; (2) union with Germany. . . . Dr. Beneš would no doubt ask what guarantees he would receive either (1) for the rump, in the event of a plebiscite favourable to Germany, or (2) for the integral State, in the event of a plebiscite unfavourable to Germany. The answer must be that no such guarantees can be offered, so far as we are concerned. . . .
>
> There were, of course, the obvious difficulties about a plebiscite ; how to frame the questions ; how to delimit the polling area ; how to ensure a free vote — e.g. foreign troops. There was also the question whether the German Government would want a free plebiscite — they liked to run their own plebiscites. But these could be left aside for the moment.

Mr. Newton feared that a plebiscite would go overwhelmingly in favour of incorporation, and would destroy Czechoslovakia. The maintenance of the mixed State, be it within the German orbit, would be better for the Czechs, and might be accepted by the Germans. A

British investigator or commission of inquiry would involve Britain deeply in the Sudeten problem : but this, he thought, could hardly be avoided and " would be in keeping with the leading part we have played in this question since the beginning ". The warning given to Germany on May 21 had enhanced Britain's influence, and, " whatever we intended, we are certainly regarded as being more deeply committed in the Czech affair than before ".

In Berlin, too, Britain was " regarded as having played the chief part in frustrating Germany " ; and the Embassy thought that His Majesty's Government, having taken a hand in the Sudeten question, " must go through with it " ; in case of deadlock they should negotiate " an equitable settlement " with the German Government, to be imposed and guaranteed by France and Germany, and perhaps " witnessed " by Great Britain and Italy.

Early in June the Foreign Office, having examined the idea of neutralizing Czechoslovakia, reached the conclusion that the Czechs were bound to demand in return a guarantee from the Great Powers; that this would burden Britain with " an entirely new commitment ", fail to free France from her dilemma, and not satisfy Germany, whose real object was to sever Czechoslovakia's connexions with East and West. For the guarantors only a collective undertaking would be satisfactory which would lapse if one of them violated it — *e.g.* Germany by attacking Czechoslovakia — but the Czechs could hardly be persuaded to attach any value to it.

When the French Ambassador in Berlin, M. François-Poncet, spoke of suggesting to Hitler Anglo-French-German negotiations about Czechoslovakia and a plan to neutralize her under their guarantee, Lord Halifax, on June 9, protested against a plan " which would require Great Britain to guarantee Czechoslovakia ". (It was only too obvious that the Germans would attack a Czechoslovakia disarmed externally and internally.)

On May 31, a message having reached London from the " moderate Henlein " about the reasonable proposals he had made to the Czechoslovak Government, the Czechs were promptly informed that unwillingness to accept them as a basis of discussion " would exercise an immediate and adverse effect upon the interest taken in the problem in this country "; while the French were asked by His Majesty's Government to put " the greatest possible pressure on Dr. Beneš in person without delay ", and to warn him that if " the present opportunity to reach a settlement is missed, the French Government would be driven to reconsider their position *vis-à-vis* Czechoslovakia " — with which M. Bonnet readily concurred. Mr. Newton telegraphed back on June 2 :

> I think it very desirable that we should continue to show sympathetic appreciation of the fact that Czechoslovak Government have hitherto accepted very far-reaching and doubtless unpalatable advice and appear to have been doing their utmost of late at any rate to cope with the problems which might well baffle the wisest statesmanship.

If pressed too far they might be unable to carry their public with them. In further telegrams he explained their position : they had no intention to prolong the delay ; were ready to concede to the Sudetens the fullest equality of rights and benefits, self-administration through local councils possessed of wide powers, and cultural autonomy through a national Curia on a personal basis, but not a separate National Parliament, which concession could not be limited to them and would endanger the unity of the State; nor could they admit the creation of a distinct *Volksgruppe* governed on Nazi lines by a *Volkstag* representing Germans wherever resident in the Republic; and being democratic, the Government had to carry with it the parliamentary coalition on which it was based. There were also tactical considerations : the Sudetens (proceeding on the lines laid down for them in Berlin on March 29) tried at first not to disclose their full programme, but to raise and amplify their demands as they were being conceded; the Czechs, though pressed from London to show results, obviously could not lend themselves to such a mug's game.

The negotiations between the Czechs and the Sudetens are in themselves of minor importance : they were conducted with a maximum of chicanery and sharp practice on the part of the Sudetens, and with embarrassed solicitude by the Czechoslovak Government, who knew only too well the gang they were dealing with, but had to heed the opinions and exhortations of the Western Powers. Indeed, if any excuse can be found for the way in which these harried the Czechs, it is in the excessive meekness with which the Czechs submitted to it, or occasionally even invited it in order to overcome opposition within their own ranks. Thus, on June 26, Hodža (a Slovak who at times pursued an incomprehensible line of his own) said to Mr. Newton

> that it would . . . be useful if, of course without mention of himself, Czechoslovak Minister in London were summoned . . . and informed of the impatience felt by His Majesty's Government at the absence of results and of the grave consequences to be expected if Czechoslovak Government failed to go not merely fast enough but above all far enough.

In a subsequent telegram Mr. Newton emphasized the " most confidential nature " of that remark which, as Hodža said himself, " might be regarded as treasonable ".

M. Bonnet had agreed to take concerted action with Britain over Henlein's " reasonable proposals ", but said that representations in Prague had better be made separately, as the " French Minister will have to go somewhat further than the British ''[1] (which he did not, partly because he doubted the accuracy of Henlein's statements, as did Mr. Newton). When Lord Halifax complained that the interview had been " exploratory " in character (and not minatory), M. Bonnet replied that he had, through the Czechoslovak Minister in Paris, sent Beneš " a memorandum couched in very strong terms ". Lord Halifax hoped it would be shown to him : M. Bonnet promised to do so. But when, after a reminder, it at last reached Lord Halifax, he observed with regret that it did " not contain any specific warning that France would have to reconsider her treaty position if the Czechoslovak Government were unreasonable on the Sudeten question ". M. Bonnet was ready enough to leave the unpleasant jobs to Great Britain.

Meantime Lord Halifax had raised with M. Bonnet the subject of Czechoslovakia's foreign relations. These, he wrote to Phipps on June 17, rather than minority problems, might well be at the root of the German-Czechoslovak difficulty. He therefore suggested a remodelling of Czechoslovakia's treaty relations such as would relieve her from assisting France or Russia against Germany, and preclude her from letting her territory be used for operations against another State ; Germany should become, and France and Russia each remain, a guarantor of Czechoslovakia, only her obligations towards them being cancelled (Czechoslovakia would thus have been neutralized without a British guarantee). Lord Halifax asked M. Bonnet's opinion, which he promised to give. Reminded on July 1, he promised it " within the next few days ". But by July 20 no answer had been received. Then interest shifted to a scheme of mediation.

[1] To Osusky Bonnet is reported to have said on June 4 that he " declined making a joint démarche ", but had to tell him that " the British are much irritated, and that their irritation turns against the President of the Republic " ; see Osusky's report of June 7, 1938, in Berber, *op. cit.* pages 113-14.

On June 18 Lord Halifax instructed Mr. Newton to sound the Czechs whether, in case of a deadlock with the Sudetens, they would accept the mediation of an independent British expert. Mr. Newton thought the time not ripe for it, though the proposal might eventually be welcomed. Yet such " outside mediation " would have to be suggested tactfully — " there is . . . a certain latent suspicion among the Czechs that the British policy in Central Europe is directed to solely selfish ends ", and they might therefore hesitate " to accept purely British mediation in a matter which would affect the whole future of their independent existence ". No immediate action was taken. When at the end of the month the French were consulted, Lord Halifax added that he was anxious

> to avoid committing His Majesty's Government to the support of any particular proposals and the mediator would therefore act in a purely independent capacity, with the task of endeavouring to reconcile the two opposing points of view.

But " that the mediator, although British and appointed by British Government, would not commit His Majesty's Government to support of his views would ", Mr. Newton feared, " make the proposal less attractive to Czechoslovak Government ".

About July 8 Henlein again enlightened London on the situation : the Czechs were deliberately dilatory, he did not trust Hodža any longer, Beneš " did not take the pressure from London and Paris at all seriously and thought he could fool them ", etc. Lord Halifax told Mr. Newton on July 14 that " if the present situation were anything like Herr Henlein's description ", he intended a most pressing *démarche* ; and if a deadlock should appear imminent he would warn the Czechs that Henlein might demand a plebiscite, " which public opinion in this country would almost certainly feel to be a not unreasonable proposal ", and

His Majesty's Government might feel it their duty publicly to propose the appointment of an independent mediator, and place upon the Czechoslovak Government the responsibility of accepting or rejecting the proposal.

By July 18 Lord Halifax thought that the moment had come to broach his " offer of investigation and mediation " with President Beneš, naming Lord Runciman. Mr. Newton was to press Beneš strongly " to declare himself ready to accept in principle the proposal ", or, still better, " request our help in the matter " ; best of all, if the Czechs and Sudetens made a joint announcement of both having asked for it. When on July 20 Mr. Newton conveyed the suggestion, Beneš " seemed greatly taken aback and much upset ", and said " it was a most serious and most unexpected message ". Such a proposal was liable to put him in an impossible position ; it amounted to far-reaching intervention, and might provoke a crisis, possibly entailing the resignation of the Government and his own. If the Sudeten party " were put on an equal footing with Government, it would mean that the Government were no longer sovereign ".

> The proposal went beyond his constitutional competence and the reply must come from the Government. . . . He repeatedly begged my approach might be treated only as a preliminary sounding. I equally repeated as often as necessary . . . that I had no authority to depart from my instructions. . . .

Beneš said " he must consult the French Government before he could reply ".

The same day, July 20, Lord Halifax spoke in Paris to MM. Daladier and Bonnet on the subject.

> The French Ministers expressed their agreement with the action that we had taken. I made it plain to them that if and when we took this action we should not be prepared to assume any responsibility

for what the individual selected . . . might do.
Our responsibility would begin and end with finding
him and with turning him loose at Prague to make
the best that he could of the business. . . . Indeed,
I told the French Ministers . . . that, before I had
come to Paris, I had received a visit from the Aga
Khan, during which he had stressed the responsibility that lay upon His Majesty's Government to
accept no commitment that might involve the British
Empire in war. The same, I said, would be the
position of South Africa.

The next day Mr. Newton saw Hodža, who

said that he would try to convince his colleagues in
the Cabinet that offer should be regarded as proof of
good will of His Majesty's Government and therefore
accepted. One difficulty was how to avoid putting
Sudeten Germany Party on the same footing as
Government of State.

While the action proposed was exceptional he
personally would welcome arrival of Lord Runciman
and I gather the sooner the better.

Meantime in London a Sudeten emissary had to be
assured that the Czechoslovak Government would not
present its own scheme to its Parliament: Henlein was
about to see Hitler and had to be encouraged " to perse-
vere in his policy of moderation, which ", wrote Lord
Halifax, " he at present inclined to abandon in disgust ".
From Berlin Henderson continued in his best style — he
wrote to Sir Alexander Cadogan on July 22:

It is easy and popular to put all the blame on
Germany as Dr. Beneš is prone to do . . .
It is easy to say but impossible to prove that
Germany does not desire a settlement. . . . In my
opinion Germany's attitude has not so far been in-
correct during the past two months, in the sense that
she has left us unimpeded in our mediation at Prague.
It is also easy for Dr. Beneš to attribute all ill faith
and all difficulties to Germans and Sudeten, but I

fancy that strict impartiality would distribute blame fairly equally. Certainly those of my colleagues who know Beneš best are those who trust him least and extremists are not confined to one side of the frontier — or of any frontier, *vide* Cot and Mandel in France and the Jews and Communists everywhere.

(Mr. Churchill calls Mandel " this valiant Frenchman ", and adds : " His memory is honoured by his countrymen and their Allies ".) [1]

On July 23 Dr. Hodža handed to Mr. Newton the official reply of the Czechoslovak Government. It expressed appreciation of the constant interest shown by His Majesty's Government in the Czechoslovak situation, spoke of its own endeavours to find an " equitable solution of the Nationalities question ", welcomed

> every support which could be granted to it in this work, and believing that it is in this hope of perfect harmony of ideas with the British and the French Governments,[2] it begs His Majesty's Government to be good enough to indicate a person who would be ready with his opinion and advice to help to overcome difficulties which might eventually still arise.

[1] See *Their Finest Hour*, page 159.
[2] This passage apparently got confused in transmission. Since the above essay was written, the French text of the Czech *note verbale* has been published in the *Documents on British Foreign Policy, 1919–1939*, Third Series, vol. ii, page 10, where the passage runs :
> Il sera donc heureux de tout appui qui pourra lui être accordé dans cette œuvre et croyant d'être en cela en parfaite communauté de pensée avec le Gouvernement britannique et le Gouvernement français, il prie le Gouvernement de Sa Majesté. . . .

APPEASEMENT

WHEN early in 1948 a collection of captured German documents dealing with *Nazi-Soviet Relations, 1939–1941*, was published by the American State Department, the Russian Foreign Office, as a counter-blast, produced from its own captures two small volumes of *Documents and Materials Relating to the Eve of the Second World War*.[1] The printing of historical documents out of context and to a political purpose is, as a rule, to be deprecated, especially if there is the prospect of an early fuller and more systematic edition. But as, unfortunately, in the case of the Soviet Government there is little chance of integral publication, even haphazard disclosures are welcome in so far as documents are thereby rendered available which might otherwise remain permanently undisclosed : the careful and critical student of contemporary history will know how to fit them into the framework built up from other materials. It is therefore to be hoped that the Soviet Government will continue its publications. The authenticity of these documents can in most cases be tested by comparing them with copies captured by the Western allies, or by reference to their authors : and so far no ground has appeared for questioning it. But then only the crudest propaganda operates with forgeries, which can almost invariably be exposed. Here genuine documents are printed with meticulous scholarship, after having been selected with equally meticulous care : indeed, the purpose is so obvious as to impair the effect — a fuller and seemingly more objective publica-

[1] Ministry of Foreign Affairs of the U.S.S.R.; *Documents and Materials Relating to the Eve of the Second World War*. Vol. i, November 1937–1938. From the Archives of the German Ministry of Foreign Affairs. Vol. ii, Dirksen Papers (1938–1939). Moscow: Foreign Languages Publishing House. London: Collet's Holdings. These volumes were first published in Russian translation.

tion, whose story would leave room for human weakness, ignorance, fear, deliberate self-deception, and feeble attempts to preserve appearances, would drive home its conclusions far more forcibly than this concentrated, misleading tale of political " villainy ".

The first volume, which recounts how Czechoslovakia was sacrificed by the Western Powers and stabbed in the back by Poland, resembles a documentary film rather than a collection of diplomatic documents. But skill is shown in the dramatic grouping of the material : few will be able to re-live these transactions without distress, or even shame. Yet if spiritual atonement there shall be, what more can any nation or Government do than publish without reserve or palliation the full evidence available in its archives ? The volume of *Documents on British Foreign Policy, 1919–1939*, covering March–July 1938, makes sad reading ; even worse must be expected in those on Munich and its aftermath. But when has the Soviet Government published a single document showing a flaw in the judgment of its rulers, or any moral weakness in them ? This is done in democracies only, and renders them less vulnerable to " exposure " manipulated with hostile intent. Another purpose of this volume is to show up the hostility or distrust which in 1938 the Western Powers and Poland evinced towards the Soviet Union : ill-timed and impolitic these feelings may have been, but hardly unjustified.

The volume is marked on the title-page : " From the Archives of the German Ministry of Foreign Affairs ". But of its forty-four documents only twenty-seven answer that description : of these eighteen are German documents, while three are Czech and six Polish diplomatic reports, seized by the Germans in Prague and Warsaw, and found by the Russians in Berlin.[1] There were no

[1] Original copies of the Polish documents were found by the Russians, the Czech documents apparently in German translation only.

Polish documents among the material captured by the Western allies, while the Czech, in accordance with courtesy rules usually observed between friendly Powers, were returned by them to Prague. Eight more Czech documents are printed in this volume: one is a Czech Note to the U.S.S.R.; two are from an unpublished Czech White Book; five are reprinted from books by two Czech Ministers. But to tell a coherent story, even well-known texts, such as the Anglo-German and Franco-German Declarations of September and December 1938, are reproduced from *The Times* and the French *Yellow Book*; four documents, including the Munich Agreement, from British White Papers on Czechoslovakia (Cmd. 5847 and 5848); etc. In all, about one-third of the material included in this volume consists of reprints; and there is not much for which scholars will have permanently to rely on it.

For the British minutes of the talks which Hitler had with Lord Halifax on November 19, 1937, and with Nevile Henderson on March 3, 1938, we may have to wait a few years. But there is nothing very new or un-expected in the statements ascribed to the British repre-sentatives by the German minutes now published, while Hitler's talk, even as recorded by his own side, is sickening in its shrewd mendacity and venomous incoherence. On November 5, 1937, he had held the conference known from the so-called Hossbach notes, and rightly described by the prosecution at Nuremberg as marking "the tran-sition to planned aggression": territorial expansion was envisaged, and Austria and Czechoslovakia were specific-ally singled out for its opening stage. A fortnight later Hitler received at Berchtesgaden Lord Halifax (then President of the Council), who had come, he told Hitler, to ascertain how a comprehensive and frank discussion could be arranged of all the questions affecting their two countries; this, followed by a Four-Power agreement, would secure lasting peace in Europe. Britain, he said, did not insist on the *status quo*; changes would probably have to come — for instance, in Danzig, Austria, and Czechoslovakia; but what Britain was concerned about was that such changes should be effected by reasonable arrangement and peaceful evolution. Hitler replied that Germany must get her due, either " by the free play of forces " or by the application of " higher reason " (*die höhere Vernunft*): the result in both cases, he warned Lord Halifax, would have to be approximately the same, except that " reason " would prove cheaper.

Lord Halifax's overture was subsequently exploited by Hitler who, according to a report of the American Consul-General in Vienna, alleged in his interview with Schuschnigg at Berchtesgaden on February 12, 1938, " that everything he did with respect to Austria and the Sudeten Germans was in entire agreement with Lord Halifax. . . ." This was a crude distortion; yet from what Lord Halifax did say, Hitler was bound to conclude that he would be able to carry through his programme of aggression without interference from the Western Powers — for, having given up the substance, would they fight for what to him (and not to him alone) seemed a mere matter of form? Nor would anyone who knew and understood the European Continent (which Lord Halifax did not) have imagined that anything short of force, or of a deadly threat of force, could wring from Austria, Czechoslovakia, and Poland the suicidal concessions which alone would satisfy Germany.

Lord Halifax inquired whether, after a settlement of disputed questions, Germany would re-enter the League of Nations; what changes she would desire in the Covenant; what her attitude would be towards disarmament; and what solution Hitler envisaged of the colonial problem. But the League and disarmament never entered into Hitler's purview except as baits for

British pacifists; while colonies, a "grievance" with which to belabour the neurotic conscience this country had developed towards the German "innocents", did not engage his attention at that juncture. There was, in fact, no occasion for the talk as far as he was concerned. About the League he was evasive; on disarmament he put up a smoke-screen of petulance; as for colonies, Germany, he said, was entitled to her former possessions, but if Britain, for strategic reasons, did not think their return possible, she should suggest compensation in other areas. Still, that problem had better wait till it could be discussed in a calmer atmosphere.

Hitler harped incessantly on the malignant influence which party demagogy and the Press had on international relations. When Lord Halifax replied that if he thought no advance possible towards an understanding so long as Britain remained a democracy, further conversation between them could serve no useful purpose, Hitler fumbled: his remarks about political parties "applied primarily to France". But soon he was again declaiming about the opposition of the Conservative Party to a retrocession of the German colonies and the baleful influence of " an excited and malignant Press ": " all nations should co-operate in putting an end to journalistic filibustering ". What clearly emerges from the German minute is that further talks with British statesmen were not desired by Hitler.

But the Chamberlain Government persisted. Lord Halifax replaced Mr. Eden at the Foreign Office, and in spite of Hitler's performance during Schuschnigg's visit to Berchtesgaden on February 12, Henderson called on March 3 to discuss with Hitler " all the questions that had arisen in connexion with Halifax's visit to Germany ". He talked of limiting armaments, of appeasement in Czechoslovakia and Austria, and of a solution of the colonial problem " based on a new régime of colonial administra-

tion " in an area north of the Zambesi River, " roughly
equal to the Congo Basin ".

> The Führer replied that the most important con-
> tribution to the establishment of tranquillity and
> security in Europe would be to ban the international
> inflammatory Press . . . widely represented in Britain,
> too. . . . The British Government must have been
> in a position to influence the Press to adopt a different
> tone . . . the inflammatory Press campaign must
> cease.
> In reference to Central Europe, he had to remark
> that Germany would not allow third Powers to inter-
> fere in the settlement of her relations with kindred
> countries or countries with large German popula-
> tions. . . . If England continued to oppose the
> German effort to achieve a just and reasonable settle-
> ment here, then the moment would come when it
> would be necessary to fight. . . . Germany was not
> interfering in Empire affairs . . . everywhere the
> British Press stands in the way of Germany and
> conducts a campaign of calumny against her.

If ever " Germans were fired upon in Austria or Czechoslovakia ", Germany would intervene, and " with lightning speed ". As for the colonial problem, " instead of
setting up a complicated new system ", why not settle it
" in the simplest and most natural way " by restoring to
Germany her own colonies " lawfully acquired by pur-
chase or treaty " ? But whether Hitler contradicted or
repeated his previous declarations, he again avoided discussing concrete problems. Henderson fawned on him :
mentioned " in confidence " steps taken by Lord Halifax
to influence the British Press ; said that Chamberlain
" had taken over the leadership of the people " and
" unmasked such international phrases as collective
security " ; and when Hitler ranted about the British
Minister in Vienna having talked of the pressure exerted
by Germany on Austria, Henderson protested that this

" did not necessarily represent the views of the British Government ", and that he himself " had often expressed himself in favour of the *Anschluss* ".

For once the record of the conversation made by Dr. Schmidt was communicated to the other side ;[1] and Henderson took exception to one statement only :[2]

> I never said that I had spoken here in favour of the *Anschluss*. What I did say was that I had sometimes expressed views which may not have been in accordance with those of my Government.

The passage was accordingly deleted from the final record—or so at least Ribbentrop wrote to Henderson.[3] But whatever the meaning or value of Henderson's denial,[4] the fact that he had talked in Berlin in favour of the *Anschluss* is borne out by documents in other collections. " I was always convinced that Austria was bound to become part of Germany in some form sooner or later ", wrote Henderson to Lord Halifax on April 13, 1938 — and he did not hide his " convictions " from the Germans even when contrary to the declared policy of his Government. Thus on June 1, 1937, von Papen, then German Minister in Vienna, reported to Hitler a private talk in which Henderson assured him that Britain fully understood the necessity of the German-Austrian problem being settled in accordance with the wishes of the Reich (*im reichsdeutschen Sinne*).[5]

> And when I remarked that the British Minister in Vienna took the opposite view, and did all he could to support the thesis of Austrian independence in London and to obstruct Germany's policy, he

---

[1] *Documents on German Foreign Policy, 1918–1945.* Series D (1937–1945), vol. i, *From Neurath to Ribbentrop* (American-British-French publication), No. 138, page 240.

[2] *Ibid.* No. 139, page 249.   [3] *Ibid.* No. 141, page 251.

[4] For a denial by Henderson of a statement of his own which he himself had reported, see above, pages 174-5.

[5] *Der Hochverratsprozess gegen Dr. Guido Schmidt*, Vienna, 1947, page 415.

admitted that he was acquainted with the views of
Sir Walford Selby. " But I am of a very different
opinion, and am convinced that my view will prevail
in London — only you must not rush it. . . . But
please . . . don't give away to my Vienna colleague
that I defend this view."

About the same time Herr Tauschitz, Austrian Minister
in Berlin, reported to Vienna a talk in which Henderson
said that " he could not understand the separatist
tendencies in Austria, which ' was fully as German as
Germany ' ". Great Britain

> had the greatest interest in peace being maintained
> in Europe, and he considered that it would simplify
> matters if the two formed one State. I was to some
> extent forewarned of the peculiar views of that Briton
> . . . but this, indeed, exceeded my apprehensions.

For a moment Herr Tauschitz wondered whether he had
not gone to the wrong house in the Wilhelmstrasse — the
German Foreign Office and the British Embassy were in
the same street.[1]

A discussion of documents about the crisis of September 1938 had better be deferred till the relevant
British diplomatic and all the captured German documents are available : which should be very soon. But
we shall still have to wait a while for the British counter-
part to the Czech minute of the conversation between

[1] *Der Hochverratsprozess gegen Dr. Guido Schmidt*, Vienna, 1947, page 493.
On February 23, 1938, three days after Eden's resignation, Henderson
talked to Mastný, the Czechoslovak Minister in Berlin. " I said ", writes
Mastný, " that I knew I could congratulate him who never hid his dislike
of Eden's policy. . . ." Later on, Henderson remarked : " If there is
another change and Eden returns, you will have Eden but also war. It is
nonsense to attribute to me pro-German feelings, as was done recently when
the Austrian Minister spread stories of my having talked to him in favour
of the *Anschluss*." He went on to speak of " indispensable concessions to
Germany ", and gave Austria three months in which to make them, and
Czechoslovakia two years. See Berber, *op. cit.* page 100.

the Czechoslovak Foreign Minister, M. Chvalkovský, and the British Minister in Prague, Mr. Newton, on December 10, 1938, which dealt with the guarantee promised in part-compensation to mutilated Czechoslovakia. Mr. Newton is reported to have said :

> Britain had in mind something in the nature of a joint guarantee of the Munich Powers. The British were not prepared to give a guarantee which they could not implement, and they would be very grateful to know what kind of guarantee Prague had in view. They had learned in Berlin that Germany and Italy were thinking of giving an independent guarantee. . . . The British could not give any effective guarantee against the Central Powers, but they would be prepared to give a guarantee if at least three of the four Powers acted in favour of Czechoslovakia. Britain had no desire to give an individual guarantee, but only one in conjunction with two other Great Powers (three out of the four), because the British would not put themselves in the position which France was in last October.

Some of the disjointedness of Mr. Newton's remarks may arise from a double translation ; but is it not due also to embarrassment ? The Franco-British promise of September 19 was confirmed at Munich ; on October 3 Chamberlain in Parliament expressed the hope and belief " that under the new system the new Czechoslovakia will find a greater security than she has ever enjoyed in the past " ; and Sir Thomas Inskip declared the next day that the guarantee, though technically incomplete, morally had to be treated by Britain " as being now in force " — but he avoided answering a question " whether it was joint or several ". Now the Czechs were told that Great Britain would not give an individual guarantee, nor even one jointly with France, but only in conjunction with at least two of the Munich signatories. The condition and Mr. Newton's argument acquire clarity when collated with the Foreign Office memorandum on the neutralization of Czechoslovakia sent to him on June 9, 1938, and published in the *Documents on British Foreign Policy, 1919–1939*, Third Series, vol. i, pages 647-652. Under a joint guarantee, states the memorandum,

> according to the view which His Majesty's Government have expressed in the past, but which is not universally accepted, there is no obligation on a guarantor State to intervene to protect the neutralized State unless all the guarantor States also act, and therefore the guarantee does not operate if the violation is committed by one of the guarantor States.

And again :

> This would in practice mean (assuming the British interpretation of a collective guarantee to be accepted) that, Germany being one of the guarantors, if she violated her guarantee none of the other guarantors would be bound automatically to come to Czechoslovakia's assistance, although, of course, they would be free to do so and might by reason of their guarantee feel that they were under a certain moral, though not legal, obligation. Such a system would reduce Great Britain's new commitment and France's present commitment to a minimum.

" Three out of the four " would have included at least one Axis Power.

And here is the concluding paragraph of Chvalkovský's minute :

> In the course of the subsequent conversation the British Minister repeatedly stressed the possibility that Czechoslovakia might be satisfied with a guarantee solely from Germany, which, in his opinion, was the most important, because Prague was probably aware how unwillingly Britain gave guarantees in cases where British interests were not

directly affected, and still less willingly in cases such as the present, where she had reason to doubt whether her guarantee would be of any use to us.

The doubts were fully justified, but sadly belated.

The second volume of the Soviet publication is a selection from the papers of Herbert von Dirksen, German Ambassador in London from May 1938 till the outbreak of the war; they were found by the Russians on his estate at Gröditzberg, in Silesia. Of its thirty-five items some twenty are copies of German official documents; six are copies of Embassy papers — not all necessarily communicated to Berlin, and some possibly burnt at the Embassy; a few are miscellaneous items of minor importance; four are private letters from, or to, Dirksen; but the gem of the volume is Dirksen's survey of his Ambassadorship in London, written at Gröditzberg in September 1939:

> I considered it my duty to make a written record of Anglo-German relations as they developed during my period of service in London, in the event that the desire should arise at some future date to collect all the available material on the subject. I felt this obligation all the more keenly because just before the outbreak of the war all important documents of the London Embassy had to be burned, and because many of the details were not given in the reports to the Ministry of Foreign Affairs.

Although the survey is correctly Nazi in outlook and sentiments, a note of personal complaint against Hitler and Ribbentrop breaks through occasionally: obviously a document written by Dirksen for record rather than for communication to the German Foreign Office.

The primary aim of this volume is to suggest, by disclosing certain approaches by Chamberlain through non-diplomatic channels, that he would have made a deal with Hitler had he been given a chance. Presumably Lord Halifax knew of these activities, and through him some of the Foreign Office staff, who, however, had no part in them: little about the transactions, which were as futile as they were ill-advised, is therefore likely to be found in the Foreign Office documents. Chamberlain,

> aware of the ingrained power of passive resistance of the Foreign Office officials to a line of foreign policy with which they were not in sympathy [writes Dirksen] . . . relied in his foreign political plans more on Sir Horace Wilson, the "Secretary of State in the Reich Chancellery". Further, he dismissed from the Cabinet Foreign Secretary Eden . . . and replaced him by a man loyal to him, Lord Halifax.

A secondary aim of the volume is to cause embarrassment to a number of people, big and small, who, if correctly reported, did not observe the necessary discretion in their dealings with representatives of a foreign, unfriendly, Government: a salutary warning for the future.

If the Chamberlain Government required a testimonial for their genuine desire to reach a peaceful settlement with Germany, and British public opinion for its growing impatience with German aggression and with official appeasement, it would be supplied by this volume. "The first and most essential plank" in the platform of "the Chamberlain-Halifax Cabinet", wrote Dirksen on July 10, 1938, "was and is agreement with the totalitarian States". They are the first British postwar Government to make an agreement with Germany "one of the major points" of their programme; and they display with regard to her "the maximum understanding". In this course they persist in spite of the "sinister machinations" of Jewry, of the Communist

International, and of "nationalist groups in various countries"; in spite of the average Englishman's ready response to sentimental appeals, and his determination to oppose further German attempts to change the European balance of power by unilateral action; and of the Opposition manœuvres to draw Anglo-German relations "into the vortex of British domestic politics" — "Churchill . . . believes that the easiest way to overthrow Chamberlain and put himself in the saddle is to accuse the Cabinet of dilatoriness in building sound defences against possible attack — on the part of Germany, of course." But Chamberlain is not likely to be "in serious danger before the summer recess" — "there is no man in the Opposition equal to him".

About the middle of July Captain Wiedemann was sent to London by Göring, with the knowledge of Hitler though not of Ribbentrop, to ascertain whether a visit from Göring would be welcome. But when news about these talks leaked out in the Press the project was dropped by Berlin.

> Further negotiations with leading British figures [writes Dirksen] were conducted during the following two months through Princess Hohenlohe.[1]
>
> A few days later — approximately July 24 — I took my vacation, previous to which I paid a farewell visit, among others, to Sir Horace Wilson. He asked me whether I would like to see the Prime Minister, and a little later led me to the latter's study. In a conversation lasting twenty minutes, Chamberlain expressed his concern over the German-

---

[1] For some of the political activities of Princess Stefanie Hohenlohe-Waldenburg, see reports of action brought by her, in November 1939, against Lord Rothermere, claiming damages for alleged breaches of agreement to employ her as his foreign representative "to carry communications to, or conduct negotiations with, statesmen and royal personages on the Continent, and to clear her name when she was described in certain foreign newspapers as a spy, or 'vamp', and an immoral woman".

Czechoslovak conflict, and requested that nothing precipitate be undertaken by the German side, for any resort to force might have far-reaching consequences. Let the British Government be given time; it would do everything in its power to promote a peaceful solution. . . .

This visit, too, was indiscreetly divulged to the Press and was furnished with distorting comments. . . .

Dirksen telephoned to Sir Horace Wilson; an explanatory statement, unsatisfactory to Dirksen, was published; Ribbentrop twice telephoned to him on the subject. " I gave him the required explanations."

While on leave Dirksen received a private letter from Chamberlain about the Runciman mission, with the suggestion that he should inform Hitler about it — possibly an attempt to by-pass Ribbentrop who was notoriously intent on war. But Dirksen was unable to obtain an interview with Hitler; and even when writing the record of his London Embassy, Dirksen seems to have been ignorant of the pother caused by that letter. When a month later Dirksen saw Hitler for a few minutes at a function, and communicated to him the contents of Chamberlain's letter, Hitler replied that a British general (named by Dirksen) had told him " that Runciman was an inveterate liberal " with " a poor understanding of the problems ".

In Dirksen's absence Theodor Kordt was Chargé d'Affaires, and reported both to him and the German Foreign Office on the situation and his own activities. On August 23 he sent Weizsäcker a (missing) minute of a talk " with Chamberlain's most intimate assistant, Sir Horace Wilson . . . one of the most influential men in the British Government ". On the 29th he wrote to Dirksen: " I have reason to presume that the British Government is prepared to meet our wishes as far as is only possible "; but that the feeling of the country was such that the Government would not have " much difficulty in persuading the entire British public of the necessity of war against Germany ". On September 1, he sent Dirksen — " for your strictly confidential information " — a copy of a conversation " with our friend ", whose attitude, " I do not have to tell you, Mr. Ambassador . . . is not typical of the attitude of the British public ". But not even " a storm of public indignation " will deter Chamberlain from a course which he considers right. The " friend ", referred to as " Wo ",

> was visibly moved . . . when at the end he shook my hand and said : " If we two, Great Britain and Germany, come to agreement regarding the settlement of the Czech problem, we shall simply brush aside the resistance that France or Czechoslovakia herself may offer to the decision."

But, as appears from a document cited at Weizsäcker's trial at Nuremberg, Kordt wrote to Weizsäcker the same day that at the Foreign Office Germany had " no friends apart from a few junior officials. As reported already repeatedly by the Embassy, the Foreign Office stands in hardly disguised opposition to Chamberlain."

Although Dirksen was at Berchtesgaden and Godesberg during Chamberlain's visits, he was not present at the talks ; never saw Hitler, and Ribbentrop only once ; and after Munich was ordered back to London without having seen either. " The impression in Berlin was that the Anglo-German protocol signed in Munich would not alter the existing situation much."

When Dirksen returned to London on October 6 he found that the protocol was " looked upon as a new foundation and guiding line for the development of Anglo-German relations " ; there was a sincere wish for a friendly settlement with Germany. Even the damping effect of Hitler's Saarbrücken speech did not stop leading members of the Government from publicly asking Germany to state her demands; colonies, raw materials, and disarmament were mentioned, and " in private conversations a delimitation of economic spheres of interest ". " Appreciative and friendly things were said of the German people. . . ." But there was no response from the German side, only " discouraging official and press statements ". " I myself, in the absence of official instructions, confined myself to attributing our unreceptive attitude to our distrust of England's excessive armament, to the press campaign, to Duff Cooper's inflammatory articles, etc. . . ." The November pogrom produced a strong reaction in Britain, " partly based on emotion and inadequate understanding of the German viewpoint, and partly deliberately fostered " — " anti-German propaganda under a humanitarian guise ". Then followed the incident connected " with the draft of Chamberlain's speech at the Foreign Press Association dinner, which compelled me at the last moment to decline the invitation on behalf of all the Germans ". When another lull set in, Dirksen decided to seek relief from political tension by trying " to achieve calm and confidence " through economic co-operation. His endeavours met with a most cordial response from the British side, inclined to attribute even excessive political importance to such moves. It was suggested that the German Minister for Economic Affairs, Funk,[1] should come to London: the answer

[1] At the Nuremberg Trial Funk was condemned to life imprisonment. " In 1942 Funk entered into an agreement with Himmler under which the Reichsbank was to receive certain gold and jewels and currency from the S.S., and instructed his subordinates . . . not to ask too many questions. As a result of this agreement, the S.S. sent to the Reichsbank the personal belongings taken from the victims . . . exterminated in the concentration camps. The gold from the eye-glasses and gold teeth and fillings was stored in the Reichsbank vaults. . . . The Tribunal is of the opinion that Funk either knew what was being received or was deliberately closing his eyes to what was being done."

from Berlin was that " owing to pressure of work " he could not come, nor could even a later date be fixed. None the less Mr. Oliver Stanley's visit to Germany " was insisted on in British quarters ".

At the end of February Dirksen was in Berlin, but Ribbentrop had no time to see him ; he therefore heard nothing officially about the impending action in Czecho-slovakia, and received no instructions about the line to take (though when action was taken he knew, of course, that the Czechs were to blame, and that the fuss in this country was unjustified). " The stiffening of Britain's attitude did not originate with the Government ", but with Parliament and the constituencies; " the whole party machine . . . from considerations of election tactics, exerted pressure on Chamberlain " ; " influential anti-German elements . . . began to stir, especially in the Foreign Office ", where " the policy of encirclement was hatched ". Dirksen was recalled to Berlin " to report ". But again Ribbentrop " had no time to receive me ".

> After waiting five days, I went . . . to Gröditzberg, and held myself at his disposal. However, I was not summoned to report, but instead was invited to attend a dinner given by the Führer to guests of honour and to hear the Führer's speech of April 28 [denouncing the Naval Agreement with Great Britain]. . . . When, on May 2, I received instructions to return to my post, I declared that I could do so only after having reported to the Reichminister.

Dirksen now received " a directive " that Germany did not want war with Britain but was prepared for all eventualities. " The British should stop supporting Poland."

In the meantime " the great swing " had occurred in British foreign policy; a world coalition was being formed against Germany; " noteworthy was the dogged-ness, the fanaticism, almost the hysteria with which the political public urged on the negotiations " with the U.S.S.R. " Crisismongers " were active : " American circles working through the American Embassy in Warsaw " — " Roosevelt was interested in an aggravation of the situation, or in war, in order to secure . . . his re-election. . . ." " The excitement, anti-German feeling, determination to fight, or fatalism of the general public were growing." Still, the " front driving for war " was less firm than might seem. " Small but influential groups " began to crystallize " for whom the encirclement front was not an end . . . but a means " : armaments and allies were to enable Britain to deal on equal terms with Germany and " compel her to effectuate her further demands through negotiations " ; but there was " a growing understanding of these demands ", readiness to make sacrifices, and disillusionment with Poland and Russia. And though Dirksen was not to approach Chamberlain or Halifax officially, he had a long private conversation with Halifax, and a " detailed talk with Sir Horace Wilson (which means with Chamberlain) " ; and through a great many channels he tried " to enlighten the English . . . on the nature of the Polish State, and on our claims to Danzig and the Corridor ". The Führer being reported to have said " that he was certain that in a direct conversation conducted in German with a decent and straightforward Englishman he would have no great difficulty in finding a satisfactory settlement for existing issues ", Dirksen tried to give currency " among influential Englishmen " to the idea " of direct conversations ". Various names were considered. " Eventually, the matter took a different turn and ended in the conversations which Staatsrat Wohlthat and I had with Sir Horace Wilson."

Wohlthat, an emissary of Göring, arrived in London about the middle of July, nominally to attend a whaling conference. The actual initiative of the conversations came, according to Dirksen, from Sir Horace Wilson, who invited Wohlthat " for a talk and, consulting prepared notes, outlined a programme for a comprehensive adjustment of Anglo-German relations. The programme envisaged political, military, and economic arrangements."

> In the political sphere a non-aggression pact was contemplated, in which aggression would be renounced in principle. The underlying purpose of this treaty was to make it possible for the British gradually to disembarrass themselves of their commitments toward Poland, on the ground that they had by this treaty secured Germany's renunciation of methods of aggression.
>
> In addition, a pact of non-intervention was to be signed, which was to be in a way a wrapper for a delimitation of the spheres of interest of the Great Powers.

A limitation of armaments and economic arrangements were proposed. Sir Horace " made it perfectly clear that Chamberlain approved that programme ", and invited Wohlthat " to have a talk there and then with Chamberlain ". But Wohlthat declined (he obviously felt uncertain how his intrusion into very high politics would be viewed in Berlin).

Next, Wohlthat had a talk with Mr. R. S. Hudson, Secretary of the Department of Overseas Trade, who " developed far-reaching plans for Anglo-German cooperation " in world markets. " Financial questions were also discussed." A loan to Germany " for conversion of her war economy to a peace economy ", according to Dirksen, " played no role in the conversation " (in another context he altogether denies its having been discussed). Taking this talk as pretext, Wohlthat asked for a further conversation with Sir Horace Wilson, in which he tried " to obtain greater clarity on certain points ". The discussion, though concrete, ranged wide. And Dirksen asserts once more :

Sir Horace Wilson definitely told Herr Wohlthat that the conclusion of a non-aggression pact would enable Britain to rid herself of her commitments *vis-à-vis* Poland. As a result the Polish problem would lose much of its acuteness.

The dates of the conversations are not given, but Dirksen's memorandum, apparently drawn up for internal Embassy use only, is dated July 21. On the 24th he addressed a report to the German Foreign Office on the " Decision of the British Government to Adopt a Constructive Policy ", which, in an attenuated form, reproduces the gist of Wohlthat's reports, and concludes :

About these plans entertained in leading circles Staatsrat Wohlthat, who, on British initiative, had long talks about them during his stay in London last week, will be able to give more detailed information.

Dirksen was treading dangerous ground : Göring's foreign policy differed from Ribbentrop's ; Wohlthat was Göring's man, but Ribbentrop Dirksen's chief ; and the notoriety which the Hudson-Wohlthat conversation had achieved might easily arouse anger in Berlin. To placate it, Dirksen wrote :

The problem which is puzzling the sponsors of these plans most is how to start the negotiations. Public opinion is so inflamed, and the warmongers and intriguers are so much in the ascendancy, that if these plans of negotiations with Germany were to become public they would immediately be torpedoed by Churchill and other incendiaries with the cry " No second Munich ! " or " No return to the appeasement policy ! "

This " active and dangerous " group Dirksen accused of having divulged and misrepresented the Wohlthat-Hudson talk ; while those who favoured the negotiations realized that the preparatory steps " must be shrouded in the greatest secrecy ".

APPEASEMENT

An angry telegram from Ribbentrop duly arrived on
July 31; it was marked " For the Ambassador personally ", and demanded a telegraphic report especially on
Wohlthat's " conversations with you, since he states that
the political negotiations were conducted in agreement
with the Ambassador ". Again Dirksen was very restrained : the general tendencies " toward a constructive
policy . . . had now crystallized into a plan, based princi-
pally on economic policy, which had been worked out by
Chamberlain, or at least approved by him " ; Wilson,
like Wohlthat, was Economic Adviser to his Government ;
and Wohlthat had " played the part of polite listener ",
and " flatly declined " a talk with Chamberlain, because
he " did not think himself empowered for this ". And to
Weizsäcker's inquiry why Wohlthat had not asked whether
" these overtures presume . . . the abandonment of the
encirclement negotiations, in particular with Moscow ",
Dirksen replied that by agreement with him Wohlthat
merely listened ; but that " an adjustment with Germany
would, so to speak, chemically dissolve the Danzig
problem ", and that continued negotiations with Russia
are " regarded here with scepticism ".

" The British side ", according to Dirksen, continued
to press " that reconciliation moves be inaugurated ",
and matters put " on official lines ". Dirksen was to
meet Mr. R. A. Butler, then Under-Secretary for Foreign
Affairs, before they both went on leave, but " Butler left
prematurely " (obviously he and the Foreign Office were
not *empressés*), and merely let Dirksen know that Sir Horace
Wilson wanted to talk with him.

In order to avoid all publicity, I visited Wilson at
his home on August 3 and we had a conversation
which lasted nearly two hours. In the main, it
followed the same lines as the Wohlthat conversations. I thought it valuable to have him confirm
the proposals he had made to Wohlthat. This Wilson

225

did, so that the authenticity of the project is beyond question.

Dirksen emphasizes that Sir Horace affirmed, " and in a clearer form than he had done to Wohlthat, that the conclusion of an Anglo-German *entente* would practically render Britain's guarantee policy nugatory ".

> After recapitulating his conversation with Wohlthat Sir Horace Wilson expatiated at length on the great risk Chamberlain would incur by starting confidential negotiations with the German Government. If anything about them were to leak out there would be a grand scandal, and Chamberlain would probably be forced to resign.

He further suggested that " the Führer, who had no political attacks to fear at home ", should take the initiative and come out with a conciliatory statement. After some more sparring Dirksen declared that the Führer " would certainly not consider making pacifying or friendly declarations unless he knew what attitude he could expect from the British side towards Germany's justified demands ". While Sir Horace is reported to have said :

> The British Government must . . . be sure that its initiative met with equal readiness on the German side. There was no sense in beginning negotiations if a new crisis was in the offing. It would therefore very much like to know how the Führer had received Wohlthat's report, whether he foresaw a quiet period of negotiation in the next few months, and, lastly, whether he himself was ready to manifest a willingness for negotiations, whether by means of a public statement or confidentially. However that might be, it would be a great disappointment to the British Government if no response to the British initiative were forthcoming from our side. The only alternative would then be catastrophe.

But Dirksen himself had received no indication of how Wohlthat's reports were viewed in Berlin. Before going on leave Dirksen had on August 9 a long talk with Lord Halifax; each repeated arguments and views long familiar to the other, but not one word was said about the Wilson-Wohlthat and Wilson-Dirksen talks — the back-stair negotiations, in which the Prime Minister unwisely engaged, had not reached the Foreign Office level. It seems doubtful whether it would have been possible thus to ignore them had not Mr. Butler " prematurely " gone on leave. The business was " small beer ", in spite of Dirksen's attempts, now seconded by the Soviet publication, to work it up into a major transaction.

Dirksen on his arrival in Berlin inquired when he could go and report to Ribbentrop, who was at Fuschl, near Salzburg. " In reply to my inquiries in the next few days I was told that no information . . . had been received. . . . It was apparent that he had no time or no desire to hear my report." [1]. In Berlin Dirksen learnt that Ribbentrop still believed Great Britain would not go to war over Poland, and that the report of his con-

[1] Here is the corresponding passage from Dirksen's memoirs, from which excerpts were published in advance in the *Neue Woche* of November 27, 1948 : " To my surprise the next few days produced no reply from Ribbentrop. . . . After several days of waiting it became clear to me that Ribbentrop did not want to see me." This seems probable — but something has gone wrong in Dirksen's time-table. He says that he left London a week after his talk with Sir Horace Wilson, which would be August 10 : and this date is borne out by a note in *The Times* of the 11th. In his memorandum Dirksen writes : " I arrived in Berlin on Monday morning, August 13 "; and in his memoirs : " I arrived in Berlin on a Monday, which must have been August 13 (*an einem Montag, wohl dem 13. August*) ". But August 13 was a Sunday — and is it not peculiar that Dirksen, in a hurry to report to Ribbentrop at a time of crisis, should have taken three or four days to get from London to Berlin ? As a rule, the day of the week is easier remembered than the date, but whether it was the 13th or the 14th, there is hardly time between either date and the 16th for " several days of waiting ", repeated inquiries, and an intervention by Weizsäcker, mentioned by Dirksen, to obtain an interview with Ribbentrop for him. Possibly Dirksen arrived in Berlin on the 11th. The matter is probably unimportant in itself, but suggests uncritical negligence on the part of the writer.

versation with Sir Horace Wilson " had been taken as a further sign of British weakness ". Having received Weizsäcker's " permission to go to Gröditzberg and there await further instructions ", Dirksen left on August 16 ; wrote a memorandum on Britain's probable attitude in a German-Polish conflict, and sent it to Weizsäcker by registered mail ; and in September was still at Gröditzberg writing the story of his London Ambassadorship.

Thus Chamberlain's last attempt at appeasement met with a contemptuous rebuff from Berlin : [1] they showed not the least interest in it. But apparently they gave him credit for a measure of honest, though feeble, naivety : Sir Horace Wilson had said that " there was no sense in beginning negotiations if a new crisis was in the offing ", and had stipulated for a quiet period of a few months ; and as they were determined to have a showdown over Poland that summer, there would indeed have been no sense in starting negotiations. Still, Chamberlain's move was not free of danger, and did harm ; and though the responsibility for it is solely his, such dealings on the part of a Prime Minister cannot be treated as a matter of indifference. But there are at least two ways of remembering and recounting every talk ; and as very little, if anything, about these transactions is likely to be found in the Foreign Office archives, or even in Cabinet records, those who can testify in the matter, and correct whatever mistakes or distortions there may be in the German accounts, should do so now. These occurrences have already passed into history, and it seems incumbent on Chamberlain's friends and assistants to tell his side of the story, which they should surely be given official leave to do.

[1] Dirksen writes in the *Neue Woche* (see above) that when he inquired of Weizsäcker how his reports of Sir Horace Wilson's offer had been received, " Weizsäcker shrugged his shoulders and made a movement with the hand as if he was brushing something off the table " — the offer " was simply thrown into the wastepaper basket ".

HITLER'S FOREIGN POLICY

HERR ERICH KORDT was a *diplomate de carrière* of the pre-Nazi period, who continued in Hitler's service to the very end. Under Neurath, and then under Ribbentrop, he held till December 1940 the post of *Leiter des Minister-büros*: that is, of *chef de cabinet* to these Foreign Ministers; and as such he dealt with their official correspondence. He was sent abroad in April 1941, and at Shanghai, in 1943–1944, worked up notes previously taken into an account of Hitler's foreign policy; having returned to Germany in the autumn of 1946, he expanded that draft with the help of Dr. K. H. Abshagen, a foreign correspondent of German newspapers, into the book now published.[1] Herr Kordt's brother was at the London Embassy, and, as Chargé d'Affaires, was on September 3, 1939, the recipient of the British ultimatum. The two brothers seem to have belonged to that mild and ineffective Opposition within the German Civil Service whose members did the work of their Nazi masters, but now, regretting it, vividly remember their objections, or even their "conspiracies". Herr Erich Kordt, in his Nuremberg affidavit of September 25, 1947, mentions having under various pretexts visited London seven times in 1938–1939, to keep his brother informed about developments in Berlin; and he claims during that year to have tried several times to resign from the service. In the book he never speaks about himself; which, in a way, is a relief in these days of blatant egotism in speech and writings; though in another way it seems regrettable that the reader, and still more the student who might wish to use Herr Kordt's work as a source book, should not be told when the author speaks

[1] Erich Kordt, *Wahn und Wirklichkeit*. Stuttgart: Union Deutsche Verlagsgesellschaft.

from his own immediate knowledge and rich personal experience.

The primary motive of the book is undoubtedly an honest desire to supply the Germans with a truthful account of Hitler's foreign policy, and thus to counteract in time the rise of unhealthy legends such as grew up after the First World War. Fuller evidence, the author remarks, will merely prove still further " the decisive part which Hitler and his Government played in bringing on the war " ; and he wisely does not try to deny the responsibility which the German nation bears for the Nazi régime. But he endeavours discreetly to reduce it ; and he finishes with an equally discreet but passionate indictment of the " unconditional surrender " clause of the allies, and a rehash of the old clap-trap about the Versailles Treaty : at which one can hardly wonder, seeing how much injudicious encouragement such German propaganda received during the inter-war period in this country and America. Still, this is as impartial a book as can be expected from an intensely interested party.

The documentation of the book and even its factual reliability are extremely uneven.[1] Naturally Herr Kordt, as one who sat at the very centre, possesses exceptionally good information concerning certain transactions : thus, for instance, his detailed account of events during the week preceding the outbreak of war, and especially of communications exchanged between Hitler and Mussolini (with the exact time of dispatch and receipt), usefully fills in a number of gaps. Further, when writing the book, he had before him the text of documents concerning Nazi-Soviet relations — he quotes them with their correct reference numbers (but these are the only documents thus quoted). By now most of them are known through the American advance publication ; even so, Herr Kordt's

[1] Some of the worst mistakes have been corrected in the second edition, published in 1948, but a good many remain.

book is a useful complement supplying several documents omitted by the American editors and also background information. Some of Herr Kordt's most interesting items of information appear in footnotes — valuable detail which adds to the character of the picture. But here again the question arises to what extent such information can be accepted without further corroboration — a question which it is difficult to answer when the sources are not, and probably often could not be, named. In fact, the serious student will in each case have to decide for himself whether to treat it as evidence or as anecdote.

The picture of Hitler and of his methods, by one who experienced them, is of value : further evidence will fill in the outlines, but is not likely to change them.

His ghastly lack of proper education, his imperfect mastery of the German language, especially of written German, and his complete disregard of logic, were patent. No well-thought-out document ever came from his pen, merely vague directions. He fought shy of committing himself. By his order, minutes of conversations were as a rule withheld from the other party. Conferences were bound to break down over his monologues. It was exceedingly difficult to obtain decisions. . . . If made, they were mostly unclear, leaving scope for arbitrary interpretations . . . and there was no appeal. The " Führer " has decided ; to resort to him once more would be blasphemy. . . . No adviser could gain permanent influence. Hitler's reactions could be skilfully manipulated by "news," but the explosive effect could not be gauged beforehand. A fairly good memory for facts and figures enabled him to bluff even experts. . . . His violent diction and the tone of his voice intimidated. . . . A smatterer in everything, he was an expert at bluffing.[1] " This last half-hour, while I was resting, I invented a new machine-gun and a contrivance for bridge-

---

[1] See also General Halder's testimony at Nuremberg, February 26, 1946 : " Whoever did not know Adolf Hitler cannot imagine what a master of deception and camouflage this man was ".

building, and composed a piece of music in my head,"
he once intimated to a late companion from Lands-
berg prison, who was duly impressed. . . . He had
not the patience to read a lengthy document, but
claimed to know Clausewitz by heart. And he often
got away with it.

It was Hitler's habit " in every domain to work with
two or more competing persons or departments, and to
play them off against each other ". In a crisis his ante-
room was thronged with party-potentates of every size
and shade, with military and with unofficial advisers,
each trying to gain the Führer's ear. But " only very
few cases are known of Hitler having called for reports
from regular diplomats " — he disliked and disparaged
them, and much rather listened to adventurers and quacks.
He would not do business in committee, nor speak to more
than two or three men at a time, unless he was addressing
monologues to large gatherings. Government lost all
collegiate character, and Ministers, with little influence
on general policy, carried on their work free of control
— except that Hitler would entrust various people with
" special tasks ", till no one knew his way through the
maze of conflicting authorities and assignments. It was
the efficiency of the well-trained middle and lower ranks
of the Services and administration which made it possible
to continue so long in spite of the utter confusion and
incompetence at the top.

Hitler imagined himself a soldier, and in these ridiculous
fancies surpassed even Wilhelm II. When during his visit
to Italy in 1938 the programme left him no time to change
into uniform for a military review, he foamed with rage
— and the chief of the protocol, von Bülow-Schwante, was
dismissed on the spot. In April 1939 he wrote to Ribbentrop: " Please invite a number of foreign guests for
my 50th birthday, and among them as many as possible
cowardly civilians and democrats whom I shall show

the most modern of armies ". But the people round him surpassed even the courtiers of the Kaiser in flattery.

When on the capture of Abbeville Hitler paid tribute to the Army commanders for its training and leadership, General Keitel replied in a big gathering : " No, my Führer, to you alone are due these magnificent achievements ! "

Finally he came to be described as " the greatest general of all times " (der grösste Feldherr aller Zeiten). But when luck turned, and his blunders became irreparable, the comic abbreviation of " der Gröfaz " gained currency. Still he went on with his fantastic operational dispositions. In April 1945, a half-demented Hitler, from his bunker in Berlin, was issuing orders to armies which no longer existed.[1]

And this is perhaps one of the most characteristic stories of Hitler. In 1936, after long negotiations, the German Foreign Office had obtained the agreement of the interested States to a change, favourable to Germany, of the international régime for the German rivers fixed by the Treaty of Versailles. When Hitler, who apparently had not been aware of restrictions on German sovereignty in that matter, or at least had shown no interest in them, heard that a settlement satisfying all legitimate German claims had been negotiated, he would have none of it, but declared that " German honour demanded a restoration of sovereignty over the rivers by unilateral action ". Consequently, on November 14, 1936, the German Government declared that Germany no longer recognized the validity of the treaty provisions concerning the German rivers. Timely publicity for such performances, which were bound to be known to the States concerned, might have promoted a healthier estimate of German policy in Western Europe.

[1] For a brilliant account of such scenes, see H. R. Trevor-Roper, *The Last Days of Hitler*, pages 176-9.

THE OTHER GERMANY?

Is it " Of the Other Germany " that Hassell's *Diaries* [1]
narrate, as is asserted in their German title? Theirs
certainly is a Germany different from the Third Reich,
but hardly a new Germany : much rather the Germany of
before 1914. The makers and leaders of the Third Reich
were Austrians, Bavarians, and Rhinelanders, of the
German *Stämme* which outside Germany have always been
preferred to the Prussians ; there was not one member of
the old ruling class among them. But most of those who
lost their lives over the unsuccessful attempt against
Hitler in July 1944 were North Germans and Conservatives, Prussian Junkers or representatives of the old military
and official class [2] (to that class belonged von Hassell
and his wife, a daughter of Admiral von Tirpitz). The
typical old Prussians — *die Stock-Preussen* — were rigid,
narrow-minded, and very often brutal ; yet there were
among them Christians and gentlemen, however out-
moded this may sound ; they had a moral code, and a
sense of law and order ; without a measure of austere
decency and selfless devotion they could never have built
up the Prussian State. Their instincts and traditions were

---

[1] *The von Hassell Diaries, 1938–1944.* Hamish Hamilton.
[2] R. Pechel, *Deutscher Widerstand* (1947), publishes a provisional list of
names of men (and a few women) murdered, executed, or suicides in connexion with the attempt against Hitler's life on July 20, 1944. 53 out of a
total of 147 were nobility or gentry (one prince, 18 counts, 7 barons,
and 27 *adelige*) ; 53 were army officers (15 generals, 14 colonels, 13 lt.-
colonels, 8 majors, and only 3 junior officers — a very significant proportion) ; 1 admiral and 1 naval captain ; 9 diplomats ; and many
high officials. — The list given by F. v. Schlabrendorff, *Offiziere gegen Hitler*
(1946), omits four of the names appearing in Pechel, and adds ten not
included in his list. — Neither list includes Kluge or Rommel ; but the
connexion between Rommel's suicide and the attempt of July 20 is established by Keitel's testimony at Nuremberg, while in the case of Kluge,
though less clearly proved, it seems probable.

outraged by the administrative corruption, the mental
chaos, the low vulgarity, and the unspeakable beastliness
of the Nazi régime: this can be seen on every page of
Hassell's *Diaries*.

No one who has read them can doubt his character:
a man with true cultural and ethical standards, not very
perspicacious, sometimes even naive, but upright and
courageous. Intellectually he had hardly outgrown the
Second Reich. He thought of a Hohenzollern restoration,
and saw in it " the one way which still offers the greatest
hope of co-ordinated action": he thought of a peace treaty
which would give back to Germany her eastern frontiers
of 1914 — not only Danzig and the Corridor, but even
Posnania and Upper Silesia — and imagined that such
terms could be accepted by the Allies. The German
working classes never entered into his schemes for the overthrow of the Nazi régime. Possibly he was right; but if
so, the fact is significant. Indeed, the *coup* as planned by
him and his associates was throughout an upper-class
affair: a counter-revolution by the old ruling class, not
for class interests, but primarily for the sake of moral
standards in which they believed, and of Bismarck's Reich
which they loved. In fact, what the generals feared when
contemplating a *coup* against Hitler — and subsequent
events proved them right — was that the junior officers,
mostly of a different class, would not follow them.

A rising which completely discounted the working
classes could be nothing but an army revolt, a conspiracy
of generals: and this is the only active theme of Hassell's
Diaries. When the plot failed, among those who had to
die were three Field-Marshals (von Witzleben, von Kluge,
and Rommel), a dozen generals, the Chief of the Military
Intelligence, a late Chief of the General Staff, besides two
ex-Ambassadors (von Hassell and Count von der Schulenburg), the Prussian Minister of Finance, and the Police
President of Berlin. It is, in fact, surprising how many of

the distinguished Army leaders were, at one time or another, approached by the conspirators, and, at least by silence, connived in their plans. In December 1939 General Beck, till 1938 C.G.S., told Field-Marshal von Brauchitsch, at that time Commander-in-Chief of the German Armed Forces, that he was ready to carry out a *coup d'état* if Brauchitsch gave him a free hand; Brauchitsch refused, but kept silent. Still, in November 1941, when disaster threatened in Russia, and he was once more approached by General von Falkenhausen, Military Commander of Occupied Belgium, he replied that if Hitler was " eliminated ", he would act. Grand-Admiral Raeder is reported to have been ready to co-operate even in December 1939—" if the Army would act ".

And this was true of most of them : someone else should start ; and Hitler, to whom they were bound by oath, should first be removed. But even then they would have needed someone to give the word of command. In October 1939 the conspirators believed that there was "the necessary number of determined generals . . . ready to proceed quickly and energetically if the order comes from the top", but " the principal factor " was " still lacking : a soldier in the position of decisive authority willing to take the initiative ". Incredible as this may seem, Hassell and his friends at one time thought that " Göring was a possibility ". " These generals who want to overthrow governments", writes Hassell in January 1940, " demand orders from these very governments before they will act ! " In the presence of Hitler they would get cold feet ; stand to attention, physically and spiritually (Halder, C.G.S., boasted that he could talk to Hitler with his hands in his trouser pockets) ; and yet, according to Hassell, the Army was the only " decent factor remaining in Germany ", and therefore they alone could save the country.

So he and his associates kept on hammering at the generals, trying to " open their eyes " to the horrors and savagery committed by their armies, and to the dangers which beset Germany's future. But whenever Hitler was victorious, the " war fever " rose among them, and they were thinking about their professional careers; and even when Hitler was clearly leading the Army to disaster, they did not dare to stand up to him. " Hopeless sergeant-majors ! " wrote Hassell on June 16, 1941. And in August 1942 : " The possessors of military power thus far have adopted a servile attitude and nothing has therefore come of these deliberations ". And in November 1942 : " We are a most curious mixture of heroes and slaves. The latter applies particularly to the generals. . . ." March 28, 1943 : " The generals are enough to drive one mad ". April 20, 1943 : " All those on whom we set our hopes are failing . . . and permit themselves to indulge in the most anti-Nazi talk, but are unable to summon up enough courage to act ".

So the chances of timely action were slipping away. " Great wonders there are in a sieve," says the beetle in a Russian story, "so many holes and no way out." And the generals were like the holes : too small and too narrow. Even when the attempt was carried out against Hitler, who by that time was reeling to his doom, and the generals in Berlin learnt that he was alive, they lost their nerve. For generations they had been trained to obey. Revolution was to them a manœuvre which they had never practised, and now it was too late to begin.

THE ANGLO-FRENCH-RUSSIAN
NEGOTIATIONS OF 1939

I

WHEN in 1942 I first set out to trace the course of the Anglo-French-Russian negotiations of March–August 1939, the official material available consisted of a few speeches and statements by Mr. Chamberlain and Lord Halifax, replies to questions in Parliament, a speech by M. Molotov and an article by M. Zhdanov, communiqués about the Moscow talks, and the *Final Report* of the Polish Ambassador to Moscow; such meagre information had to be supplemented by Press reports, especially from " Diplomatic Correspondents " in London and American correspondents in London, Paris, and Moscow. But, before my book *Diplomatic Prelude, 1938–1939*, went to press in the spring of 1947, I had more material to work on: the Nuremberg documents and depositions; the memoirs of M. Noël, in 1939 French Ambassador in Warsaw, and of M. Łukasiewicz, Polish Ambassador in Paris; an article and a speech by M. Daladier, of 1946, reviewing those negotiations; and M. Gafenco's *Derniers Jours de l'Europe*, quoting documents presumably obtained from M. Bonnet. Since then there have been two notable additions: captured German documents on *Nazi-Soviet Relations, 1939-1941*,[1] published by the American State Department, and the second volume of M. Bonnet's memoirs;[2] besides a short report by General Doumenc, in August 1939 chief of the French Military Mission to Moscow; a book by Herr Erich Kordt,[3] in 1939 *chef de cabinet* to Ribbentrop; and incidental material in the

---

[1] See below, pages 259-80.   [2] See above, pages 58-77.
[3] See above, pages 229-33.

memoirs of men who, while not directly engaged in the negotiations, have authoritative information about them. But to this day no documents have been published officially on the Anglo-French-Russian negotiations of 1939. Publication of the British documents for 1938–1939 has been started, but another year or two must pass before March–August 1939 is covered; the French are collecting their own documents to replace those burnt in May–June 1940, but it will take some three or four years before publication can begin; while the Soviet Government are not likely to publish theirs, at least not with a frankness which would make them truly serviceable. In the absence of official texts, no detailed, scholarly account of those negotiations can as yet be written.

Still, the available material is sufficient for tracing their course in broad outline; and additional information is not likely to change that outline in any vital point. What is wanting is day-to-day evidence about the thoughts and intentions of the three Governments such as might be derived from their internal correspondence, memoranda, or minutes; hence also about the development, oscillations, and deflections of their policy. The layout of the field and the nature of the game can be traced, but not the motions, still less the motives, of the players. The effects of professed obsessions and of cherished misconceptions can be gauged, but not of ignorance and of genuine error, two potent factors in human affairs: to determine these, most precise information is required, for guess-work is bound to stray in the uncharted realms of the irrational. Historical narrative logically proceeds from the elements of a situation, across the motives of the actors, to the resultant course of events; but with regard to the Anglo-French-Russian negotiations of 1939, a thorough exploration of that elusive, essentially subjective, middle zone of thoughts and aims can hardly be attempted at the present stage, least of all in the case of the Soviet Government, which finished by holding the key position in Europe.

Since 1919 a permanent peaceful settlement of Europe had been the aim of the British Government — their paramount aim as the danger to peace grew acute; and they clung to the hope of being able to achieve it through an " equitable " agreement with the Dictators. Meantime, avoidance of war had become the supreme purpose of the French Government; having failed to take timely preventive action, they did not talk equity to man-eating tigers, but envisaged the problem in terms of price, victims, and security. The European coalition required to check Hitler, if at all attainable, was impeded by doubts concerning Soviet Russia as an ally: militarily she was rated low, especially after the army purges; politically she was the declared enemy of every non-Communist ideology and society, and consorting with her seemed to call for regretful apology. But half-hearted, uneasy associates are quickly put out of countenance, and Hitler traded on the fears of the *bourgeois*, or the genteel feelings of men unhardened to power politics. The Western Powers had the choice between a Four-Power Pact with the Dictators, and a new Triple Entente with the U.S.S.R.; either entailed the sacrifice of at least some of the smaller States in East-Central Europe which, in 1919–1920, they themselves had helped to create or aggrandize at the expense of Germany and Russia, and on which the French " system " of the 'twenties was based. An agreement with the Dictators was bound greatly to increase their military power and resources; an agreement with the U.S.S.R., to favour the spread of Bolshevism. The one alliance was unpleasant and unsafe, and the other even more abhorrent — but nothing was gained by a refusal to acknowledge and face the dilemma. The Western Powers swayed uneasily between the two alternatives, and even when the pendulum swung away from the Dictators they would hardly admit, *pace* the Franco-Soviet Pact of 1935, that it was swinging towards the Bolsheviks.

Munich was a surrender to which Chamberlain, in his joint declaration with Hitler, gave a sham façade that was to disguise its nature and shut out its consequences. But shams in a crisis are like a paper umbrella in a thunderstorm. Prague produced a swing towards Russia, followed by an almost immediate recoil when Poland refused joint action with her. And so revulsion against Berlin and repugnance to Moscow landed Chamberlain in the ditch of guarantees to Poland and Rumania. But dislikes, however justified, are as little serviceable in a crisis as shams. An Albanian Moslem whom I once taunted with a policy which I knew to be uncongenial to him, replied : " There are times when you call a pig your uncle ".

After 1918 France concluded alliances with Poland and the Little Entente against Germany, Russia, Italy, Hungary, and Bulgaria ; Britain refused to endorse a policy which she deemed short-sighted and, in the long run, exceedingly dangerous. In time its insufficiency became patent ; France veered towards Britain and gradually accepted her lead even in Continental affairs. And then : after Czechoslovakia had been lost and Yugoslavia estranged, Chamberlain made the Polish-Rumanian rump of the French system — two countries allied against Russia — into the base of his defensive system against Germany, without ascertaining whether, or how, their interests and policies could be squared with those of Russia. (He cannot be taxed with having devised that policy : he tumbled into it.) But next, appealing to Stalin's declaration of March 10, 1939, that it was the policy of the Soviet Union " to support States which might be victims of aggression provided that they were prepared to defend their independence ", he invited Russia to countersign the Anglo-French guarantees to Poland and Rumania.

Chamberlain wrote in his Diary on March 26, 1939 : [1]

> I must confess to the most profound distrust of
> Russia. I have no belief whatever in her ability to
> maintain an effective offensive, even if she wanted
> to. And I distrust her motives, which seem to me
> to have little connection with our ideas of liberty,
> and to be concerned only with getting every one else
> by the ears. Moreover, she is both hated and sus-
> pected by many of the smaller States, notably by
> Poland, Roumania, and Finland.

And here is Mr. Churchill's account of a talk with M.
Stalin : [2]

> At the Kremlin in August 1942, Stalin, in the
> early hours of the morning, gave me one aspect of
> the Soviet position. " We formed the impression,"
> said Stalin, " that the British and French Govern-
> ments were not resolved to go to war if Poland were
> attacked, but that they hoped the diplomatic line-up
> of Britain, France, and Russia would deter Hitler.
> We were sure it would not."

Stalin went on to recount a conversation (without naming
the person, or the date and place) : he had asked how
many divisions France would send against Germany on
mobilization? " About a hundred." And England?
" Two and two more later."

> " Ah, two and two more later," Stalin had re-
> peated. " Do you know," he asked, " how many
> divisions we shall have to put on the Russian front if
> we go to war with Germany ? " There was a pause.
> " More than three hundred."

Sense and a measure of truth there were in the reasonings
of both Chamberlain and Stalin, but a poor prospect for
the Anglo-French-Russian negotiations.

What were at that juncture Soviet Russia's interests

[1] K. Feiling, *The Life of Neville Chamberlain*, page 403.
[2] *The Gathering Storm*, page 305.

and views ? She needed peace to strengthen her political, economic, and military system. She was obsessed by the perennial fear of a hostile coalition of " capitalist Imperialist Powers " : these were at present divided, but they might make up their differences at her expense. Therefore, with war in sight, she would try to be in with the one side or the other, and to prevent their coming together. The Western Powers were " non-aggressive " (thus Stalin described them in his speech of March 10) ; the Dictators were out for conquests, Hitler was dangerously near and a professed anti-Marxist fanatic ; moreover an Austrian : he continued the anti-Russian policy of the Habsburgs. If a new Triple Entente would have sufficed to restrain him, it might have been to Russia's interest to re-create it. But would it ? Even if the question may not have loomed quite as large in Stalin's reasoning as he chose to make it appear to Churchill, the answer certainly mattered more to him than to the Western Powers, who stood to lose neither way by Russia endorsing their guarantees. If Hitler persisted, Stalin feared another Munich ; and not he alone. (" In these final weeks " [before the outbreak of war], writes Mr. Churchill, " my fear was that His Majesty's Government, in spite of our guarantee, would recoil from waging war upon Germany if she attacked Poland." [1]) But, anyhow, the defensive strategy of the French and the " four divisions " of the British were hardly reassuring. Germany's territorial disjointedness in the East and the proximity of the Poles to Berlin predetermined the first move : which would have carried them on against Russia had she joined the Western line-up.

Victors and vanquished alike fight their previous war : to repeat their performance, or not to repeat their mistakes. Britain thought in terms of blockade ; France of a continuous defensive line ; while Russia remembered

[1] *Op. cit.* page 300.

her 1918 "defeat in victory" (so did in 1941–1942 the Poles: hoping that Russia would once more be defeated by Germany, and Germany by the West, to Poland's all-round gain). Was there any reason to suppose that France would make an all-out effort on behalf of Russia? (which she did not make even for Poland in September 1939). Might not defeat result in the overthrow of the Soviet system? Would any non-Communist regret it? Might not then an amicable agreement be reached by the "capitalist Imperialist Powers" at Russia's expense? For lack of evidence it is impossible to say for how much such thoughts counted in Soviet policy; but they did undoubtedly.

What, on the other hand, could Russia expect from victory? Obviously territorial gains: therein nationalist States or revolutionary Governments hardly differ from the monarchs of yore. Russia was out to reopen Peter the Great's Baltic "window", and to gather in the White Russian and Ukrainian lands held by Poland and Rumania. Mr. Byrnes noticed at Yalta the emotion with which Stalin insisted on the Curzon Line.[1] Ukrainian nationalism was indeed a problem for Moscow: it had to be satisfied by reunion of all Ukrainian lands, and to be purged of separatist tendencies by their inclusion in the U.S.S.R. The Western Powers were unaware of the military strength of Russia, overrated that of Poland, and had committed themselves to Poland and Rumania — would they, and could they still, admit Russia's claims?

To sum up: to gain Russia's co-operation the Western Powers would have had to convince her of their determination to resist Hitler; of their will to make a timely all-out war effort; of their joint capacity to win; of their readiness to acknowledge Russia's primacy in Eastern Europe and to acquiesce in the use which she would make of it; altogether of a *bienveillance* which she

[1] James F. Byrnes, *Speaking Frankly*, page 30.

had no right to expect, nor herself any reason to feel. Hitler alone could have brought the two sides together; but in 1939, with Poland replacing Czechoslovakia, the lay-out of the field was much more unfavourable to an Anglo-French-Russian understanding than in 1938. It is not certain that any one could have achieved it; but least of all men with the record and outlook of the Chamberlain and Daladier Governments: which does not, however, excuse either their inept handling of the negotiations, or the end which the Russians put to them.

Britain had guaranteed Poland and Rumania without having an army to pit against that of Germany, and France without having the will or the means to conduct an offensive campaign, necessary to relieve an Eastern ally. They now urged Russia to add her guarantee, while rating low its value, and while knowing that neither Poland nor Rumania desired it or would admit the entry of a Russian army. If they persisted in such refusal, Russia was affably to supply them with war material, or at the utmost be allowed to help in the air — unless, on being invaded, Poland and Rumania reconsidered their position: then Russia could take the risk which the Western Powers took in the Low Countries in 1940. The thing sounds ludicrous: but then the Western Powers had not thought out the military concomitants either of their own guarantees or of Russia's. They had meandered into a hopeless situation, and, without facing it squarely, tried to retrieve it by a " diplomatic line-up ", not devoid of bluff. They sought to avert war by bolstering up Poland, whose fate was certainly no concern of Russia.

Poland's foreign policy was acrobatics, which are performed by shutting out thought of danger — wherein the Poles excelled. An alliance with either Germany or Russia implied for them territorial cessions and loss of independence, which they would not voluntarily admit. An alliance between the two meant death to them: what use thinking of it? Even in matters of strategy and armament they were feckless — a highly militarized State which did not seem to take war seriously: they behaved as if they did not believe in its coming. They watched the Anglo-French-Russian negotiations with a distaste tempered by the conviction that they would fail: Poland was not, and did not wish to be, a party to them, however closely concerned. It is hard to see how any concrete military arrangements could have been reached while Poland preserved a negative attitude. But the French refrained from probing so delicate a question: Gamelin, who says that he would have " preferred to have no precise talks with the Poles . . . before having had them with the Russian General Staff ",[1] spent a week in May 1939 talking to the Polish army leaders without ever touching on the question of Russia; nor did Bonnet (who blames that reticence[2]) ever press it on the Polish Ambassador before August 1939; while the British Government tried throughout to preclude the Anglo-French-Russian Treaty from imposing obligations on third parties, such as the use of their territory by foreign troops. Here was a contradiction and absurdity which the Russians could put up with or exploit, whichever suited them best.

A German diplomatic official said to the Russian Chargé d'Affaires in Berlin on July 27, 1939:[3]

> What could England offer Russia? At best, participation in a European war and the hostility of Germany, but not a single desirable end for Russia. What could we offer . . .? Neutrality and staying out of a possible European conflict and, if Moscow wished, a German-Russian understanding on mutual interests which, just as in former times, would work to the advantage of both countries.

[1] *Servir*, ii., *Le Prologue du drame* (*1930–août 1939*), pages 418-19.
[2] *Fin d'une Europe*, pages 230-32.
[3] *Nazi-Soviet Relations, 1939–1941*, page 34.

Obviously Germany would have no difficulty in satisfying Russia's territorial claims; the agreement would be made with a view to war, which would set the non-Communist Powers " by the ears " (" war guilt " would not trouble the Kremlin); the Western Powers would have to meet the first impact of the German attack (and though the Russians knew France's unwillingness to carry on an offensive campaign, they probably, in common with most German generals, overrated her defensive strength); Russia would be in a position to watch and prepare. On the other hand, a victorious Germany would be a most redoubtable neighbour for Russia; and a war, once unleashed, runs its own, hardly predictable, course. Formidable dangers lurked either way; and we neither have, nor are likely to obtain, insight into the Soviet Government's calculations and reasonings : but their "realistic" approach, and their attitude equally hostile to both sides, would bid them consider either arrangement, if feasible.

At what stage the U.S.S.R. ceased to treat the negotiations with the Western Powers seriously may for ever remain a moot point : " the change is more likely to have been a gradual shifting of interest and emphasis than a sudden *volte-face* ".[1] For months Moscow and Berlin manœuvred for positions : they would throw out hints about " normalizing relations " or reopening commercial negotiations, and then quickly withdraw in intense mutual suspicion — each feared that the other side was merely out to obtain material with which to blackmail the Western Powers into an agreement unfavourable to it. And on both sides such suspicions were justified.[2] Moscow feared lest premature political talks with Berlin enabled Hitler to pull off a second Munich

---

[1] See *Diplomatic Prelude*, page 159. Mr. Churchill expresses a similar view in *The Gathering Storm*, page 284.
[2] See below, pages 262-3 and 265.

followed by an anti-Russian coalition. But they knew
that Hitler could not safely open a campaign against
Poland later than September 1, and that if he wanted an
agreement with the Soviet Government, they could have
it on their own terms, without any lengthy negotiations.[1]
Therefore, at whatever stage the Russians may have come
to prefer an arrangement with the Germans, they would
still have to play for time, and neither commit themselves to the Germans, nor put them off, but try to cut as
fine as possible the margin between their closing with
Hitler and September 1. Similarly, even if their preference
was still for the Western Powers, they would accompany
every move toward them with some parallel move toward
the Germans, so as not to cut off that line either. The
approach to Germany on April 17 coincides with Russia's
offer of a Triple Alliance to the Western Powers; the
reopening of the commercial talks with Germany, late
in July, with the practical completion of the political
negotiations with the Western Powers; and, on August
12, agreement in principle to receiving a Nazi political
negotiator, with the arrival of the Allied Military Missions
in Moscow. Thus evidence for the date at which Stalin
finally determined to close with Hitler is lacking, and it
is not even possible to trace how the two parallel negotiations affected each other.

II

Hitler's entry into Vienna opened up the problem of
Czechoslovakia, his entry into Prague that of the Baltic.
Memel, as he had foreseen, could be reclaimed by
" registered letter "; [2] but Poland was less amenable to

[1] See *Diplomatic Prelude*, pages xvii-xviii and 189-90.
[2] Hassell recounts in his *Diaries* under date of December 16, 1938, a
conversation with Weizsäcker, who told him that " the Memel problem . . .
in Hitler's opinion, would not require a resort to arms, but merely a
registered letter addressed to Kaunas ! "

persuasion or blackmail than he had expected, or even than the Western Powers had come to fear now that they felt at last compelled to face the question they had so feebly and glibly shirked a year earlier — where and how to stop Hitler's aggression.

At first Rumania was thought most immediately threatened, and on March 18 Lord Halifax inquired of the Russian Ambassador, M. Maisky, what the Soviet Government would do if she were subjected to an unprovoked attack. But the idea of joint action with Russia was shelved because of Poland's negative, actuated by distrust of Russia and by fear of provoking Hitler; and during the fortnight after Prague the British Government was more concerned to secure Poland's help for Rumania than help for Poland. Only after a common front of these two countries had been formed did the British Government propose to approach Moscow once more. Then followed the scare which, on March 31, produced the precipitate British guarantee to Poland, and an inquiry addressed to M. Maisky whether Russia would endorse it. Still, the idea of a Polish-Rumanian bloc continued to preoccupy the British Government, and it was pressed on Beck during his visit to London (April 3-7): but while Poland and Rumania were at one in their hostility to Russia, Poland would not endanger her good relations with Hungary because of Rumania, nor Rumania her relations with Germany because of Poland.

M. Bonnet claims in his memoirs that even in the first half of April he had advocated, in Cabinet and in talks with the Russian Ambassador, M. Souritz, a closer Franco-Soviet alliance ;[1] but in the documents which he adduces in evidence he is seen merely trying to make Russia promise aid to Poland and Rumania, and that in precise terms (which France herself never did). "After

[1] *Fin d'une Europe. De Munich à la guerre*, pages 176-80. See also above, pages 59-60.

that we should have to decide what attitude to take if Rumania or Poland refused such aid." [1] Technical talks might start immediately, but given the mentality which, in spite of imminent danger, "we still encounter in the rulers of Poland and Rumania, it would be advisable to conduct such talks with the greatest discretion". Thus from the outset Bonnet realized that the aid solicited by the Western Powers was not welcome to the intended beneficiaries.

Had Bonnet truly wanted to strengthen the Franco-Soviet Pact (*élargir et préciser*, as he now puts it), and define the resulting military obligations (a thing the Russians had repeatedly asked for), he could have done so without Britain's participation; which was sought, as during the Rhineland and Czech crises, in order decorously to hinder the French Government from doing what they were not over-anxious to do. At first negotiations were conducted by means of concurrent but separate communications to Russia; only when, at the end of May, they were shifted to Moscow, did the diplomatic action of the Western Powers assume a joint character. The French were throughout a few steps ahead of the British (though not nearly as far as is now claimed by M. Bonnet): the prospect of a Continental war weighed heavier on them, and they were consequently keener to divert its brunt on to Russia, at whatever cost to third parties.

After the guarantees to Poland and Rumania had been announced, on April 15 Britain asked Russia to promise aid should the Western Powers become involved in war in discharge of their obligations; the French suggested

[1] See Bonnet's wire to the French Embassy in Moscow, April 10, 1939, claiming to reproduce what he had said to the Russian Ambassador. But in the summary given in the book (page 178) by way of introduction to the wire, he supplies another version without apparently realizing the difference: " Should these two countries refuse an aid which we deem indispensable, the French Government would have a right to reconsider the attitude to be adopted toward them ".

the same thing in a nicely balanced formula [1] promising mutual help if either the Western Powers or the U.S.S.R. became involved in war by aiding and assisting Poland or Rumania — scrupulously "reciprocal" commitments over countries which were the concern of the Western Powers but no friends of Russia. The Russian counter-proposal of April 17 was for a Triple Alliance between the three Great Powers, coupled with immediate military conversations and a promise not to conclude separate peace; the pact was to cover also the Baltic States, Britain was to declare that her guarantee to Poland was only against Germany, and Poland and Rumania were to cancel their anti-Russian alliance. [2] On April 29 the French produced an amended formula to cover war resulting from "action undertaken to prevent a modification by force of the *status quo* in Central or Eastern Europe", and not merely if incurred through assisting Poland or Rumania. This was wide and vague, and satisfied neither Britain nor Russia. The British attitude was indicated in the Prime Minister's speeches, and clearly defined in an *aide-mémoire* to the French Government (April 29): no chance was to be neglected of obtaining Russian help, but due care was to be taken not to offend the susceptibilities of Poland and Rumania or anti-Communist world opinion, and not to provoke Germany. [3] Consequently the next British note of May 8 was merely

[1] See *Diplomatic Prelude*, pages 152-3, footnote, and Bonnet, *op. cit.* page 180.

[2] See Bonnet, page 182. His date (April 19) is wrong, and his formulation of the last two points differs from that given to me by a reliable source (see *Diplomatic Prelude*, page 178) and reproduced above: it sounds more likely that the Russians asked for an assurance as to the character of the guarantee than that they demanded a "limitation" of a guarantee whose exact terms were not known; and the *Final Report* of M. Grzybowski, Polish Ambassador in Moscow, dated November 6, 1939, and published in the Polish White Book, seems to confirm that Russia demanded a cancelling of the Polish-Rumanian alliance, and not its extension "against *all* aggressors", as alleged by Bonnet.

[3] See *Diplomatic Prelude*, page 157.

explanatory of the previous proposal. Meantime M. Litvinov had been replaced by M. Molotov, and on May 15 the Russians similarly restated their previous demands. Further talks followed, and the note of May 27, presented by the Western Powers in Moscow, marked an advance : they were willing to discuss a triple pact ; but action under it was to conform with Article 16 of the League Covenant ; immediate aid had been promised by the Western Powers to Belgium, Poland, Rumania, Greece, and Turkey, but in the case of the Baltic States there was first to be consultation, if asked for ; help to third parties was to be conditional on their asking for it, nor were any obligations to be imposed on them by the treaty (*e.g.* to allow the passage of foreign troops) ; and military talks were to be started after the political pact had been concluded. The restrictive stipulations arose from a well-founded fear of the use which the Soviet Union might make of the treaty, but such scruples were not helpful in an anyhow very difficult negotiation ; while the Russian refusal to guarantee Holland and Switzerland, because they had not recognized the Soviet régime, was formalism hardly indicative of a desire to reach a speedy conclusion. Russia insisted on absolute " reciprocity " ; on the same kind of guarantee to the two groups of countries ; League procedure was deemed by her too slow and cumbrous for dealing with Hitler ; and in view of his methods, provision was required also against " indirect aggression ". In the negotiations which followed the concessions all came from the Western Powers which were seeking assistance in the discharge of obligations they had assumed, while the Soviet Union still had the choice of policy.[1]

By the beginning of July only two serious difficulties remained : how to define " indirect aggression ", and

[1] For the Soviet note of June 2, see *Diplomatic Prelude*, page 182 ; and for the further negotiations till July 4, see *ibid.* pages 183-94, and Bonnet, *op. cit.* pages 186-93.

how to correlate the political and military agreements. The British definition ran : " the word ' aggression ' is to be understood as covering action accepted by the State in question under threat of force by another Power and involving the abandonment by it of its independence or neutrality " ; while the Soviet Government desired " indirect aggression " to cover even an internal *coup d'état* or a political change favourable to the aggressor : which would have admitted of intervention in the internal affairs of the countries concerned. Complete agreement was never reached on this point.[1]

According to Bonnet, Molotov, on July 8, having suggested a compromise formula for " indirect aggression " (not reproduced by Bonnet), demanded insertion of an article (VI) whereby the political agreement would come into force only when " an implementing military convention is concluded ".[2] This seems to have greatly upset Bonnet, who now urged the British Government to accept Molotov's formula but reject Article VI. Surely, he argued, Russia could not suspect the Western Powers of trying to involve her politically, and then wishing to shirk military commitments.[3] " To enter that path," wrote Bonnet to M. Corbin, French Ambassador in London, " would mean to risk being placed in August, when the international crisis will be at its worst, before the alternative of either submitting to all Soviet military demands . . . or of letting . . . both the military and political agreements be wrecked." [4] And he added : " That game could the more easily be played against us as the execution of the military agreement to be effective

[1] For " indirect aggression ", see Bonnet, page 194, and *Diplomatic Prelude*, pages 195-7.
[2] See Bonnet, pages 194-5.
[3] But compare how in May 1939, Bonnet, and also the French High Command, juggled with their political and military pacts with Poland ; see *Diplomatic Prelude*, pages 454-64, and above, pages 68-72.
[4] Bonnet, page 196.

in the east, requires, as you know, the concurrence of Poland. . . . Here, too, we can foresee difficulties which the Soviet Government will undoubtedly raise to justify limiting its assistance. It is therefore essential that the question of Article VI be settled in our sense." But the British Government were sick of giving in to consecutive Russian demands, and would have neither Molotov's formula nor his article. The French were thus faced with the possible failure of the negotiations; and on July 19,[1] Bonnet appealed to Halifax to avert it as France's "diplomatic and strategic position in Central and Eastern Europe" and "the efficacy of the help promised to Poland and Rumania" would be compromised. Finally the British Government accepted Article VI, but persisted in their refusal to give way over "indirect aggression."

Still, Molotov himself is reported to have described the divergence as of minor importance; and at the end of July all was sunshine. In an appendix,[2] Bonnet publishes the draft treaty as it then stood (though again without the Russian formula). Article I stipulated for mutual assistance in case of aggression against one of the Contracting Parties, or against a European State whose independence or neutrality the interested Contracting Party would feel obliged to defend against direct or indirect aggression; the guaranteed States were enumerated in a secret protocol: Estonia, Finland, Latvia, Lithuania, Poland, Rumania, Turkey, Greece, and Belgium; action under the Treaty was to conform with League of Nations principles but not necessarily with its procedure. By Article IV the Contracting Parties undertook to inform each other of promises of assistance they had given to

[1] Bonnet in his book dates the letter sent to Halifax through the British Ambassador "July 19", but in an article which he published in the *Revue de Paris* in November 1947, "July 17"; and the communication through M. Corbin is stated in the book to have been sent "the same day".

[2] *Op. cit.* pages 401-3.

third parties, and not to assume any such new engagements without previous consultation ; and by Article V not to conclude a separate armistice or peace. Article VI made the treaty conditional on a military convention being concluded.

" The arrival in Moscow, at the request of the U.S.S.R., of Franco-British military experts ", wrote, on July 24, the French Ambassador, M. Naggiar, " is fit publicly to range the U.S.S.R. on our side . . ."[1] (which was perhaps the reason why counter-balancing steps were taken by the Soviet Government towards Germany). And on the 28th Naggiar warned the French War Office : the military " should know that the Soviet authorities will not be satisfied with a perfunctory examination of the problem, but will probe it to the bottom in discussions which will be extremely close ".[2] But the Western Powers were aware of Poland's attitude to a military agreement with Russia, and according to M. Noël, French Ambassador in Warsaw, General Doumenc, Head of the French Military Mission, " before leaving Paris, was apparently warned that he would have to try to avoid letting that question be put by the Russians ".[3]

Here is General Doumenc's account of his Moscow negotiations.[4] In the first session, on August 12, Marshal Voroshilov presented his authority to sign a military agreement, and Doumenc an order authorising him " to deal with all military questions ". " But Admiral Drax [Head of the British Mission] had to state, *après avoir quelque peu toussé*, that he had no such document, though

---

[1] Bonnet, page 202. [2] *Ibid.* page 204.
[3] Noël, *L'Agression allemande contre la Pologne*, page 423.
[4] On May 15, 1947, M. Marcel Cachin, the Communist leader, wrote in the *Humanité* : " When as Chairman of the Foreign Affairs Commission I asked to be shown that report, I was told at the Quai d'Orsay that the dossier Doumenc was burnt at the time of the German advance on Paris, in May 1940 ". Thereupon Doumenc published in the *Carrefour* of May 21 his record of the report.

there could be no doubt as to his Government's intentions."

Next, Voroshilov asked for the concrete plans of the Western Powers. Doumenc claims to have supplied " sincere and accurate information while giving it a sufficiently general character *pour que personne n'eût l'impression d'aller au delà de ce qui pouvait être divulgé* ".[1] The Russians stated that on the European front they would mobilize 120 infantry and 16 cavalry divisions,[2] and 5000 airplanes; and should the Germans attack in the west, 70 per cent of these forces would go into action. They expected a corresponding effort from the Western Powers if the attack turned against the east. Doumenc would have preferred a vague formula : that the Allies should " act with all their forces, on all fronts on which they could actively fight, till the German power was broken "; but he had to agree to a concrete discussion.

Then, on August 14, the Russians demanded that the Western Powers should obtain from the Baltic States agreement to a Russian occupation of their islands and main ports, and from Poland and Rumania to the passage of Russian troops across their territory. Bonnet calls this " The Thunderclap of August 15 ".[3] He now tried to put the utmost pressure on the Poles : " We cannot believe that by refusing to discuss the strategic conditions of Russian intervention Poland will assume responsibility for a failure of the military negotiations with Moscow,

[1] I do not venture to translate this, to me incomprehensible, sentence. A clearer account appears in Noël (*op. cit.* page 420) : Voroshilov "inquired of the French and British what engagements their countries were prepared to assume on land, sea, and in the air. General Doumenc answered with prudent generalities. Voroshilov — I have it from a witness — replied with haughty insolence that Doumenc's declaration was meaningless."

[2] The figures given by Stalin to Churchill (see above, page 242) were probably an exaggeration; but these are an obvious underestimate to suit the highest possible equivalent on the part of the Western Powers.

[3] The news reached Bonnet in the small hours of August 15.

and for all its consquences ".[1] But Beck was adamant:
" This is a new Partition we are asked to sign; if we are
to be partitioned, we shall at least defend ourselves. . . ."[2]
And on August 19: " I do not admit any discussion of
the use of any part of our territory by foreign troops. This
is for us a question of principle: we neither have, nor
wish to have, a military agreement with the U.S.S.R." [3]
On August 17 the military conversations were adjourned
to the 21st (and on the 19th the Soviet Government
agreed to receive Ribbentrop in Moscow on the 26th or
27th, which date was, on the 21st, advanced to the 23rd).
On the 19th Bonnet again warned the Polish Government
" to measure the extent of their responsibilities should
their attitude produce a breakdown of the negotiations
with the U.S.S.R." Next day Naggiar asked Bonnet to
authorize Doumenc *de traiter et de signer au mieux dans l'intérêt
commun* — they argued that " M. Beck's objections should
not be taken altogether literally, and that perhaps he
merely wishes not to know anything about the matter ". [4]
With Daladier's concurrence [5] the authorization was given
on August 21.[6] When on the 22nd, after Ribbentrop's
forthcoming visit had been announced, Doumenc told
Voroshilov that France gave the desired assurance *aux
lieu et place de la Pologne*, Voroshilov replied that Poland
was a sovereign State and France could not speak for
her; if the Polish and Rumanian Governments express
their agreement and " political circumstances remain
unchanged, it will be easy to draft the military conven-

[1] Bonnet, pages 279-80.   [2] Noël, page 423.   [3] Bonnet, page 282.
[4] See Gafenco, *Derniers Jours de l'Europe* (1946), pages 233-4.
[5] For a conversation which Daladier alleges to have had that morning
with Łukasiewicz, but which Łukasiewicz denies ever having taken place,
see *Diplomatic Prelude*, pages 209-10.
[6] Bonnet writes (page 284, note 3): " The same day we asked London
to give analogous instructions to the British delegation, which was done ".
If M. Bonnet means to imply that the British Delegation was authorized to
sign for Poland, his statement cannot be accepted.

tion ".[1]   In the afternoon of August 23, Beck at last
agreed to let Doumenc say: " We have acquired the
certainty that in case of common action against German aggression, collaboration between Poland and the
U.S.S.R., under technical conditions to be determined, is
not excluded (or is possible). . . ." [2] But in a wire to
Łukasiewicz he added that this move " could have only
tactical significance ".[3] At that hour Ribbentrop was
already at the Kremlin.

Bonnet had carefully avoided probing the military
contradictions or impossibilities of the diplomatic line-up
which he so zealously pursued — hence his excitement
when the Russians insisted on tying up the political with
the military pacts. The Military Missions to Moscow were
placed in an absurd position which the Soviet Government could exploit: it suited them to do so.

[1] See Daladier's speech in the French Chamber of Deputies, reported in
the *Journal Officiel* of July 19, 1946; also *Diplomatic Prelude*, page 292.
[2] See Bonnet, page 290.
[3] See Łukasiewicz, " Wspomnienia i uwagi ", in the *Dziennik Polski* of
December 5, 1946, and *Diplomatic Prelude*, page 292.   This time Bonnet's
dating seems correct, and Łukasiewicz's out by one day.

NAZI-SOVIET RELATIONS, 1939-1941

WHILE the documents presented at Nuremberg were selected to prove guilt rather than to delineate policy, the collection published from the German archives by the American State Department sets out to tell the story of *Nazi-Soviet Relations, 1939–1941*.[1] But this, too, is a selection : thus for the four months May–August 1939, twenty-eight telegrams exchanged between the Berlin Foreign Office and the German Embassy in Moscow are printed out of a traceable total of nearly 400 ; and though a fuller publication will hardly change the outlines of the story, the student who tries to follow it step by step in the material now offered is acutely conscious of its fragmentary character. Moreover, it comes from one side only : and few men will retail their mistakes or the rebuffs they may have met with ; they posture for their own records, and the picture is retouched. Besides, opposite accounts of the same conversation are apt to differ widely ; but a frank publication of the corresponding documents by the Soviet Government can hardly be expected.

The story of Nazi-Soviet approaches does not open on April 17, 1939, the date of the first document in this collection ; nor with Stalin's speech of March 10, 1939, as it suited Ribbentrop to suggest in Moscow on August 23 — a post-prandial compliment which the Russians could ill refuse. Stalin spoke of " the military block of aggressors " who, unresisted, infringed " upon the interests of the non-aggressive States, primarily Britain, France, and the United States of America ". Russia desired closer trade relations with all countries and " close and friendly rela-

---

[1] *Nazi-Soviet Relations, 1939–1941.* Documents from the Archives of the German Foreign Office. Edited by R. J. Sontag and J. S. Beddie. Department of State, Washington.

tions " with such as had common frontiers with her —
that is, with the States intervening between her and
Germany. Further: " We stand for the support of
nations which are victims of aggression and are fighting
for the independence of their country ". He spoke of
the British, French, and American Press foretelling, and
indeed desiring, a German march against the Soviet
Ukraine. He defied would-be aggressors of Russia, but
added that she would not allow herself " to be drawn into
conflicts by warmongers who are accustomed to have
others pull the chestnuts out of the fire for them ". The
speech was not flattering to the Western Powers, but it
requires more zeal than sense, or else a purpose, to discover in it a distinct approach to Germany.

Appeasing efforts were made, not by the West alone,
during the post-Munich period. Erich Kordt, *chef de
cabinet* to Ribbentrop, mentions in his book *Wahn und
Wirklichkeit*[1] an agreement concluded in October 1938
between M. Litvinov and Count von der Schulenburg,
German Ambassador in Moscow, which in either country
prohibited Press attacks against the leading personalities
of the other. And in January trade negotiations were
started whose course subsequently provided M. Molotov
with material for recriminations: first, a German trade
delegation was to have gone to Moscow; next, it was only
Dr. Schnurre, of the Trade Department of the Foreign
Office; but he got no farther than Warsaw, and in
February the negotiations were broken off.

After Hitler's entry into Prague Russia proposed a Six-
Power Conference in Bucharest, Britain a Four-Power
Declaration.

> During this period [wrote Count Raczyński,
> Polish Ambassador in London, on April 26, 1939]
> the two Governments were in comparatively frequent
> touch, but when the British Government abandoned

[1] Page 155, note 2.

their own proposal, and decided to give Poland a guarantee, the contacts were broken off, to the great dissatisfaction of the Soviets.

The Anglo-Polish *rapprochement* seems to have had its effect on German-Russian relations: for when, on April 17, M. Merekalov, Russian Ambassador in Berlin, called on the State Secretary, Herr von Weizsäcker, and asked him point-blank what he thought of Russian-German relations, Weizsäcker could already point to an improvement in the tone of the Press in both countries; further, " as everybody knew, we had always had the desire for mutually satisfactory commercial relations with Russia ". Merekalov replied that Russia saw no reason why she should not live on a normal footing with Germany; and " from normal, relations might become better and better ". He added that he was about to go to Moscow " for a visit ".

He went, and never returned; till September 1, 1939, there was only a Chargé d'Affaires in Berlin, M. Astakhov, late chief of the Press Department in Moscow, a singularly talkative Soviet diplomatist. After M. Litvinov's dismissal he assured M. Coulondre, French Ambassador in Berlin, that there was no change in Russian foreign policy, but that Litvinov " no longer saw eye to eye with M. Molotov, and M. Stalin, though valuing him, did not like him "; Astakhov also talked of Litvinov's " well-known hostility to Poland ".[1] But when rumours started circulating in Berlin of German proposals to Russia for a partition of Poland, Astakhov, on May 9, excitedly asked Coulondre: " Have you heard that the Soviet Government has decided to change its policy? " " I pointed out ", writes Coulondre, " that it was much rather myself who should ask him that question. . . ." Whereupon Astakhov volunteered the statement that Merekalov, in his talk with Weizsäcker on April 17, " did not discuss political

<hr>

[1] See Bonnet, *Fin d'une Europe*, page 184.

matters ".[1] Similarly he asked Schnurre on August 10, 1939, whether the Germans " had not heard anything from Moscow regarding M. Merekalov " ; but added that " it made no difference in our talks who was acting as the official representative of the Soviet Government in Berlin". In short, here was *un jeune ingénu*, fitted for a peculiar part. In reality the dominant note in Nazi-Soviet relations was intense mutual distrust : for several months each side was holding out vistas of improved relations in order to render the other less inclined to an agreement with the Western Powers, while it avoided commitments which the other could have utilized in negotiating with them.

Merekalov talked to Weizsäcker about " better and better " relations on the day the Soviet Government proposed a Triple Alliance to the Western Powers : a significant " re-insurance ". Nor does the summoning of Merekalov and Maisky to Moscow at that juncture seem accidental. How far the reorientation in Russian policy had gone is not known even now. But it clearly appears from the new documents that the moves towards a Nazi-Soviet *rapprochement* were as yet of a most tentative and vague character. None the less, on May 6 a close associate of Göring's, General Bodenschatz of the Luftwaffe (referred to in the French *Yellow Book* as " X "), told Captain Stehlïn, Assistant Air Attaché of the French Embassy,[2] that, before leaving, the Soviet Ambassador was received by Ribbentrop (which was not accurate) and " fully informed of the views of the Reich Government " (which was untrue) : " You will learn some day that something is brewing in the East " — and he finished by foretelling a Fourth Partition of Poland. Coulondre thought that Bodenschatz, having got excited, had said

---

[1] French *Yellow Book*, page 165. For other samples of Astakhov's talk, see Bonnet, *op. cit.* pages 207 and 289.

[2] Referred to in the *Yellow Book* as " C ". M. Reynaud names M. François Conty as the recipient of Bodenschatz's " confidences " (see *La France a sauvé l'Europe*, i. 582, note 2). That identification is wrong.

"much more than he was authorized to say".[1] But on May 29, at Lammers's birthday party, Bodenschatz gave similar warnings to the Polish Military Attaché, Colonel Szymański. Nor were these the only recipients of his " confidences ". It would seem that Göring, exploiting the first glimmer of a Nazi-Soviet *détente*, attempted blackmail in the war of nerves over " Danzig ".

The Russians, though they may not have known about this manœuvre, wondered whether Germany's changed attitude was not a move in a political game. And when, on May 20, the Germans offered to send Schnurre for trade talks to Moscow, Molotov told Schulenburg that the Soviet Government could resume them only " if the necessary ' political bases ' for them had been constructed "; but he would not be drawn to define his meaning in concrete terms. Berlin thereupon told Schulenburg to sit tight and wait; and he himself suspected that the Kremlin might have merely fished for German proposals " to exert pressure on England and France ".

A letter from Weizsäcker to Schulenburg of May 27 discloses wavering at the top. On May 22 the " Pact of Steel " had been signed, and the next day Hitler decided " at the first suitable opportunity " to attack Poland. The time had come to clear up Germany's relations to Russia, and some time between May 23 and 26 instructions were drafted for a " far-reaching " step towards her,[2] apparently

[1] See *Yellow Book*, page 154.
[2] A. Rossi, *Deux Ans d'alliance germano-soviétique, août 1939-juin 1941*, quotes from that draft which is among the German documents captured by the Western Allies. It is apparently of considerable length and, judging by the passages quoted in Rossi, seems to have served subsequently as a text for German negotiators. The following is in para. 7: " Should, however, contrary to our wishes, an armed conflict occur with Poland, even this, we are firmly convinced, need in no way lead to a conflict of interests with the Soviet Government. So much we can say even today, that in a clarification of the German-Polish problem — in whatever manner it is brought about — we would pay the utmost regard to Russian interests." And in para. 9: " We are also of opinion that Britain is in no position . . . to offer anything in exchange to Soviet Russia which could be of real value ".

also in order to "disturb and impede" Anglo-Russian negotiations.[1]   But, next, the view prevailed that it would not be easy to prevent that combination, and that "a very open statement in Moscow" might do more harm than good, "and perhaps produce a peal of Tartar laughter". Therefore on May 26 a negative telegram was sent to Schulenburg (again omitted from the American collection of documents).   Germany now meant to wait and see how far the Western Powers and Russia "are willing to pledge themselves to each other".   Additional information can be gathered from other sources.   Gaus, legal adviser to the German Foreign Office, says in his Nuremberg affidavit that he and Weizsäcker were ordered to draft those "far-reaching" instructions, which were not sent "as Hitler found them, after all, 'too explicit'"; and Kordt suggests that Hitler was put off by Chamberlain's statement in Parliament that agreement had practically been reached with Russia.[2]

But on May 30 a telegram to Schulenburg states: "Contrary to the policy previously planned, we have now decided to undertake definite negotiations with the Soviet Union".   The same day Weizsäcker had a talk with Astakhov on instructions from Ribbentrop, to which, as usual, he "strictly adhered".   They are contained in two memoranda, one in Ribbentrop's confused style, and both aggressive.   Having declared that the German Government thought the Soviet Government "very little interested" in trade relations with Germany and inclined to support the British policy of "encirclement", Weizsäcker was to aim at "clarification".   He did so by quoting Merekalov on better relations; said that the change with

[1] In personal letters, produced by the prosecution at Weizsäcker's trial at Nuremberg, he wrote on May 31, 1939, to Ambassador Moltke in Warsaw and Ambassador Mackensen in Rome: " The problem whether and how one could try to put a spoke in the wheel of the Anglo-Russian conversations, has turned to and fro in the last days ".

[2] See *Wahn und Wirklichkeit*, page 157.

regard to Poland had freed German policy in the East; that Germany would be neither narrow-minded nor importunate toward Russia; that the handing over of the Carpathian Ukraine to Hungary refuted her alleged intentions with regard to the Soviet Ukraine; and that Russia had the choice of anything from a " normalization " of relations with Germany to " unrelenting hostility ". Astakhov explained that Molotov had talked " with the customary Russian distrust " but without intention to stop further Russian-German discussions; and he referred incidentally to a Soviet offer of alliance rejected by Germany before she concluded her treaty with Poland (was this perhaps the background to Souritz's mission to Berlin at the end of 1933, and Nadolny's to Moscow?).

On May 31 Molotov gave in the Supreme Soviet a critical review of the negotiations with the Western Powers and referred to a possible resumption of trade talks with Germany. He " at once utilized tactically our offer . . ." wrote Schulenburg to Weizsäcker on June 5. " Caution . . . was and is therefore necessary, but it seems clear . . . that the way is open for further negotiations." " The Soviet Russians are full of distrust towards us, but they do not much trust the democratic Powers either." The Germans continued to press their offer to send Schnurre to Moscow, and the Russians to suspect a political game behind it; Schulenburg thought they did not want the stir which would be caused by a resumption of trade negotiations, " and above all by repeated journeys of a special plenipotentiary to Moscow "; and he therefore suggested inviting a Russian delegate " with all necessary powers " to Berlin. The Führer, however, ordered an answer which would have ended the talks with Russia; but next agreed that it " be delayed for a few days " — a characteristic performance.

Had the matter rested with Hitler, Ribbentrop, and their subservient Weizsäcker, the negotiations would probably have failed. But in Count von der Schulenburg they had an excellent ambassador of the old school, a Junker with the Bismarckian belief in German-Russian friendship, who, moreover, dared to stand up to Ribbentrop and even to Hitler.[1] In a talk with Molotov, on June 29, Schulenburg again emphasized Germany's wish for normal relations with Russia, and dwelt on her non-aggression pacts with the Baltic States and her wish to resume trade talks. Molotov was reserved and even brusque: the Soviet Government desired good relations with all countries, therefore also with Germany; Germany's non-aggression pacts did not concern Russia, while Poland's recent experience made him doubt their permanence; and as for the Anglo-Polish Agreement (the Nazi excuse for denouncing that with Poland) this was "a purely defensive instrument". But a hint skilfully dropped by Schulenburg that the German-Russian Treaty of 1926 (of friendship and neutrality) "was still in force", aroused Molotov's interest. Schulenburg concluded that the Soviet Government was "greatly interested in knowing our political views and in maintaining contact with us"; and he thought that it would be possible to resume trade talks without a prior political basis. But Ribbentrop replied that "in the political field enough had been said until further instructions". And here the curtain drops in the American documents: to rise on July 22 on a Soviet announcement that trade negotiations between a Soviet representative and Schnurre had "recently been resumed" in Berlin.

During the next three weeks the Germans tried to force the pace, while the Russians played for time. The Germans argued that once the trade talks were concluded, political relations should be normalized and an arrangement made, taking account of "the vital political interests of both parties"; these nowhere conflicted: "there was

[1] He was executed after the attempt against Hitler of July 20, 1944.

no problem from the Baltic to the Black Sea that could
not be solved " between them; Germany's policy was
directed against Britain, not against Russia; and " in
any development of the Polish question " the Germans
would safeguard Russia's interests. But they pressed
Russia to state her claims, and to define her attitude
towards Poland. The Russians were amiable but reserved; they were spinning out trade negotiations, and
now would not link them up with political matters :
Moscow, for once, seemed to believe in the inevitability
of gradualness. While the Germans discoursed on future
friendship, the Russians indulged in recriminations about
the past; and Molotov, "this remarkable man and difficult
character ", told Schulenburg that peace or war with
Poland depended on Germany alone.

" I had the impression," wrote Schnurre on July 27,
after a dinner with Astakhov, " that Moscow had not yet
decided what they meant to do ", and pursued " a policy
of delay . . . toward us as well as England ". And
Schulenburg on August 4 :

> My over-all impression is that the Soviet Govern-
> ment is at present determined to sign with England
> and France if they fulfil all Soviet wishes. I believe
> that my statements made an impression on Molotov ;
> it will nevertheless take a considerable effort on our
> part to cause the Soviet Government to swing about.

The questions asked by the Russians show that the German
offers were not indifferent to them ; but material is lacking
even now for tracing hesitations and changes in Soviet
policy.

Then, on August 12, the day on which talks with the
allied military missions started in Moscow, Astakhov told
Schnurre that the Soviet Government was prepared to
discuss

> besides the pending economic negotiations, ques-
> tions of the Press, cultural collaboration, the Polish

question, the matter of the old German-Soviet political agreements of 1926. Such a discussion, however,
could be undertaken only by stages.

The Soviet Government proposed Moscow as the place
for these discussions, and left it open to the Germans to
conduct them through their Ambassador " or another
personage, to be sent out ". Schnurre's report reached
Berchtesgaden while Ciano was with Hitler. He was told
that a " telegram from Moscow " agreed " to the dispatch
of a German political negotiator to Moscow ". Ciano
does not mention the incident in his minute of the conference,[1] nor even in his *Diary*; and he was taken aback
when informed, on the night of August 21, of Ribbentrop's
forthcoming journey to Moscow.

Possibly the Russians themselves were taken aback by
the German reaction to their message. On August 14
Ribbentrop sent Schulenburg a long and fatuous memorandum to be read out to Molotov but not to be given in
writing, which, none the less, was to reach Stalin " in as
exact a form as possible ". It spoke of closing the period
of conflicts in German-Russian relations and of settling
them " for generations " on a basis of friendship ; of " the
natural sympathy of the Germans for the Russians ",
which had " never disappeared ", and their common
hostility to " the capitalistic Western democracies " ; and
of the need of speedily clarifying German-Russian relations and perhaps also " the territorial questions of Eastern
Europe ". Ribbentrop was prepared to come to Moscow.

[1] Ciano decided to omit it from the minute after having taken counsel
with his brother-in-law, Magistrati, and Attolico (they talked in Ciano's
bath-room, with the taps running, to defeat German microphones).
According to Toscano, " Fonti per la storia della guerra ", *Rivista Storica
Italiana*, Vol. lx, No. 1, 105-6, " having had so many proofs of bad faith ",
they suspected a trick to manœuvre Italy into agreeing to an attack
against Poland ; but even if the statement was true, they feared that it
might induce Mussolini to decide prematurely in favour of intervening in
the war. Still, the omission from the *Diary* and Ciano's subsequent surprise
suggest that he attached insufficient importance to the communication.

On August 15 Schulenburg saw Molotov, who was quite unusually affable, but said that before answering he would have to refer to his Government; that Ribbentrop's visit to Moscow would require most careful preparation; and he asked whether Germany was prepared to conclude a non-aggression pact with Russia. The Baltic States and Russo-Japanese relations were mentioned, but no concrete demands were formulated. Ribbentrop replied the next day by conceding anything Molotov had adumbrated; asked for a " rapid clarification " of German-Russian relations as Germany was " determined not to endure Polish provocation indefinitely "; and offered to fly to Moscow. Schulenburg was told it was " of very special interest " that the trip should take place in the next few days.

On the 17th Schulenburg was given Stalin's reply to his communication of the 15th : it starts by recalling Germany's previous hostility to the Soviet Union ; declares Russia's readiness to establish " new and improved relations "; points to a trade agreement as the first step, to be followed, shortly afterwards, by a non-aggression pact accompanied by a " special protocol " defining " the interests of the signatory parties ". As for Ribbentrop's journey, Molotov repeated that it would require thorough preparation. " The Soviet Government did not like the publicity that such a journey would cause. They preferred that practical work be accomplished without so much ceremony."

It was obvious that Ribbentrop's visit would commit the U.S.S.R. to Germany and end their negotiations with the Western Powers; and it is not certain even now whether Stalin had already made his choice; but even if he intended to close with Hitler he would not do so in a way which might give time to the Germans to pull off another Munich, followed, the Russians feared, by a coalition of the " capitalist Imperialist Powers " against the Soviet Union; and as Hitler, because of the season, could not postpone his Polish campaign beyond September 1, this was the date which Stalin had to approximate in spinning out negotiations.

On August 18 Ribbentrop again insisted on a method which would yield " quick results " ; " incidents " might render war with Poland unavoidable; Germany had accepted whatever Molotov had suggested on the 15th; " all factual elements " for personal negotiations and " for final accord were therefore present " ; Ribbentrop " would come with full powers from the Führer " ; he sent a draft of the non-aggression agreement. He added:

> Please conduct conversation . . . by pressing emphatically . . . for a rapid realization of my trip and by opposing . . . possible new Russian objections. . . . An early outbreak of open German-Polish conflict is probable and . . . we therefore have the greatest interest in having my visit to Moscow take place immediately.

But on August 19 Molotov told Schulenburg

> that for the present it was not possible even approximately to fix the time of the journey. . . . The German draft of the non-aggression pact was by no means exhaustive. . . . Further, the content of the protocol was a very serious question and the Soviet Government expected the German Government to state more specifically what points were to be covered in the protocol. . . .
> Molotov remained apparently unaffected by my protests, so that the first conversation closed with a declaration on the part of Molotov that he had imparted to me the views of the Soviet Government and had nothing to add to them.

Still, half an hour later he recalled Schulenburg, gave him the Russian draft of the non-aggression treaty, and agreed to Ribbentrop coming about a week after the signing of the economic agreement [1] — therefore at the earliest on August 26 or 27 (Schulenburg ascribed even this concession to Stalin's having intervened); but Molotov refused to accept any earlier date.

Then, on August 20, Hitler sent a personal telegram to Stalin: he accepted the Russian draft; said that the supplementary protocol could best be settled by personal negotiations in Moscow; spoke of the " intolerable tension " with Poland; and asked Stalin to receive Ribbentrop on August 22, or " at the latest " on the 23rd. Schulenburg was to give the telegram to Molotov " in writing, on a sheet of paper without letterhead ' He asked for a reply the same day (August 21); Stalin now agreed to Ribbentrop coming on the 23rd.

When they met an understanding was quickly reached; its most vital, territorial clauses were embodied in a Secret Additional Protocol.[2] Russia's demand that the entire coast of the Baltic States be included in her sphere was referred to Hitler, and conceded; the demarcation line in Poland, suggested by Stalin, was accepted immediately; and Germany declared her " complete political disinterestedness " in South - Eastern Europe (which Ribbentrop was authorized to extend to Constantinople and the Straits — but these " were not discussed "). Stalin showed concern about Italian aims in the Balkans; spoke with dislike of Britain (similarly to Matsuoka in March, 1941 : " Soviet Russia never got along well with Great Britain, and never would "); described the French Army as " worthy of consideration "; and when the irrepressible Ribbentrop declared that " all strata of the German people, and especially

---

[1] It was signed the same night, August 19-20.

[2] According to Rossi, *op. cit.*, a sealed envelope in the archives of the German Embassy in Moscow contained the declarations of fourteen Embassy officials, dated August 27, 1939, promising to preserve absolute silence about the existence of that protocol, whose contents were known to only very few among them.

the simple people, most warmly welcomed the understanding with the Soviet Union ", replied that this
was because " the Germans desired peace ". But " indignation against Poland ", interrupted Ribbentrop,
" was so great that every single man was ready to
fight ".

Stalin believed that the " simple people ", even in
Germany, wished for peace; yet, having decided not to
join the Western Powers in an anti-aggression *bloc*, he
deliberately opened the door to war. He and Hitler
became uneasy partners, exceedingly suspicious of each
other; but every time the Nazis were about to double-
cross the Bolsheviks they spoke of the " cordial relations "
existing between them. When the Germans quickly
advanced in Poland, Stalin, on September 18, asked
Schulenburg whether they would, " at the appropriate
time ", withdraw to the agreed line. By the end of the
month Ribbentrop was again in Moscow to negotiate a
final agreement. The line of August 23 cut across Polish
ethnic territory and the Russians proposed an exchange
of such territory included in their sphere for Lithuania;
which was accepted by the Germans (although warned
by one member of their delegation that the new frontier
practically coincided with the Curzon Line and deprived
Germany and Russia of a common anti-Polish interest).[1]
While Ribbentrop was still in Moscow Russia started
forcing the Baltic States into " military alliances "; and
when they turned to Germany they were completely cold-
shouldered.

None the less, relations between Moscow and Berlin
did not improve. Indeed, in Russia's attitude there was
" a distinct shift " unfavourable to the Germans : Schulenburg ascribed it to fear of getting involved in the war
when allied action in Scandinavia was apprehended; but

[1] The change was accepted by Hitler over the telephone, after a few
minutes' consideration; see Kordt, *op. cit.* pages 219-20.

the occupation of Norway by the Germans produced a new turn in their favour. Next, in view of German victories and conquests, Russia hastened to gather in her own spoils: in June 1940 the three Baltic States were Sovietized, and on the 23rd Molotov informed Schulenburg that the solution of the Bessarabian question " brooked no further delay ", and that " the Soviet claim likewise extended to the Bukovina which had a Ukrainian population ". This claim was finally limited to the northern, genuinely Ukrainian, part of the province, and on June 27 Rumania was advised by the Germans " to yield to the Soviet Government's demand ".

But although " the Soviet Government . . . had no intention of encouraging other States (Hungary, Bulgaria) to make demands on Rumania ", these followed, and were settled by the Axis Powers in the Vienna Award of August 30, 1940; and only on the following day Ribbentrop, " in view of the friendly relations between our countries ", informed Molotov of it: " Hungarian-Rumanian negotiations were running into very great difficulties "; there was the danger of " military complications "; for economic reasons, the Axis Powers had a primary interest in peace being maintained in those regions; both parties had requested their arbitration; and " the meeting in Vienna was agreed upon a few days ago on very short notice ". Lastly, as Russia's claim on Rumania had been, and Bulgaria's was being, satisfied, the Axis Powers agreed to guarantee Rumania's remaining territory. But Molotov failed to display the affability with which Mussolini was wont to receive such announcements from Hitler: he told Schulenburg that the German Government by confronting the Soviet Government with accomplished facts " had violated Article 3 of the Non-Aggression Pact, which provided for consultation ".

Before the end of September a new communication was made " in view of the cordial relations existing between

Germany and the Soviet Union " : the Axis Powers were about to sign a military alliance with Japan " directed exclusively against American warmongers " — an article would safeguard " the existing political relations " with the Soviet Union. Molotov answered by claiming that (in view of Articles 3 and 4 of the Non-Aggression Pact) his Government should be shown the treaty and any secret protocols before they were signed. He also inquired about an agreement whereby Finland allowed the passage of German troops to Norway, and a report that these had landed in Finland. Ribbentrop replied that the German-Finnish agreement was " a purely technical matter . . . without political implications ". And on October 10, " in view of the friendly relations ", he informed Molotov that " a German military mission with certain instruction units " was proceeding to Rumania : to protect German " oil and grain interests " against England. Molotov inquired about the number of the German troops ; and he thought that Britain had more pressing worries than to interfere in Rumania.

The position was becoming tense ; and a directive was issued by Göring " to avoid shipments to Russia which would . . . strengthen her war potential ". Then, on October 13, 1940, Ribbentrop addressed to Stalin one of his long, nonsensical letters : having surveyed the events of the past year, he restated the German argument about the transactions complained of by Russia, and finished with " the historical mission of the Four Powers — the Soviet Union, Italy, Japan and Germany — to adopt a long-range policy and direct the future development of their peoples into the right channels by delimitation of their interests on a world-wide scale ". For that purpose Molotov was invited to Berlin : " a direct contact between the responsible personalities . . . is indispensable from time to time in authoritarian régimes such as ours ". The invitation was accepted, and in the first conference on

November 12, 1940, Ribbentrop gave Molotov an *exposé* of the situation.

> . . . no power on earth could alter the fact that the beginning of the end had now arrived for the British Empire . . . the country was led by a political and military dilettante . . . Churchill, who throughout his previous career had completely failed at all decisive moments and who would fail again this time. . . . The entry of the United States into the war was of no consequence at all for Germany. Germany and Italy would never again allow an Anglo-Saxon to land on the European Continent. . . . Because of the extraordinary strength of their position, the Axis Powers were not . . . considering how they might win the war, but rather how rapidly they could end the war which was already won . . .
>
> The Führer now was of opinion that it would be advantageous . . . if the attempt were made to establish the spheres of interest between Russia, Germany, Italy, and Japan along very broad lines.

Japan had turned South; Germany having settled Western Europe, " would also find her *Lebensraum* expansion . . . in a southerly direction, *i.e.* in Central Africa. . . ." Italy's expansion was to the South, to Africa. And Ribbentrop

> wondered whether Russia in the long run would not also turn to the South for the natural outlet to the open sea that was so important for her.

When Molotov inquired which sea he meant, Ribbentrop pointed to the Persian Gulf : Germany " was completely disinterested " in that part of Asia. But he agreed that the Montreux Convention about the Straits should be revised.

Molotov replied that " the concept of a ' Greater East Asian Sphere ' was quite vague, at least for one who had not participated in the preparation of the Pact " ; that precision was necessary in a long-term delimitation of spheres of influence; and that Russia wanted an understanding with Germany first, and only later on with Italy and Japan, after having obtained precise information about the Tripartite Pact.

Then on November 12 and 13 followed two long talks between Molotov and Hitler in Ribbentrop's presence; both broken off in the evening because of possible English air attacks. Hitler discoursed on political collaboration between their two countries which " had been of considerable value " to both, and should be secured " beyond the life span of the present leaders "; spoke of a " Monroe Doctrine " against the United States which " had no business in Europe, in Africa, or in Asia "; and described the British Empire " as a gigantic world-wide estate in bankruptcy ".

> All the countries which could possibly be interested in the bankrupt estate would have to stop all controversies among themselves and concern themselves exclusively with the partition of the British Empire. This applied to Germany, France, Italy, Russia, and Japan.

Even the United States merely tried to pick up suitable bits from it.

Molotov " voiced his agreement " with the Führer, but tried to discuss concrete problems. The Russians were troubled by the presence of German troops in Finland and Rumania, and by its political repercussions; objected to the Axis guarantee to Rumania; and desired to include Bulgaria in their own sphere, and to discuss Turkey and the Straits. Hitler explained that war requirements made Germany act in regions in which she was not interested politically, and insisted that there must be no new war between Russia and Finland; Molotov argued that there was no such danger if Germany adopted a clear line: there must be neither German troops in Finland, nor any political encouragement of the Finns. The discussion tended to assume an acrid character and no progress was made. In Ribbentrop's concluding talk with Molotov, in an air-raid shelter that night, Ribbentrop produced a vague draft for a Four-Power Pact: they were " to respect each other's natural spheres of influence ", and not join any combination directed against one of them; but he resented being " queried too closely on concrete points ". Molotov concluded by saying that " the questions raised should now be further dealt with through diplomatic channels ".

On November 26 the Soviet Government declared their readiness to accept the pact provided the German troops were immediately withdrawn from Finland; the security of the U.S.S.R. was assured in the Straits by a pact with Bulgaria and a lease by Turkey of bases for Soviet "light naval and land forces " in the Straits; the area south of Batum and Baku and towards the Persian Gulf was acknowledged as a centre of Soviet aspirations; and Japan renounced certain concessions in Northern Sakhalin. Molotov said he " would appreciate a statement of the German view " on these matters.

It never came; instead, on December 18, Hitler issued a secret directive for an invasion of Russia (on which work had proceeded since July). Considerable German forces were concentrated in Rumania. On January 17 the Russian Ambassador called on Weizsäcker and, having mentioned the report that these troops were to occupy Bulgaria, Greece, and the Straits, gave warning that his Government would " consider the appearance of any foreign armed forces on the territory of Bulgaria and of the Straits a violation of the security interests of the U.S.S.R." The Germans replied that they would march through Bulgaria if action had to be undertaken against England in Greece; and on March 1 Schulenburg informed Molotov (without reference to " cordial relations ") that Bulgaria had joined the Tripartite Pact, and that German troops would enter Bulgaria. Molotov received the communication "with obvious concern", and reiterated Russia's objections.

When, at the end of March, the Japanese Foreign Minister, Matsuoka, arrived in Berlin, Ribbentrop expatiated to him on Germany's might.

> A huge army, which was practically idle, was at Germany's command and could be employed at any time and at any place the Führer considered necessary. . . .
> . . . Should Russia some day take a stand that could be interpreted as a threat to Germany, the Führer would crush Russia. Germany was certain that a campaign against Russia would end in the absolute victory of German arms and the total crushing of the Russian Army and the Russian State . . . there would in a few months be no more Great Power of Russia.

And Hitler told Matsuoka that "the Axis Powers had become the dominant combination. Resistance to their will had become impossible."

The Yugoslav Government, which on March 25 had joined the Tripartite Pact, was overthrown on the 27th; and on April 4 Molotov informed Schulenburg that the Soviet Government, "actuated solely by the desire to preserve peace", had agreed to conclude a treaty of friendship with Yugoslavia. On the 6th, Schulenburg had, in turn, to inform Molotov that Germany felt "compelled to proceed to military action against Greece and Yugoslavia": which Molotov described as "extremely deplorable". So far the Russians had kept up their end in dealings with Germany, using at times very direct language. But the power and speed of the German advance in the Balkans seems to have shaken their impervious equanimity, a compound of Marxian determinism and of indifference to the possible sufferings of their people. They now did their best to avert war with Germany; and so did the German diplomatists of the old school, who were anti-British rather than anti-Russian. On April 28 Schulenburg told Hitler that Russia, whom the Western Powers had failed to win over in 1939 when they were still strong, would not " make such a decision today, when France was destroyed and England badly battered "; but that Stalin was prepared to make still further concessions to Germany. And Weizsäcker wrote the same day, commenting on a memorandum by Schulenburg [1]:—

> If every Russian town reduced to ashes were as valuable to us as a sunken British warship, I should advocate the Russian-German war for this summer; but I believe that we would be victors over Russia only in a military sense, and would . . . lose in an economic sense . . .
>   . . . the sole decisive factor is whether this project will hasten the fall of England. . . . England is close to collapse . . . we shall encourage England by taking on a new opponent. Russia is no potential ally of the English. England can expect nothing good from Russia. . . . With Russia we do not destroy any English hopes.

When on May 7, 1941, Stalin took over the chairmanship of the Council of the People's Commissars, and thus officially became head of the Soviet Government, Schulenburg wrote that the reason lay

> in the recent mistakes in foreign policy which led to a cooling-off of the cordiality of German-Soviet rela-

[1] Weizsäcker's memorandum, addressed to Ribbentrop and opposing the latest tendencies of Hitler's policy, seems to have been a sincere and courageous expression of his own opinions: as a nationalist of the old school and a late officer in Tirpitz's navy, he was apparently more anti-British than anti-Russian, irrespective of Russia's internal régime. The memorandum further shows with what foresight he worked for the cause he served. As the prosecution stated at his trial at Nuremberg, controverting some of his own assertions, " his fervent nationalism made him a willing partner to the Nazis' plans of aggrandizement ".

tions, for . . . which Stalin had consciously striven, while Molotov's own initiative often expended itself in an obstinate defence of individual issues.

And, again, on May 12 : " Stalin personally has always advocated a friendly relationship between Germany and the Soviet Union ". (But in the days of friendship with the Western Powers Stalin would, before their representatives, jocularly tax Molotov with the Nazi-Soviet treaties.) Still, all Russian endeavours were to prove of no avail : soon the unavoidable " frontier incidents " made their appearance, and in the night of June 21-22 the Russians were told that their attitude was threatening, and that the Führer had therefore ordered the German armed forces to oppose this threat with all the means at their disposal. Ribbentrop, blaming the Russians, remarked to their Ambassador that " the ideological conflict between the two countries had become stronger than common sense. . . ."

DOCUMENTS

I. LETTER FROM PRESIDENT BENEŠ, WITH EN-CLOSED DOCUMENTS ON NEGOTIATIONS BETWEEN CZECHOSLOVAKIA AND POLAND, SEPTEMBER 21–NOVEMBER 1, 1938

I print below a letter which I received from President Beneš after he had read my articles " Coloured Books ", published in the Political Quarterly *between July 1941 and January 1944 (and subsequently republished, as Chapters I–III, in my book* Diplomatic Prelude, 1938–1939). *Some of the material contained in his letter I used in the book — for instance, in the footnote on pages 14-15, naturally without naming my source. To-day there is, I feel, no reason to withhold this letter, nor even the enclosure which at that time I was asked to treat as confidential. Indeed, in view of the scarcity of Czech diplomatic documents, now behind the iron curtain, there is good reason for publishing whatever is available.*—L. B. N.

PRESIDENT OF THE CZECHOSLOVAK REPUBLIC

LONDON, 20th April, 1944

MY DEAR MR. NAMIER,

I have read through your articles on " Coloured Books " and really do not know what I could add thereto. I can only say that I congratulate you very sincerely on your observations, which are brilliantly written and deserve to be issued as a book as early as possible. It will be one of the best treatises regarding the diplomatic background of the present catastrophe.

Nevertheless, I should like to offer you the following observations:

1. In the autumn of 1933 Hitler sounded me in Prague as to whether Czechoslovakia would conclude with him a pact of the type which he subsequently offered to Poland. I rejected this proposal and immediately informed Paris, London, *Warsaw*, Belgrade and Bucharest of the situation.

When Hitler found he could achieve nothing in Prague, he turned to Beck. I learnt of the offer made by Berlin and of the negotiations between Berlin and Warsaw in the Christmas of 1933. In January 1934 I was in Geneva for a meeting of the League. Minister Beck also attended the session. I visited him on the 15th January in the Hotel Beau Rivage and asked him directly whether he was negotiating with Berlin. He denied everything categorically. Before I left Geneva I telegraphed to Berlin to our Minister, Dr. Mastný, asking him to seek out the Polish Minister Lipski, and to attempt to discover whether it was true that a Polish-German Pact was being prepared. Lipski for a long time avoided making contact. Finally Mastný got hold of him on the eve of the signature of the Polish-German Pact of the 25th January. In reply to a direct question as to whether a Polish-German Treaty was involved he received a categorical reply that nothing of the sort was being contemplated. . . . At this moment Lipski was already in possession of Hitler's invitation to sign the Pact on the following day, 26th January, 1934.[1]

[1] *I have received from M. Lipski the following comment on President Beneš's letter*:

1. Pilsudski considered that Germany's withdrawal from the League of Nations and the Disarmament Conference deprived Poland of an element of security, and instructed me to speak to Hitler about it, which I did on November 15, 1933. The upshot of our talk was his offer of a non-aggression pact to Poland.
2. On the 16th, M. Mastný called on me and inquired about my talk with Hitler. I told him that I looked upon Hitler's reply as a declaration of non-aggression, which may result in a written agreement.
3. After the German Ambassador, von Moltke, had on November 27 presented to Marshal Pilsudski the German draft of a non-aggression pact, I was instructed by Colonel Beck to keep the matter strictly secret, and that also towards the *corps diplomatique*. Pilsudski, who personally dealt with the problem, would not sign a pact with the Germans before sounding Paris once more about jointly taking decisive action against Hitler: which was a further reason for his instructing me to preserve absolute silence.
4. The Polish-German talks were not resumed till January 9, 1934, when I presented the Polish counter-proposal to Neurath. When on January 13 Beck passed through Berlin on his way to Geneva, the fate of the agreement was as yet undecided. Serious difficulties arose in my talk with Gaus on January 16, which made Pilsudski summon me to Warsaw. The German Government, too, at that time insisted

2. On the other side three times in the course of 1932 and 1933 I officially offered Beck a treaty between Poland and Czechoslovakia, which would have developed into military co-operation. I never received any reply.

3. When Poland concluded the Treaty with Germany in January, 1934, two days after signing it she began an unbelievably sharp campaign against the Czechoslovak Republic with respect to the situation of the Polish minority therein. There was no justification for it, as we had done nothing to them. This campaign simply began, and continued right up to Munich. In its intensity it rivalled the German campaign which Goebbels began in 1936, and which was also continued up to Munich.

4. We had a Treaty of friendship, arbitration and non-aggression with Poland, which had been signed after my visit to Warsaw in 1924. It was to last ten years and to be automatically continued unless either of the two parties concerned repudiated it. Should this happen it automatically became void six months after such repudiation. When Germany's preparations against Czechoslovakia culminated in 1937 Poland, without giving any reasons and without receiving any provocation thereto on the part of Czechoslovakia, repudiated it just in good time to be able to carry out her attack against Czechoslovakia at the time of the crisis in September 1938.

5. When General Gamelin went to Warsaw in August 1936 I put into his hands a *written* proposal for military co-operation between Czechoslovakia and Poland, asking him

on strictest secrecy. There was in Germany, especially among the Prussian nationalists, serious opposition to a *détente* with Poland, and Hitler himself, as I was told by Goebbels, met with resistance and dissent on that point.

5. In these circumstances it was difficult for me to reply to M. Mastný's inquiry about the pact, especially as it was made, rather indiscreetly, at a dinner in Horcher's restaurant, in the presence of other diplomats. That talk did not, however, take place, as is stated by President Beneš, on the eve of signing the declaration (January 25), but a few days earlier. After it had been signed on the 26th, I called on M. Mastný at his Legation, and explained why I had been unable earlier to inform him about the negotiations.

to hand it over in Warsaw. He gave it to Rydz-Smygly and spoke about it with the President.[1] He received an evasive reply and the Polish Government did not return to the subject.

6. You are doubtless aware of the negotiations regarding the so-called Eastern Pact. When finally after the negotiations in 1934 and 1935 Germany and Poland smashed the whole plan, Poland did so by a Note one of the chief arguments of which was directed against the Czechoslovak Republic ; she declared that Poland could not sign the Pact because she could not submit to any obligations relating to the Danube Basin. This, she said, was not in her interests.

7. Finally, I am sending you herewith in confidence the chief diplomatic documents relating to the action taken by Poland against Czechoslovakia in 1938. They have not so far been published anywhere. I call attention to the following main points :

(a) The letter to President Mościcki of 22nd September I sent him when I signed the decree for our mobilization; *I believed that within two or three days it would come to war with Germany*, and I wanted therefore to secure at least the neutrality of Poland. The reply sent me by Poland provided me with the last and decisive reason for the fact that, in spite of the insistence of Moscow, I did not provoke war with Germany in 1938. But it was clear to me already in September 1938 that Poland would pay a terrible price for what she had done.

(b) Read the ultimatum of Beck to our Government from September 30th, 1938, regarding the handing over of

[1] Here President Beneš made a mistake which he repeats in his memoirs, *Paměti*, pages 57-8. Gamelin received Beneš's memorandum not on his way to Warsaw but, as he himself states (*Servir*, ii. 233), on his way back, with a view to communicating it to General Rydz-Smigly during his forthcoming visit to Paris. The memorandum is published in full in Gamelin, *op. cit.* pages 235-6 ; and although it is undated, the point in question is proved by its opening sentence :

Vu la visite de M. le général Rydz-Smigly à Paris et vu les conversations antérieures de M. le général Gamelin avec l'inspecteur général de l'armée polonaise à Varsovie, le président É. Beneš donne au général Gamelin les informations et les assurances suivantes. . . .

the Těšín territory ; its text is almost identical with the ultimatum which Hitler sent to Beck himself a year later with respect to the solution of the question of Danzig. This is certainly characteristic. Perhaps the chief difference lay in the fact that the ultimatum of the Polish Government to Czechoslovakia was limited *to only twelve hours.*—

I think that these notes, even if they may not be of any use to you in connection with the publication of your book, will at east throw a clearer light upon certain matters about which you are writing.

Yours very sincerely,

DR. EDVARD BENEŠ

ENCLOSURE

Diplomatic correspondence between Czechoslovakia and Poland was carried on in French, and the French texts are printed below as given to me by President Beneš. The notes and minutes of the Czechoslovak Foreign Ministry were of course in Czech, and the copies given to me contain both the Czech texts and an English translation. I print below their English text only.—L. B. N.

No. 1

Minute of Conversation between Dr. Krno, of the Czechoslovak Foreign Office, and the Polish Minister, M. Papée

PRAGUE, 21st September, 1938

The Polish Minister came this morning to obtain information concerning the latest developments. He led the conversation to the Polish minority in Czechoslovakia, observing expressly that he spoke for himself only.

That question, he said, is of wholly different character and of relatively less importance than the other problems of the minorities in Czechoslovakia. A solution had originally been arrived at after the World War which, in his opinion, was equitable and satisfactory for both parties, on the basis of resolutions passed by the local Czech and Polish National Councils. Unfortunately, however, the forcible occupation by the Czechoslovak army took place shortly after this.

I replied that the present state of affairs — following the unsuccessful attempt at a plebiscite — is based on the arbitration decision made by the Great Powers which had also been accepted by the Polish Government.

M. Papée replied that the decision at Spaa was made during the period when the Russian army was before Warsaw, that is, in a situation in which Poland had been compelled to accept anything whatsoever in order to obtain the assistance of the Western Powers.

I remarked that if we took up this point of view, then the present time is absolutely unsuitable for a fresh discussion of this question, because to-day Czechoslovakia is again in a situation analogous to that of Poland in 1920.

M. Papée concluded with the observation that in spite of this it would perhaps be good if Czechoslovakia made a gesture by the voluntary cession of the Těšín [Teschen] district as reparation for that injustice and so definitely to regulate Polish-Czechoslovak relations.

KRNO

No. 2

Note from the Polish Minister, M. Papée, to the Czechoslovak Foreign Minister, Dr. Krofta

POLISH EMBASSY

PRAGUE, le 21 septembre 1938

MONSIEUR LE MINISTRE,

D'ordre de mon Gouvernement j'ai l'honneur de communiquer à Votre Excellence ce qui suit :

I. Se référant à la déclaration du Gouvernement de

la République Tchécoslovaque aux termes de laquelle le Gouvernement tchécoslovaque s'est engagé à ne pas faire des discriminations entre la communauté nationale polonaise et aucune autre communauté nationale se trouvant au dedans des frontières de la République Tchécoslovaque, ainsi qu'en rappelant le point de vue du Gouvernement polonais connu du Gouvernement tchécoslovaque et qui n'admet aucune discrimination entre les intérêts de la Pologne et ceux des autres États intéressés, — le Gouvernement polonais attend une décision du Gouvernement tchécoslovaque au sujet des territoires habités par la population polonaise, décision immédiate et analogue à celle que le Gouvernement tchécoslovaque a pris à l'égard du problème allemand.

II. Étant donné ce qui précède le Gouvernement polonais considère que le règlement concernant la situation de la population polonaise en Tchécoslovaquie prévu à la partie III de la Convention polono-tchécoslovaque signée à Varsovie le 23 avril 1925 est devenu sans objet, et en conséquence le Gouvernement polonais dénonce la dite partie de cette Convention.

Veuillez agréer, Monsieur le Ministre, les assurances de ma très haute considération.

KAZIMIERZ PAPÉE

No. 3

Minute concerning Polish Note of September 21, 1938

PRAGUE, September 22, 1938

To-day, the 22nd September, I telephoned the Envoy, M. Papée, at 10.05 A.M. that I had handed his note of yesterday to the Minister, Dr. Krofta, who informs him that he is laying the matter immediately before the Czechoslovak Government and as soon as a decision concerning the reply is made, he will inform M. Papée of it. M. Papée repeated my telephone message and said that he would notify his Government immediately.

DR. KRNO

No. 4

Dr. Krofta to M. Papée

PRAGUE, le 25 septembre 1938

MONSIEUR LE MINISTRE,

Par votre note en date du 21 septembre 1938 vous avez bien voulu me faire connaître que votre Gouvernement, se référant à des déclarations du Gouvernement tchécoslovaque concernant le traitement des nationalités, attend concernant les territoires habités par une population polonaise une décision immédiate et analogue à celle que le Gouvernement tchécoslovaque a prise à l'égard du problème allemand.

Je me permets de faire ressortir que la déclaration du Gouvernement tchécoslovaque dont il s'agit n'a pu avoir trait qu'au traitement des différentes nationalités dans le cadre de l'État. Les négociations avec les Gouvernements de France et de Grande-Bretagne concernant le problème allemand se sont déroulées sur une base différente.

Cependant, dans son désir de placer les relations des deux États sur une base solide et durable et de trouver des solutions pratiques équitables pour les deux États, et vu les conversations et discussions entre nos deux pays qui durent depuis des longues années au sujet de nos rapports mutuels, le Gouvernement tchécoslovaque est disposé à engager des négociations amicales immédiates avec le Gouvernement polonais sur toutes les questions, afin d'arriver à une entente véritable entre la Pologne et la Tchécoslovaquie.

Veuillez agréer, Monsieur le Ministre, l'expression de ma très haute considération.

[No signature on the copy]

A Son Excellence
Monsieur Kazimierz Papée
Envoyé Extraordinaire et Ministre
   Plénipotentiaire de Pologne
à Prague

No. 5

President Beneš to President Mościcki

PRAGUE, le 22 septembre, 1938

MONSIEUR LE PRÉSIDENT,

Au moment où le destin de l'Europe se joue et où nos deux nations ont un vrai intérêt de poser des bases durables pour une collaboration confiante entre nos deux pays, je m'adresse à Votre Excellence avec la proposition de rétablir des relations amicales et une collaboration nouvelle entre la Pologne et la Tchécoslovaquie.

Je propose donc à Votre Excellence au nom de l'État Tchécoslovaque une explication franche et amicale sur le règlement de nos différends au sujet des questions touchant la population polonaise en Tchécoslovaquie. Je voudrais régler cette question sur la base de l'acceptation du principe de rectification de frontière. L'accord sur la question de nos rapports mutuels serait évidemment la conséquence logique et immédiate de cet arrangement. Si nous nous mettions d'accord — et je suis convaincu que ce sera possible — je considérerais cela comme le commencement d'une période nouvelle des rapports entre nos deux pays.

J'ajoute, comme ancien ministre des affaires étrangères et actuel Président de la République, que la Tchécoslovaquie n'a, en ce moment, aucun engagement ni aucun traité secret ou public — et n'en a jamais eu — qui aurait le sens, le but ou la tendance d'endommager les intérêts de la Pologne.

D'accord avec les ministres responsables, je présente cette suggestion à Votre Excellence confidentiellement, mais en même temps personnellement, pour lui donner le caractère d'un engagement ferme. Je voudrais en faire ainsi la question entre nos deux nations seules.

Connaissant la délicatesse de nos rapports mutuels, sachant combien il a toujours été difficile de les changer pour le bien dans les temps normaux et par les moyens diplomatiques ou politiques normaux, j'essaie de me servir de la crise actuelle pour briser les obstacles de dizaines d'années précédentes et pour créer une atmosphère nouvelle d'un seul coup. Je le fais en toute sincérité. Je suis convaincu que l'avenir de nos deux nations et la collaboration future entre elles ne peut qu'en être définitivement assurée.

Veuillez agréer, Excellence, l'expression de mes sentiments les plus distingués.

Dr. Edv. Beneš

A Son Excellence Monsieur Ignacy Mościcki
Président de la République Polonaise
Varsovie, Pologne

No. 6

Note from the Czechoslovak Foreign Minister to the Polish Minister concerning the President's letter

25. ix. 1938

Monsieur le Ministre Papée a mentionné à plusieurs reprises qu'un geste du côté tchécoslovaque pourrait contribuer efficacement à la solution de la question.

M. le Président envoie donc par M. Slávik [1] à M. le Président de la République Polonaise une lettre personnelle qui complète la note d'aujourd'hui et contient le principe de la rectification de la frontière. Ainsi le geste sera plus solennel qu'une simple note diplomatique.

Pour l'avenir des relations mutuelles, il importe qu'il ne puisse y avoir des recriminations du côté tchécoslovaque que la solution a été imposée dans une situation difficile. On veut donc traiter le problème indépendamment de la question sudète, ce qui explique le début de la note.

Il serait indispensable que toute campagne de presse et tout acte inamical soient évités à l'avenir.

No. 7

President Mościcki to President Beneš

Varsovie, le 27 septembre, 1938

Monsieur le Président,

En réponse à la lettre de Votre Excellence qui m'a été remise le 26 courant, je m'empresse de vous communiquer

[1] Czechoslovak Minister in Warsaw.

que j'ai soumis à l'examen le plus sérieux les propositions de Votre Excellence.

Je partage entièrement l'opinion de Votre Excellence que les rapports entre nos pays ne sauraient être améliorés que dans le cas où décisions sérieuses et effectives seraient rapidement prises.

Je suis également d'avis que, au premier plan des préoccupations de l'heure actuelle, se dresse uniquement aujourd'hui une décision courageuse en ce qui concerne les questions territoriales qui pendant presque vingt ans rendaient impossible l'amélioration de l'atmosphère entre nos pays.

En transmettant à mon Gouvernement les suggestions de Votre Excellence, je suis persuadé qu'il sera possible d'élaborer, à bref délai, le projet d'un accord qui pourrait répondre aux exigences de la situation sérieuse d'aujourd'hui.

Veuillez agréer, Excellence, l'expression de mes sentiments les plus distingués.

Mościcki

Son Excellence
Monsieur Edvard Beneš
Président de la République Tchécoslovaque

No. 8

M. Papée to Dr. Krofta

Prague, le 27 septembre 1938

Monsieur le Ministre,

J'ai pris connaissance de la note de Votre Excellence en date du 25 courant, ainsi que de la déclaration orale faite à cette occasion par Elle, et ayant été informé par Son Excellence Monsieur le Président de la République sur les propositions de la lettre de Son Excellence Monsieur le Président de la République Tchécoslovaque, j'ai l'honneur de proposer à Votre Excellence, au nom de mon Gouvernement, de conclure immédiatement un accord en vue de régler le fond du problème qui se pose entre nos deux États, et notamment celui des territoires habités par une population de nationalité polonaise.

Votre Excellence a bien voulu souligner dans sa note la nécessité d'améliorer définitivement les relations entre nos deux pays. Cependant l'examen de la situation actuelle nous prouve incontestablement que toute action entreprise en vue d'une pareille amélioration ne pourrait aboutir à des résultats positifs qu'à condition qu'une solution radicale et courageuse du problème des territoires en question soit entreprise, et que l'on procède à cet effet à une rectification indispensable de la frontière entre la République de Pologne et la République Tchécoslovaque, — ce qui d'ailleurs a été reconnu et proposé dans la lettre de Son Excellence Monsieur le Président Beneš.

La gravité de l'heure présente force le Gouvernement polonais à rechercher des solutions définitives, basées sur le principe de l'équité et de la volonté de la population locale, et qui tiendraient en même temps compte des mesures dont le caractère serait à même d'apaiser l'opinion publique polonaise, si profondément boulversée et qui devraient être prises d'urgence.

L'accord à conclure, pour répondre au but envisagé, devrait de l'avis du Gouvernement polonais, statuer sur deux catégories de problèmes :

(1) Il devrait stipuler les principes en vertu desquels la population dans les régions au delà de notre frontière sud-ouest, habitées par une forte proportion de la population polonaise, pourrait exprimer sa volonté quant à l'union de ces territoires à l'un de nos deux pays, et fixer des delais de cette consultation populaire.

Le droit de vote lors de cette consultation serait limité aux personnes qui l'auraient pu exercer dans l'hypothèse où le plébiscite, prévu par l'accord polono-tchèque de 1919, aurait eu lieu, ainsi qu'aux descendants directs de ces personnes.

(2) Il devrait contenir également un arrangement exécutoire qui, par la cession immédiate des territoires habités par une majorité polonaise indiscutable, et dont l'étendue est délimitée sur la carte ci-jointe, préviendrait d'un côté les graves conséquences résultants de l'état de choses existant

actuellement dans ces territoires, et manifesterait d'autre part à l'opinion polonaise d'une manière évidente la réalité des efforts entrepris par les deux Gouvernements pour l'établissement entre nos deux pays de relations durables de bon voisinage.

Les modalités de la consultation populaire, prévue dans le point (1) ci-dessus, seraient réglées par un accord entre les deux Parties intéressées.

Vu le développement des événements en cours, la prise des territoires mentionnés sous le point (2) serait effectuée par les troupes polonaises. Le commandant en chef de ces forces d'occupation y exercerait le pouvoir administratif suprême.

Du moment que les principes de l'accord susmentionné seraient acceptés, le Gouvernement polonais serait à même de faire des propositions sur les détails techniques d'application de sa proposition. Le Gouvernement tchécoslovaque précisera, pour sa part, ses désiderata quant à l'exécution pratique de l'accord proposé.

Afin d'éviter toute friction possible, et pour prévenir au développement ultérieur d'événements redoutables dans les territoires habités par une population polonaise, le Gouvernement polonais insiste sur une réponse urgente du Gouvernement tchécoslovaque, surtout en ce qui concerne le point (2) de la présente note.

Je tiens à ajouter que mon Gouvernement m'a muni de pleinpouvoir pour entrer immédiatement à Prague en négociations préliminaires.

Veuillez agréer, Monsieur le Ministre, les assurances de ma très haute considération.

KAZIMIERZ PAPÉE

A Son Excellence
Monsieur le Dr. Kamil Krofta
Ministre des Affaires Étrangères de la
    République Tchécoslovaque
à Prague

No. 9

Dr. Krofta to M. Papée

No. 139350/II–1/38

PRAGUE, le 30 septembre 1938

MONSIEUR LE MINISTRE,

J'ai pris connaissance du contenu de la note en date du 27 septembre par laquelle Votre Excellence propose, au nom du Gouvernement, de conclure immédiatement un accord réglant les questions en suspens entre nos deux États et notamment au sujet du territoire habité par une population de nationalité polonaise.

Le Gouvernement tchécoslovaque sait gré au Gouvernement de la République Polonaise d'avoir exprimé sa façon de voir sur le mode de procéder, susceptible, à son avis, de mener à l'accord désirable.

Mené par le désir de voir cet accord complet, permanent et qu'il ne laissât pas de sentiment d'amertume, chez aucune des deux parties, il se permet de recommander la procédure suivante, tout en faisant remarquer que, pour les motifs qui viennent d'être mentionnés, il voudrait éviter que le milieu tchécoslovaque ait l'impression que l'on tire profit des difficultés où se trouve actuellement la Tchécoslovaquie, juste au moment où se discute la question concernant le territoire habité par la population allemande. Le Gouvernement tchécoslovaque désirerait souligner par toute la façon de procéder qu'il s'agit ici d'un acte de bonne volonté, venu de sa propre initiative et de sa libre décision. Il considère cela comme très important pour les relations entre les deux peuples et les deux États dans l'avenir, relations qu'il désirerait les plus amicales possibles.

D'abord, le Gouvernement tchécoslovaque se permet de faire remarquer que dans les négociations relatives à la population allemande de la République, nous avons été forcés de refuser tant le plébiscite que les cessions territoriales avant la fixation définitive des frontières. Pour ces motifs, le Gouvernement tchécoslovaque ne peut, non plus dans le cas de la Pologne, se départir de ce principe d'autant plus qu'il pourrait en résulter un précédent pour la solution de la question allemande des Sudètes, ce qui ne saurait être l'intention du Gouvernement de la République Polonaise.

Le Gouvernement tchécoslovaque, s'inspirant de ces considérations, se permet de proposer pour la solution des questions dont il s'agit les principes suivants :

(1) Le Gouvernement tchécoslovaque donne au Gouvernement polonais l'assurance solennelle que la rectification de frontières et la remise consécutive du territoire, dont il sera décidé par la procédure stipulée, seront réalisées dans toutes les circonstances, quelque tournure que prenne la situation internationale. La République Tchécoslovaque est prête à donner une déclaration à cet égard aussi à la France et à la Grande-Bretagne et d'accepter ces deux États comme garants de cet accord.

(2) La répartition du territoire se ferait la base du principe que les districts en question seraient territorialement divisés suivant le rapport numérique existant entre la population polonaise et la population tchèque.

(3) Il serait immédiatement constitué une commission paritaire polono-tchécoslovaque qui élaborerait la procédure de détail sur la base de ce principe. Elle pourrait être convoquée pour le 5 octobre 1938. Cette commission réglerait notamment encore les questions concernant l'option des habitants, les déplacements et échanges réciproques de la population, ainsi que toutes les questions économiques et financières qui en dependent.

(4) Il serait fixé la date à laquelle la commission devrait avoir terminé ses travaux. Nous proposons celle du 31 octobre.

(5) Il serait immédiatement fixé la date à laquelle doit s'effectuer la remise des territoires. Cette date serait fixée en déterminant les limites extrêmes : la date la plus proche possible et la dernière date possible.

(6) Un communiqué commun pourrait immédiatement faire connaître au public polonais et tchécoslovaque qu'une entente est intervenue sur le principe d'un accord polonais-

tchécoslovaque des frontières et que toute la procédure sera terminée dans un délai sur lequel les deux parties se sont entendues.

(7) Pour ne laisser aucun doute sur la portée de l'accord et sur la ferme volonté qui anime les deux Gouvernements, la commission, comme il a été dit plus haut, entamerait ses travaux au plus tard le 5 octobre et la remise du territoire et [*sic*] au plus tard le 1er décembre, suivant la date où la commission compétente aura terminé ses travaux. La date du premier décembre ne saurait être dépassée.

Le Gouvernement tchécoslovaque pense qu'il s'agit des dispositions si précises, concrètes et fermes, qu'il serait possible de les accepter et de les mettre en œuvre dans un esprit de bonne volonté et d'entente.

Il croit qu'il est possible d'arriver sur cette base à un accord qui assurera aux deux peuples dans l'avenir le sentiment que le conflit se trouve définitivement réglé, qu'il ne restera entre eux ni amertume ni sujet de récriminations et qu'il se créera immédiatement après, entre les deux États, même en ce qui concerne les autres questions politiques, une atmosphère, grâce à laquelle leur collaboration amicale sera pleinement assurée.

Veuillez agréer, Monsieur le Ministre, l'expression de ma très haute considération.

Dr. K. Krofta

Son Excellence
Monsieur Kazimierz Papée
Envoyé Extraordinaire et Ministre
    Plénipotentiaire de Pologne
à Prague

No. 10

Note on conversation between Dr. Krno and M. Papée

29. ix. 1938

The Envoy, M. Papée, visited me at 13 hours on 29.ix. He had come, he said, to make a last appeal, that Czechoslovakia should give Poland a favourable answer in the shortest time, and if possible, during the course of to-day. Only so, he said, would it be possible to ward off the inevitable. He said it is inevitably necessary that a solution of the Polish-Czechoslovak dispute should be reached outside the scope of the Munich conference. I hinted to M. Papée that the Czechoslovak reply will probably be handed over to-day and will contain basic agreement with the Polish demands and the constitution of a Parity Commission which is to decide all the modalities of execution. M. Papée declared that a declaration was insufficient to-day and that it is necessary to proceed to actions, by which he obviously alluded to evacuation. M. Papée further expressed the desire to speak with the President of the Republic on the matter.

KRNO

No. 11

M. Papée to Dr. Krofta

POLISH EMBASSY

PRAGUE, le 30 septembre 1938

MONSIEUR LE MINISTRE,

Le Gouvernement polonais considérant la réponse du Gouvernement tchécoslovaque en date du 30 septembre 1938 à sa note du 27 septembre 1938 comme complètement insuffisante et dilatoire, j'ai l'honneur d'ordre de mon Gouvernement de vous communiquer ce qui suit :

Le Gouvernement polonais a depuis plusieurs mois, attiré l'attention du Gouvernement tchécoslovaque sur l'état des choses impossible à maintenir existant sur le territoire habité en Tchécoslovaquie par le groupe national polonais. Une correspondance diplomatique suivie a été le résultat de cette démarche. Tout récemment à un moment critique de cet échange de vue, il a été constaté de part et d'autre que la normalisation des relations entre la Pologne et la Tchécoslovaquie ne pourrait s'effectuer qu'en premier lieu par la voie d'une cession territoriale en faveur de la Pologne, des territoires habités par la population polonaise, facilement définissables sur la base des données existantes et au deuxième lieu par un plébiscite sur l'autres territoires habités par une population mixte. Son Excellence Monsieur le Président de la République Tchécoslovaque, le Docteur Édouard Beneš, dans sa lettre en date du 22 courant, et remise le 26 courant, à Son Excellence Monsieur le Président de la République de Pologne, a accepté ce principe. Les déclarations du Gouvernement tchécoslovaque l'ont confirmé.

A la suite de ces déclarations le Gouvernement polonais par sa note en date du 27 septembre 1938 a formulé des propositions concrètes, par lesquelles il exigeait le règlement définitif du problème.

En vue de la situation dramatique et menaçante dans la région de frontière en Silésie de Teschen, le Gouvernement polonais a mis en avant la demande d'une cession territoriale immédiate de deux districts indiqués sur la carte annexée à la note susmentionnée.

Il est digne d'être mentionné que Son Excellence Monsieur le Président de la République Tchécoslovaque a bien voulu confirmer personnellement au Ministre de Pologne à Prague la promesse d'une réponse positive, et que les représentants diplomatiques du Royaume Uni et de la République Française ont communiqué au Gouvernement polonais le 29 courant que le Gouvernement tchécoslovaque avait complètement accepté la demande polonaise et ont même fait part des termes fixant l'exécution technique. Ces informations n'ont pas trouvé de confirmation et les promesses n'ont pas été réalisées.

Il est évident qu'étant donné toutes les circonstances et vu que le Gouvernement polonais ne peut plus accorder de confiance aux déclarations faites au nom de la République Tchécoslovaque, et tenant compte de la gravité de la situation, il se voit obligé de la façon la plus catégorique de demander l'exécution du point (2) de sa note en date du 27 septembre courant, et notamment :

(1) L'évacuation immédiate par les troupes et la police
tchécoslovaques du territoire défini par la note susmentionnée,
et délimité dans la carte y annexée, et la remise du dit territoire, d'une façon définitive, aux autorités militaires polonaises.

(2) L'évacuation dans le cours de 24 heures, à compter
de midi 1 octobre 1938, du territoire indiqué dans la carte
ci-annexée.

(3) La remise du reste du territoire des districts de Teschen
et de Frysztat doit être définitivement effectuée au cours d'une
période de dix jours, à compter de la même date.

(4) L'évacuation des dits territoires doit avoir lieu sans
que les entreprises et objets d'utilité publique ainsi que les
voies de communication de toutes sortes soient endommagés,
rendus inutilisables ou enlevés. Tous les ouvrages d'art et
constructions servant à la défense militaire doivent être
désarmés.

(5) Les modalités et les délais de l'évacuation du reste du
territoire mentionné au point 4 ci-dessus, seront communiqués
avant midi du 2 octobre 1938.

(6) Les autres questions soulevées par la note polonaise
du 27 septembre, c'est-à-dire la question du plébiscite dans
d'autres regions, sont laissées à l'entente ultérieure entre les
deux Gouvernements intéressés, sans en exclure la possibilité
de la participation des facteurs tiers.

En ce qui concerne les questions qui résulteront du trans-
fert des territoires susmentionnés, le Gouvernement polonais
est prêt à régler avec le Gouvernement tchécoslovaque par
des négociations.

(7) Le Gouvernement tchécoslovaque prendra des mesures
immédiates afin que tous les ressortissants tchécoslovaques de
langue polonaise, originaires des deux districts, de Teschen et
de Frysztat, faisant actuellement le service dans l'armée
tchécoslovaque, soient libérés de ce service et autorisés de
rentrer dans leurs foyers.

Le Gouvernement tchécoslovaque prendra également de
mesures pour élargir tous les detenus politiques d'origine
polonaise.

(8) Le Gouvernement polonais attend une réponse non-équivoque, acceptant ou rejetant les demandes formulées dans la présente note, jusqu'à midi du 1 octobre 1938. En cas de refus ou d'absence de réponse, le Gouvernement polonais tiendra le Gouvernement tchécoslovaque pour seul responsable de la suite des événements.[1]

Veuillez agréer, Monsieur le Ministre, l'expression de ma très haute considération.

KAZIMIERZ PAPÉE

A Son Excellence
Monsieur le Dr. Kamil Krofta
Ministre des Affaires Étrangères
 de la République Tchécoslovaque
à Prague

No. 12

Minute about the handing over of the Polish Note of 30.ix.1938

To-day, the 30th September, 1938, at 11.40 P.M., the Polish Envoy, M. Papée handed to the Minister of Foreign Affairs, Dr. Krofta, the Polish Government's note of the 30th of this month, referring to the cession of the greater part of the Těšín district. The Foreign Minister, Dr. Krofta, who had been confidentially informed in advance of its contents, referred to the impolite passage in the note stating that the Polish Government can no longer place faith in the Czechoslovak Government's declarations and referred also to to-day's reports of the Polish Press Agency PAT which create the impression of alleged aggressiveness on the Czechoslovak side. He also stated that he regarded it as ignoble to strike a fatally wounded nation with a dagger at the moment when they are endeavouring to regain consciousness. Dr. Krofta made no reference to the contents of the note itself; he said that he would only take

[1] [Note in handwriting of President Beneš] : On nous a fait dire inofficiellement le même jour que Varsovie concentre sur les frontières de Teschen dix divisions.

cognisance of it and that he would discuss it at the Cabinet meeting.

DR. FRÁGNER

30.ix.1938.

No. 13

Dr. Krofta to M. Papée

No. 139373/II–38

PRAGUE, le 1ᵉʳ octobre, 1938

MONSIEUR LE MINISTRE,

En réponse à votre note du 30 septembre j'ai l'honneur de porter à votre connaissance que dans toutes les négociations au sujet de la population polonaise de Tchécoslovaquie le Gouvernement tchécoslovaque avait l'intention de se placer sur le point de vue que ce problème devrait être réglé par des pourparlers directs, amicaux et rapides entre les deux Gouvernements.

Tandis que l'accord de Munich du 29 septembre avait prévu pour les négociations entre les deux Gouvernements un délai de trois mois, la note du Gouvernement tchécoslovaque du 30 septembre a proposé des délais sensiblement plus courts.

Tant au point de vue objectif qu'au point de vue de l'esprit dans lequel a été conclu l'Accord de Munich, le Gouvernement tchécoslovaque considère les propositions de sa note du 30 septembre toujours comme justes et équitables.

Vu cependant la note du Gouvernement polonais du 30 septembre et forcé par les circonstances, le Gouvernement tchécoslovaque accepte les propositions de cette note.

Dans l'intérêt de la population polonaise locale elle-même et pour rendre possible une évacuation sans danger d'incident quelconque, le Gouvernement tchécoslovaque propose que des experts militaires polonais et tchécoslovaques se réunissent immédiatement pour arriver à une entente en ce qui concerne la procédure de détails à suivre.

Il demande en outre que même après l'occupation par les

troupes polonaises, le trafic sur la ligne Bohumín-Žilina soit maintenu et que la commission qui aurait à fixer les autres questions, puisse définitivement régler ce problème, cette ligne étant la seule jonction entre les districts tchécoslovaques importants.

Veuillez agréer, Monsieur le Ministre, l'expression de ma très haute considération.

[No signature on the copy]

A Son Excellence
Monsieur Kazimierz Papée
Envoyé Extraordinaire et Ministre
  Plénipotentiaire
à Prague

No. 14

Minute about delivery of Czechoslovak reply of 1.x.1938 to Polish Note of 30.ix.1938

After the conference at the President of the Republic I telephoned the Polish Envoy, M. Papée, at 11.45 hours that the Czechoslovak Government accepts the proposals of the Polish note of 30th September, 1938. I requested the Envoy to come to me at the Černinský Palác in about half-an-hour for the written reply. M. Papée arrived at 12.30 and took over from me the note signed by the Minister of Foreign Affairs, Dr. Krofta. He also remarked that General Krejčí had already got into contact with the Polish Colonel Noel with regard to a meeting of military specialists.

DR. KRNO

PRAGUE, 1st October 1938

No. 15

Note on conversation between Dr. Krofta and the British Minister, Mr. Newton, October 1, 1938, 12.30 P.M.

After the telephonic conversation with me yesterday evening, the British Minister telegraphed immediately to London.

Even before this he had been informed by London of the instructions telegraphed to the British Ambassador at Warsaw. According to these, the Ambassador was to inform the Foreign Minister, Colonel Beck, that he should acquaint himself with the Munich decisions which implicitly expressed the need for agreement on the Polish and Hungarian questions in Czechoslovakia. It was pointed out that it would be very short-sighted on the part of the Polish Government to attempt a unilateral solution of those questions by its own power in place of remembering that the Four Powers had already bound themselves to a peaceful solution of the Polish question. The British Government hopes that the Polish Government will not take an unconsidered and irretrievable step. If that Government speaks of an ultimatum and if it threatens an occupation by force, then the British Ambassador was to say that the Polish Government would be in the wrong should Poland occupy part of the Czechoslovak territory before reaching an agreement on these matters on the lines of the agreement on the Sudeten German question. The British Government had offered the services of a mediator to Germany and offers them now also to Poland. The British Ambassador is to inform Beck that the British Government is also taking steps in Prague in this sense.

––––––––––

Shortly before midnight London telegraphed to Newton that a report had been received from the Ambassador in Warsaw stating that the situation there had worsened. Beck had summoned him in order to give him urgent news. The Ambassador feared that an ultimatum was intended.

London instructed the Minister Newton to report at Prague the hints given to the Ambassador in Warsaw and to offer us the mediation of Great Britain in the quarrel with Poland.

DR. KROFTA

No. 16

M. Papée to the Czechoslovak Minister for Foreign Affairs, Dr. František Chvalkovský

POLISH EMBASSY

PRAGUE, le 1ᵉʳ novembre 1938

MONSIEUR LE MINISTRE,

Par la note du 1ᵉʳ octobre 1938, le Gouvernement tchécoslovaque avait accepté les propositions contenues dans la note du Gouvernement polonais du 30 septembre, qui dans son point 6 traitait notamment des autres questions laissées à l'entente ultérieure entre les deux Gouvernements.

Par la suite, ces deux Gouvernements sont tombés d'accord de fixer dans des négociations directes les questions ayant trait à la mise en pratique du point susmentionné.

Ils ont établi des traces de la ligne frontière entre la Tchécoslovaquie et la Pologne suivant les cartes annexées.

Une commission mixte de délimitation, composée de techniciens, sera chargée de tracer cette ligne en détail dans le terrain frontière :

Iº—Au nord, du point de rencontre de l'Odra avec son affluent l'Olza, une ligne longeant l'Odra vers le sud, laissant de côté Hruszów, traversant le pont ferroviaire entre Hruszów et Wierzbica, englobant la ligne du chemin de fer au sud du lac innommé et du lac Hermański Rybnik ; de là, au sud de l'intersection de la voie ferrée avec la route Rychwałd-Hruszów, visant la lettre H de l'inscription Hermanice, tout en laissant de côté la localité même d'Hermanice.

De ce point, vers le sud, visant les lettres Ch de l'inscription Michałkowice, tout en laissant de côté la localité de Michał-kowice et englobant la côte forestière 276 ; de là, par le point de jointure de la voie ferrée avec la route sur Radwanice, par le chemin forestier sur Podlesie, laissant de côté la maison du garde forestier, aboutissant à la bifurcation des chemins d'Orłowa et de Szumbark-Radwanice.

De ce point, longeant du côté est la route Frydek-Orłowa

jusqu'au ruisseau Datyniak ; de là, vers l'est, jusqu'à l'extré-
mité nord de la forêt Bobczak, puis longeant la lisière est de cette
forêt jusqu'au point situé 300 mètres au nord de la côte 308.

De ce point, deux kilomètres directement vers l'est,
englobant Dolna Datynia et la partie sur le Błedowice ; de
là à la hauteur de l'inscription Oberhof, vers le sud, le long
du ruisseau Lucyna, jusqu'à la bifurcation des routes sous
Vojkovice ; de là, vers le sud, sous la côte 317, suivant la
ligne du ruisseau Raczek jusqu'à sa source, laissant de côté
Lhota Górna avec la côte 446, 3 et la route sur Dobra,
aboutissant à la rivière Morawka.

De ce point, vers le sud-est, suivant la ligne de la rivière
Morawka, jusqu'à la côte 748 à un demi-kilomètre à l'ouest
de Kozi Grzbiet, puis par la crête de Polczany, englobant
Mały Połom, Trojaczka — côte 1058, aboutissant au sommet
Uhorsk, côte 1028, qui reste du côté tchécoslovaque.

Carte annexée.

IIo—Dans la région de Čadca :

du sommet Uhorsk, vers l'est, longeant à la distance d'un
kilomètre l'ancienne frontière polono-tchécoslovaque, jusqu'à
la hauteur de Dejówka, côte 627.

De ce point, toujours vers l'est, englobant et dépassant d'un
kilomètre vers le sud la bifurcation des voies ferrées Čadca-
Jabłonków et Čadca-Zwardoń ainsi que la bifurcation ana-
logique des routes.

De là, suivant la ligne des crêtes, englobant et dépassant d'un
kilomètre vers le sud le sommet Kycera, côte 580, Slunkov
Vrch, 793, Tri Kopce, 826, Liskovec, 850, descendant sur
Svancari Vrch, 847, remontant par la ligne des crêtes nord
sur le sommet Kikula, 1076, jusqu'au point de la frontière
actuelle située à 5·5 kilomètres au sud de Zwardoń.

(2) Dans la région de Jaworzyna :

du sommet Rysy, côte 2499·2, suivant la ligne du partage
des eaux : par la ligne des crêtes vers le sud-est, par les
sommets Wysoka, Złocisty et Batirowski Szczyt (côte 2458)
au passage de montagne Polski Grzebień ;

de là, vers le nord-est, suivant la ligne des crêtes par les
sommets Mała Wysoka (côte 2428), Swiszczowy Szczyt,

Jaworowy Szczyt, Mały Lodowy, Lodowy (côte 2630) et Baranie Rogi (côte 2536) ;

de Baranie Rogi vers le nord, suivant la ligne des crêtes par les sommets Kołowy Szczyt, Jagnięcy Szczyt, le passage de montagne Pod Kopą, au Szalony Wierch ; de là, par le sommet Płaczliwa Skała (côte 2148), englobant Hawrań (côte 2154) et par la Stara Polana, englobant Okulary (côte 1464), au contour de la route Jaworzyná-Ždiar ;

de ce point, vers le nord, par la côte 1216, englobant Rzepisko (côte 1267), de là, par la Kozwińska Polana, suivant toujours la ligne du partage des eaux jusqu'à la frontière actuelle au sommet Wielka Bryja (côte 1011).

(3) Dans les monts Pieniny :

à partir de l'intersection de la frontière actuelle avec le fleuve Dunajec au sud-ouest de Szczawnica Niższa, jusqu'à son point d'intersection avec la route à l'est de Niedzica, la frontière nouvelle sera ramenée du Dunajec de façon à laisser toute la route longeant Dunajec du côté polonais.

(4) Dans le secteur où, à un kilomètre à l'ouest de la station Wierchomla, la frontière actuelle abandonne le cours du Poprad sectionnant, au 117ème kilomètre la ligne du chemin de fer Zegiestów-Piwniczna et laissant du côté tchéco-slovaque 218 mètres de voie ferrée — la frontière nouvelle devra être refoulée jusqu'au cours du Poprad.

(5) Dans la région de Zegiestów :

la frontière suivant le cours du Poprad sera dirigée de façon à ce que l'espace contourné en cet endroit par le fleuve se trouve du côté polonais.

(6) Sur la ligne du chemin de fer Łupków-Cisna le secteur allant du kilomètre 15,915 au kilomètre 17,050, qui se trouve dépassé par un demi-km^2 de territoire tchécoslovaque devra se trouver entièrement du côté polonais.

Cartes annexées.

Les commissions mixtes de délimitation commenceront leurs travaux immédiatement après l'échange des présentes notes et termineront ces travaux :

(1) la commission ad (I) — le 15 novembre 1938,
(2) la commission ad (II) — le 30 novembre 1938.

L'occupation de la nouvelle ligne-frontière par les autorités tchécoslovaques, respectivement polonaises, aura lieu après la clôture des travaux susmentionnés le 16 novembre, respectivement le 1er décembre 1938.

Un accord spécial réglant la question de l'exploitation de la gare de Hruszów par les autorités polonaises sera conclu dans le cadre d'une commission mixte de techniciens ferroviaires.

Par le présent échange de notes les Gouvernements tchécoslovaque et polonais déclarent d'avoir terminé définitivement les questions de la rectification des frontières respectives.

Veuillez agréer, Monsieur le Ministre, les assurances de ma très haute considération.

KAZIMIERZ PAPÉE

A Son Excellence
Monsieur le Dr. František Chvalkovský
Ministre des Affaires Étrangères de la
    République Tchécoslovaque
à Prague

No. 17

M. Chvalkovský to M. Papée

PRAGUE, le 1er novembre 1938

MONSIEUR LE MINISTRE,

En accusant réception de votre note en date du 1er novembre 1938, j'ai l'honneur de vous confirmer ce qui suit :

[Here follows, word for word, the text of the preceding Polish note.]

Veuillez agréer, Monsieur le Ministre, les assurances de ma très haute considération.

DR. FRANTIŠEK CHVALKOVSKÝ

A Son Excellence
Monsieur Kazimierz Papée
Envoyé Extraordinaire et Ministre
    Plénipotentiaire de Pologne
à Prague

II. CORRESPONDENCE BETWEEN M. G. BONNET
AND M. J. ŁUKASIEWICZ, MAY 26 AND 27, 1939

I am indebted to M. J. Łukasiewicz, late Polish Ambassador in Paris, for the text of the following two letters.—L. B. N.

MINISTÈRE DES AFFAIRES ÉTRANGÈRES

PARIS, le 26 mai 1939

MON CHER AMBASSADEUR,

Je vous ai indiqué les conditions dans lesquelles j'ai eu à m'assurer, comme je devais le faire, d'une suffisante concordance de textes français et anglais avant la signature du projet de protocole franco-polonais.

Je vous ai pleinement renseigné sur l'état où j'ai trouvé le travail de préparation poursuivi au Foreign Office, sur les échanges de vues que j'ai eus à ce sujet avec Lord Halifax en présence de M. Daladier, et sur l'étude commune qu'à Genève, avec mon collègue britannique, j'ai eu à cœur de pousser aussi loin et aussi rapidement que possible pour me trouver en mesure d'échanger à bref délai avec vous les signatures dont l'intervention entre nous a dû être momentanément ajournée.

Cette étude a fait apparaître tout d'abord l'impossibilité pour le rédacteur anglais d'adopter, dans les termes que vous m'avez proposés, la formule de conclusion du projet de protocole franco-polonais, sous peine de trop s'écarter des éléments de base déjà arrêtés entre M. Beck et Lord Halifax. M'attachant du moins, sur ce point capital, à réduire toute divergence entre conceptions anglaise et française, j'ai été heureux de pouvoir réussir à faire dégager de l'étude franco-anglaise une nouvelle formule de conclusion qui s'écarte le moins possible, sur le fonds comme dans la forme, de la rédaction que vous m'aviez proposée, les termes essentiels de votre rédaction étant repris eux-mêmes dans un autre ordre.

Cette formule nouvelle est en ce moment soumise à l'approbation du Gouvernement britannique, qui me fera connaître d'autre part les autres dispositions du projet d'accord anglo-polonais.

Sans même attendre les conclusions de Londres, et pour éviter toute perte de temps qui puisse retarder encore la signature du protocole franco-polonais, je crois devoir dès maintenant, à titre officieux, et pour vous faciliter d'avance l'étude que vous aurez à faire vous-même de ma proposition officielle, vous communiquer personnellement la formule qui a été provisoirement arrêtée à Genève d'accord avec le juriste britannique.

Dès que j'aurai reçu les premières indications de Londres — et vous pouvez compter que j'aurai soin d'en faire hâter l'envoi — je m'empresserai de vous les faire connaître, pour hâter, s'il y a lieu, tous échanges de vues que vous pourriez souhaiter entre nous.

En attendant la signature du protocole d'interprétation franco-polonais, qui ne fera que confirmer explicitement la portée extensive déjà donnée publiquement aux engagements d'assistance mutuelle existants entre la France et la Pologne, je ne puis que vous rappeler la situation de droit et de fait qui couvre déjà, entre la Pologne et la France, toutes préoccupations possibles du Gouvernement polonais: à savoir que la garantie d'intervention immédiate et directe de l'assistance française à la Pologne lui a été, et lui demeure, pleinement assurée par la déclaration solennelle du chef du Gouvernement français, à la date du 13 avril dernier.

Veuillez agréer, mon cher Ambassadeur, l'assurance de ma haute considération.

GEORGES BONNET

Copie

" En même temps, ils (les Gouvernements français et polonais) déclarent entendre désormais les dits accords comme comportant l'engagement pour la France et la Pologne de se prêter sur le champ toute aide et assistance en leur pouvoir si l'un des deux pays est l'objet d'une action menaçant manifestement son indépendance directement ou indirectement et si ce pays, pour la défense de ses intérêts vitaux, résiste par les armes à cette action."

AMBASSADE DE LA RÉPUBLIQUE DE POLOGNE

PARIS, le 27 mai 1939

MON CHER MINISTRE,

Dans votre lettre du 26 de ce mois vous avez bien voulu retracer certaines phases de l'évolution de notre négociation ayant pour but la signature d'un Protocole d'interprétation des Traités d'alliance qui lient nos deux pays.

Permettez-moi de vous communiquer aussi quelques remarques sur le même sujet et de récapituler certains points importants de nos conversations.

Le premier projet de Protocole que je vous ai remis le 28 avril 1939 s'inspirait, comme je vous l'avais alors signalé, des déclarations officielles faites par M. le président Daladier et par le Premier britannique, M. Chamberlain. Comme il s'agissait d'un accord qui devait être conclu entre les Gouvernements français et polonais, dans l'élaboration de son projet mon Gouvernement s'est basé surtout sur la déclaration du chef du Gouvernement français du 13 avril dernier en insérant dans le projet de texte de Protocole presque textuellement la phrase suivante de cette déclaration :

" La France et la Pologne se garantissent immédiatement et directement contre toute menace directe ou indirecte qui porterait atteinte à leurs intérêts vitaux " (Texte de la propositon polonaise: " La Pologne et la France se garantissent mutuellement et directement de porter sur le champ toute aide et assistance en leur pouvoir à la Partie contractante dont les intérêts vitaux seraient directement ou indirectement menacés ").

Le 3 mai vous m'avez proposé certaines modifications de mon projet de protocole, en laissant pourtant intacte la phrase susmentionnée. En me remettant ce texte de projet de Protocole, revu par vous, vous avez souligné que c'est un texte

déjà approuvé par le Gouvernement français et, qu'en conséquence, il serait désirable de ne plus apporter de nouvelles
modifications.

Le 12 mai je vous ai apporté le consentement de mon
Gouvernement d'accepter votre texte, en ajoutant seulement,
qu'au moment de la signature, je ferai une déclaration sur
Dantzig, jugée nécessaire par mon Gouvernement en raison
de la situation actuelle et de l'attitude prise par mon Gouvernement dans cette question, avant la début de notre négociation.
Je vous demandais de bien vouloir prendre note de cette
déclaration.

Le 17 mai vous m'avez fixé la date du 19 mai comme celle
de la signature du Protocole en m'informant que vous n'aviez
pas d'objections en ce qui concerne la déclaration sur Dantzig.
Ensuite la date de la signature avait été différée. Dans notre
conversation officielle du 25 mai, rectifiant votre communication téléphonique du samedi 20 mai, vous m'avez informé que
la question de la déclaration concernant Dantzig ne soulève
aucune objection de votre part et que c'est seulement sur une
formule de la rédaction du Protocole d'interprétation que
vous n'avez pas réussi à vous mettre d'accord avec votre
collègue anglais.

D'autre part, pour éviter des malentendus sur les méthodes
de négociation, dont il est question dans votre lettre, je
voudrais préciser que le Gouvernement polonais en entre-
prenant avec le Gouvernement français une négociation —
qu'il espérait voir aboutir à bref délai — n'avait pas en vue de
poursuivre indirectement et par anticipation une négociation
avec le Gouvernement anglais et de créer, en marge d'une
interprétation d'un Traité d'alliance existant, des formules
fixes pour le nouveau Traité polono-anglais. Une telle éventua-
lité n'était pas envisagée et vous n'aviez pas fait, au cours de
nos conversations avant le 20 mai aucune allusion en ce sens.

J'ai mis mon Gouvernement au courant de la situation
dans laquelle se sont trouvées nos négociations et je lui ai
transmis la nouvelle formule suggérée par vous officieusement,
sous réserve de l'approbation de la part du Gouvernement
britannique. En même temps, je n'ai pas manqué de l'in-

former de l'assurance catégorique que vous m'avez donnée le 25 mai que la déclaration sur Dantzig, que je me propose de faire au moment de la signature du Protocole, ne soulève pas d'objections de votre part et qu'une fois le texte du Protocole fixé, vous accepterez ma déclaration. J'ai tâché aussi de présenter à mon Gouvernement, d'une manière la plus détaillée et la plus précise, les arguments et informations que vous m'avez communiqués dans nos dernières conversations.

J'ai pris bonne note de la référence que vous faites dans votre lettre aux déclarations solennelles du président du Conseil, M. Édouard Daladier, en date du 13 avril at aux engagements qui en résultent, sur la base des obligations d'assistance mutuelle, pour le Gouvernement français. Le ministre des Affaires Étrangères de Pologne a confirmé pour sa part cette déclaration, entre autres, dans son discours du 5 mai. Je ne manquerai pas de porter à la connaissance de mon Gouvernement vos constatations à ce sujet.

Veuillez agréer, mon cher Ministre, l'assurance de ma très haute considération.

J. ŁUKASIEWICZ

INDEX

Abbeville, 233

Abetz, Otto, German Ambassador to Vichy (1903–), Laval and, 98; and Laval's arrest, 102

Abshagen, Dr. K. H., German journalist, 229

Abyssinia, France and Italian designs on, 16-17; Mussolini and, 111; Britain and recognition of Italian rule, 119; Italian need to pacify, 141; Churchill and, 156

Acquarone, Count, Italian Royal Chamberlain (1890–), 148

Aga Khan (1877–), 203

Agression allemande contre la Pologne, L' (Noël), 255 n., 256, 257

Air Defence Research, Committee on, 157

Albania, Mussolini and, 111, 115; Ciano and, 139; invasion of, 139

Albert I, King of the Belgians (1875–1934), 51-2

Alexander, A. V. (1885–), 94 n.

Algiers, 9

Alsace-Lorraine, and French territorial integrity, 3; Pétain and fortifications in, 37; Ribbentrop and, 62; annexation of, 98

Alto Adige, German-Italian relations and, 131, 136, 143

Amery, L. S. (1873–), 169

Anfuso, Filippo, Ciano's *chef de cabinet* (1901–), 113, 114

Anglo-French Entente (1904), 3

Anglo-German Naval Agreement (1935), Flandin and, 12; conclusion of, 156; its denunciation by Hitler, 221

Anglo-Polish Agreement (1939), 68, 70, 266

Anschluss, 120 ff., 129, 132

Anti-Comintern Pact, 117, 130; converted into alliance, 128, 136 ff., 142-3; German-Italian discussions on, 131, 132, 133, 140

Arras, 87

Astakhov, Russian diplomatist, and Nazi-Soviet relations, 261, 264, 265, 267

Attolico, Bernardo, Italian Ambassador in Berlin (1880–1942), and Ribbentrop, 122; and Munich, 124; his dispatches, 130; and German-Italian alliance, 131-43 *passim*; and Ciano, 268

Aube, 62

Austria, Flandin and 1938 crisis, 23, 25 ff.; Schuschnigg ordered to take Nazis into govt., 25, 173; the *Anschluss*, 173 ff.; aggression against, planned by Hitler, 207; Henderson and, 211-12

Badoglio, Pietro, Italian Marshal (1871–), 17

Baku, 43, 44, 277

Baldwin, Stanley (later Earl) (1867–1947), Flandin and, 18; break with Churchill, 151-2; his premiership, 153; and German rearmament, 155; Churchill's appraisal of, 155

Baltic States, Anglo-French-Soviet negotiations and, 251, 252, 254, 256; Nazi-Soviet negotiations and, 269, 271, 272

Bari, 110

Barthou, Louis, French politician (1862–1934), 15, 35

Batum, 43, 44, 277

Baudouin, Paul, French politician (1894–), becomes Under-Secretary, 48; and Tours meeting of Supreme Council, 54-5, 56-7; his early career, 78; his 1938 article in *Revue de Paris*, 78-80; and Germany, 79-80, 85; and his diaries, 81; and Reynaud's govt., 82; and Gamelin, 83; and Weygand, 84-5, 87; and battle of France, 87; and armistice, 90, 91; refuses Ministry of Finance,

313

Brauchitsch, Walter von, German Field-Marshal (1881–1948), 99, 236

Bressy, French diplomatist, 77

Briand, Aristide, French politician (1862–1932), 13

Briare, 49

Britain, Battle of, Flandin and, 32

British Empire, Ribbentrop and, 275; Hitler and, 276

Bukovina, 273

Bulgaria, and Rumania, 273; Russia and Germany and, 276, 277, 278

Bülow-Schwante, von, 232

Butler, R. A. (1902–), 225, 227

Byrnes, James F., U.S. politician (1879–), 244

Cachin, Marcel, French politician (1869–), 255 n.

Cadogan, Sir Alexander, British diplomatist (1884–), 203

Caillaux, Joseph, French politician (1863–1944), 3, 78

Campbell, Sir Ronald, British Ambassador in Paris (1883–), 92, 93, 94

Cangé, 50

Carlsbad, 183

Castellane, Marquis de, French Chargé d'Affaires in London, 93

Cavallero, Ugo, Italian General (1880–1943), 143

Chamberlain, Lady (Austen) (d. 1941), 119

Chamberlain, Sir Austen (1863–1937), 13

Chamberlain, Neville (1869–1940), and Munich, 6; and resignation of Eden, 26; and Bonnet, 60; and Anglo-German Declaration, 61; his guarantee to Poland, 68, 69; and French declaration of war, 75; his policy towards Italy, 118-19; his visits to Hitler, 122-3; at Munich, 124 ff.; secure in power, 133; visits Paris, 135; and Churchill, 151-2; Churchill's appraisal of, 158; and Halifax's

German visit, 158; asks Churchill to join Cabinet, 164; Churchill's only intimate social talk with, 166; Labour refuses to serve under, 169; resigns, 169-70; and Czechs, 177, 186-8, 189; and guarantee to Czechs, 213; Dirksen and, 215-16, 218-19; speech to Foreign Press Association, 220; and stiffening of British attitude, 221; Wohlthat and, 225; and secret negotiations with Germany, 226; his last attempt at appeasement, 228; and negotiations with Russia, 238, 242, 245, 251, 264; his guarantees to Poland and Rumania, 241

Chamberlain, The Life of Neville (Feiling), 158, 242

Charles-Roux, François, French diplomatist (1909–), 93

Chautemps, Camille, French politician (1885–), and armistice, 51, 90

Chauvineau, Narcisse Alfred, French General, 39

China, 12

Choc, 109

Christič, Yugoslav Minister in Rome, 113

Churchill, Winston (1874–), and France in 1918, 4; and France in 1940, 5; and Munich, 6, 160-163; and Gen. Georges, 8; and Flandin, 9; and Finnish war, 43; correspondence with Reynaud, 48; and need to preserve R.A.F., 49, 88; and defection of France, 50; and union with France, 51; urges right action but comes to power too late, 52; at Tours meeting, 53 ff.; and Rougier agreement, 81; and Gamelin, 83; and Battle of France, 87; and French need for armistice, 89; and French fleet, 94-5; Ciano's letter to, 106, 111, 116; The Gathering Storm, 150-70; and rearmament of Germany, 150-51, 153-4; his exclusion from office, 151-3; and rearmament, 153-5;

INDEX

Baudouin and situation of, 79-80 ;
hopelessness of military position,
84; need for armistice, 89;
Britain and release of, from undertakings, 92; her fleet, 92-5;
Italian designs against, 110;
Mussolini and, 117, 129; re-
arms, 133; Churchill and military power of, 153-4; and
Czechs, 162-3, 177, 195, 197;
Documents and Materials and sacrifice of Czechs by, 206; Hitler and
political parties in, 209; Anglo-
French negotiations with Russia,
238 ff. ; avoidance of war the aim
of, 240; her alliances in eastern
Europe, 241; her views about
likely course of war, 243; Stalin
and French army, 271
France a sauvé l'Europe, La (Reynaud),
24 n., 34, 44 n., 46 n., 52-3;
quoted, 24, 33-8 *passim*, 42, 46-52
passim
Franco-German Declaration (1938),
61 ff., 135
Franco-Italian Agreement (1935),
47 n.
Franco-Polish Alliance (1921), 68 ff. ;
Bonnet and, 74
Franco - Soviet Pact (1935), 3;
Flandin and, 9, 14; ratification
of, 19; and Locarno, 19; de-
nounced by Right, 20; French
politicians and, 35-6; Bonnet
and, 59-60, 65, 249-50; Franco-
German Declaration and, 63
François-Poncet, André, French Am-
bassador in Berlin (1887-),
Ciano and, 124; and Czech
crisis, 197
Frank, Hans, German Governor of
Poland (1900–1946), 113
Free French, arrest Flandin, 9
French Policy, 1919–1940 (Flandin).
See *Politique française*
French Revolution, meaning of, 2
Front Populaire, and Russian alli-
ance, 15; and 1936 election, 25;
Riom and, 85; Pétain and, 86
Frossard, Charles, French General
(1807–75), 38

Funk, Dr. Walter, German Minister of Economics (1890-), 31,
220 and n.

Gafenco, Grigore, Rumanian For-
eign Minister (1892-), 72, 73
Gamelin, Maurice Gustave, French
General (1872-), his memoirs,
2; and French confusion, 7; and
Poland, 7, 246; and Italian attack on Abyssinia, 17; and the
Rhineland, 18-19, 22-3; and
Maginot Line, 37; and Rey-
naud's plea for reorganization of
army, 41; his accumulation of
functions, 41; and lack of help to
Poland, 43; Daladier and, 82;
Baudouin and, 83; replaced by
Weygand, 84; Riom and, 85;
Beneš and visit of, to Warsaw,
283-4 and n.
Gathering Storm, The (Churchill),
150-70; quoted, 4, 8, 150-70
passim, 242, 243, 247, 256; re-
veals author's character, 166
Gaulle, Charles de, French General
(1890-), his *Vers l'armée de
métier*, 40
Gaus, Friedrich, German Foreign
Office official (1881-), 264,
282 n.
Genoa, 131
Gensoul, Marcel Bruno, French
Admiral, 95
George V, funeral of, 18
Georges, Alphonse Jacques, French
General (1875-), 8, 42, 44,
46
German-Russian Treaty (1926),
266, 268
Germany, disunity of, 2; as a
neighbour, 3; her army in 1939,
8; and Flandin, 9; and Rhineland, 11; dams to imperialism of,
removed, 12-13; Flandin advo-
cates rapprochement with, 26 ff. ;
and Czechs, 28, 121 ff., 176 ff. ;
invades Norway, 44; invades
Low Countries, 45; and Franco-
German Declaration, 61 ff. ;
Laval and, 97; Ciano and, 111

319

and responsibility too late, 52;
summary of his character and his
book, 52-3; and Allied Supreme
Council Meeting at Tours, 53-7;
Baudouin and, 54-6; Bonnet
cites, 60; and Anglo-French-
Soviet negotiations, 72; and
Baudouin, 80, 82; and armistice,
90, 91; and German numerical
superiority, 168; and Bodenschatz " confidences ", 262 n.
Rhine, River, plan to mine, 167
Rhineland, remilitarization of, 5, 6,
9, 10-11; Flandin and, 17-18,
20-21; German troops enter, 19, 41
Ribbentrop, Joachim von, German
Foreign Minister (1893–1946),
Flandin and his note of Aug. 30,
1939, 30-31; visits Paris, 62; and
Franco-German Declaration, 63,
64; Laval and, 100; Ciano and,
112, 113; proposes alliance to
Italy, 120, 130, 131, 132, 136,
140, 142; and German designs
on Czechoslovakia, 122; and
Munich Agreement, 124; and
Italian Central European aims,
127; his bellicosity, 131, 133;
his 1938 visit to Rome, 132-3;
thanks Ciano for friendship, 138;
meets Ciano, 141-2; informs
Ciano of imminence of war, 144;
Halifax and, 173; and *Anschluss*,
173-4; Henlein and, 182-3; and
settlement of Sudeten problem,
190-91; and Henderson's talk
with Hitler, 211; Dirksen and,
215, 218, 221, 227; and Wohlthat's mission, 225; believes
Britain will not go to war, 227;
invited to Moscow, 257, 258, 268;
and Nazi-Soviet approaches, 259,
264, 266, 268; Schulenburg and,
266; his Moscow visit, 269, 271,
272; his letter to Stalin, 274; and
Molotov, 274-7; and Matsuoka,
278
Riom Trials, 1; defeatists and, 34;
Bonnet not on trial, 77; screen
Pétain, 84-5; Pétain and, 97
Rist, Charles, French economist, 78

Rome, ancient, 2
Rome Agreement, Flandin and, 9
Rommel, Erwin, German Field-
Marshal (1891–1944), 234, 235
Roosevelt, Franklin Delano, U.S.
President (1882–1945), Reynaud
appeals to, 49; his proposal for
Washington conference, 159;
Dirksen and, 222
Rossi, A., 263 n.[2], 271 n.[2]
Rougier, 81, 99, 100
Rousseau, Jean-Jacques (1712–
1778), 12
Rouvier, Maurice, French poli-
tician, 3
Royal Air Force, prevented from
bombing Ruhr, 43; not yet re-
formed, 48; need to preserve, 49,
88 and n.
Royal Navy, at outbreak of war, 165-6
Ruhr, defended by neutrality of
Low Countries, 41; R.A.F. pre-
vented from bombing, 43
Rumania, remilitarization of Rhineland and, 11; Franco-Soviet
Pact and, 59, 60; Beneš and,
113; guarantees offered to, 139;
Iron Guard in, 187, 188; Chamberlain's guarantee to, 241, 245;
hatred for Russia, 242; thought
to be threatened, 249; Russia
and, 251; Anglo-French-Soviet
negotiations and, 254, 256, 257;
Russian claims on, 273; and
Vienna Award, 273; German
military mission to, 274; Russia
and German troops in, 276;
German troops concentrated in,
277
Runciman Mission, responsibility
for, 28; suggested, 202; Beneš and,
202; Hodža and, 203; accepted
by Czechs, 204; Dirksen and, 218
Russia, and French predominance,
2; source of strength of, 3;
British and French approaches to,
7, 139; Flandin and, 12, 14-15,
29-30; Reynaud and, 35; and
pact with France, 36; 1939
negotiations with, 59, 69, 71,
72-3, 221-2, 238 ff.; Mussolini

THE END